There have been other distinguished biographies of William Wilberforce, rich in historical scholarship and awesome facts. What Kevin Belmonte provides in his study of Wilberforce is the humanity of the man, the total self-sacrifice undertaken for the love of his fellow sisters and brothers whose fate he reckoned emanated from the greed and inhumanity of mankind. The elegance and simplicity of his writing, and the wealth of source material researched and sifted with such evident love of his subject, make this a compelling book – a must for all associating themselves with the Bicentenary of the Abolition of the Slave Trade Act of 1807.

LADY DAVSON,
third great-granddaughter of William Wilberforce

Having been brought up with the weight of this saintly ancestor, Kevin Belmonte has, for the first time for me, brought home the humanity of William Wilberforce – his capacity to amuse, charm, converse on any subject, sing, break off deep conversations to run in the garden with his children; his extensive reading and correspondence, and the wide range of causes he supported both with his time and his resources. Here is a portrait of a man driven by his Christian beliefs, not only to wage war on slavery, but also to improve the moral life of Britain; not in a judgmental or sanctimonious manner but with true compassion for his fellow beings and in a humble and self-doubting way.

THE HON. SAMUEL WILBERFORCE,
third great-grandson of William Wilberforce

Since Wilberforce is arguably not merely one of the greatest Christian philanthropists in the history of the church but one of the greatest philanthropists in all history, it would be understandable for a Christian biographer to lapse into hagiography. Kevin Belmonte, however, provides just the right combination of praise and analysis. He carefully catalogues his subject's extraordinary range of achievements while sensitively introducing us to the attractive, though at times idiosyncratic, humanity of so great a "hero."

RANALD MACAULAY,
author and cultural apologist

William Wilberforce – who probably did as much for humanity as any man has ever done – deserves the best, and he has got it. Kevin Belmonte has done a superb job, meticulously researched and beautifully written.

JOHN JULIUS, LORD NORWICH,
the distinguished author and BBC presenter

WILLIAM WILBERFORCE

A HERO *for* HUMANITY

KEVIN BELMONTE

FOREWORD *by* CHARLES COLSON

ZONDERVAN®

ZONDERVAN.com/
AUTHORTRACKER
follow your favorite authors

We want to hear from you. Please send your comments about this book to us in care of zreview@zondervan.com. Thank you.

 **ZONDERVAN®**

William Wilberforce
Copyright © 2002, 2007 by Kevin Belmonte

Requests for information should be addressed to:
Zondervan, *Grand Rapids, Michigan* 49530

Library of Congress Cataloging-in-Publication Data

Belmonte, Kevin Charles.
    William Wilberforce : a hero for humanity / Kevin Belmonte.
        p.   cm.
    "Much of this book was previously published as Hero for Humanity: A Biography of William Wilberforce, published by NavPress Publishing Group, Colorado Springs, 2002."
    Includes bibliographical references.
    ISBN-13: 978-0-310-27488-9
    ISBN-10: 0-310-27488-5
    1. Wilberforce, William, 1759-1833. 2. Legislators — Great Britain — Biography.
3. Abolitionists — Great Britain — Biography. 4. Philanthropists — Great Britain —
Biography. 5. Great Britain — Politics and government — 1760-1820. 6. Great
Britain — Politics and government — 1820-1830. I. Belmonte, Kevin Charles. Hero for
Humanity. II. Title.
    DA522.W6B45   2007
    326.092 — dc22   [B]

                                                                              2006033485

Much of this book was previously published as *Hero for Humanity: A Biography of William Wilberforce*, published by NavPress Publishing Group, Colorado Springs, 2002.

The frontispiece image was drawn by W. M. Craig and engraved by Thomson, originally published in 1819.

All Scripture quotations are taken from *The Holy Bible: King James Verson*.

Interior design by Beth Shagene

Printed in the United States of America

---

08 09 10 11 12 • 23 22 21 20 19 18 17 16 15 14 13 12 11 10 9 8 7 6 5 4

for Kelly and for Sam

CONTENTS

WILBERFORCE

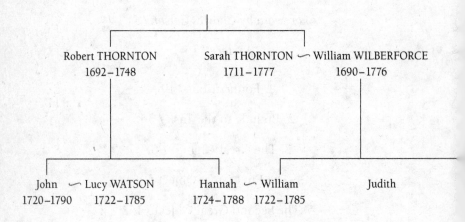

Robert THORNTON ∕ Sarah THORNTON ∕ William WILBERFORCE
1692–1748   1711–1777   1690–1776

John ∕ Lucy WATSON   Hannah ∕ William   Judith
1720–1790   1722–1785   1724–1788   1722–1785

Sarah ∕ 1. Revd. Thomas CLARKE
1758–1816   2. James STEPHEN MP
                1758–1832

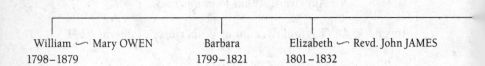

William ∕ Mary OWEN   Barbara   Elizabeth ∕ Revd. John JAMES
1798–1879   1799–1821   1801–1832

FAMILY TREE

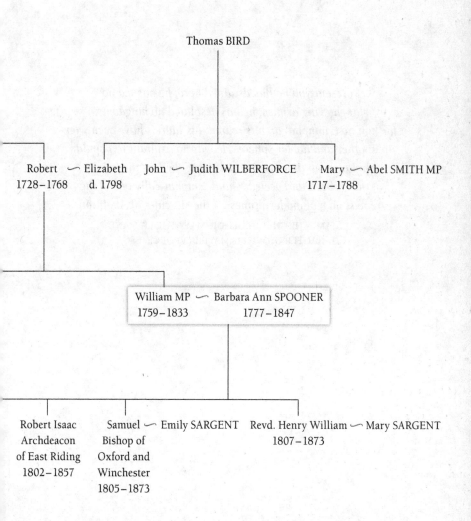

Thomas BIRD

Robert   Elizabeth   John   Judith WILBERFORCE   Mary   Abel SMITH MP
1728–1768   d. 1798   1717–1788

William MP   Barbara Ann SPOONER
1759–1833   1777–1847

Robert Isaac   Samuel   Emily SARGENT   Revd. Henry William   Mary SARGENT
Archdeacon   Bishop of   1807–1873
of East Riding   Oxford and
1802–1857   Winchester
               1805–1873

*I present you no bloodstained hero; he has led no
slaughtering armies, he has desolated no kingdoms;
· for him no triumphal arch is reared; his laurels have been won
in another and nobler sphere. He was no aspirant to popular
applause; no time serving politician; he was the friend
of the "robbed and peeled;" [and] emphatically one of the
greatest men of modern times ... the Hercules of Abolition.*

BENJAMIN HUGHES, "EULOGIUM ON THE LIFE AND
CHARACTER OF WILLIAM WILBERFORCE. ESQ."

FOREWORD BY CHARLES COLSON

Had William Wilberforce remained content with the life that Providence had given him, he might easily have become prime minister of Great Britain and, consequently, the most powerful political leader of his day. He was wealthy, well educated, witty, a fine singer and brilliant speaker, with no peers at having fun or attracting a crowd, as Kevin Belmonte's carefully researched and well-written study reveals. But his life, at one pivotal moment, took a very different turn. For God, it seems, had other plans for William Wilberforce.

The Great Change in his life was brought about in part by an "accidental" encounter with the young scholar and evangelical Isaac Milner, whose "clear grasp of the intellectual heart of Christianity" had a profound effect on the young politician. On their long travels together in Europe during the summer of 1785, the two men debated the claims of Christianity. Together they read an influential treatise written by Philip Doddridge, *The Rise and Progress of Religion in the Soul*, which had a transforming effect.

Wilberforce had long been skeptical of religion. More comfortable with Unitarians, he had attended church irregularly but with a serious aversion to those who took the Christian faith too seriously. Over time, however, and with the steady encouragement of Milner and other friends, including the hymn writer and former slave trader John Newton, Wilberforce was persuaded to give himself fully to Jesus Christ. It was no casual commitment.

Wilberforce feared that his close friendship with Prime Minister William Pitt would be damaged by his conversion, and he met with Pitt to discuss the change. For a time Wilberforce considered giving up his seat in Parliament, fearing that his newfound beliefs would be incompatible with the rowdy and often dirty business of politics, but Pitt and others persuaded him to stay. Where else, they reasoned, could he do more good or have more influence than in government service?

Conflicts did, of course, come in abundance, particularly when the young statesman took on the ultimate challenge of his life: the eradication of slavery in the British colonies. Ultimately, he was deserted by many who once called him friend. His health failed repeatedly, and on four occasions he came within a whisper of death. If it had not been for the support and prayers of the small circle of believing friends who met with him faithfully for many years at Clapham, this small, frail man would not have survived to achieve his life's work. But survive he did, learning of the abolition of slavery in the British colonies just days before his death.

From beginning to end this is a remarkable and powerful story. In his deep convictions, his perseverance, his industry, and his imagination, William Wilberforce provides an unparalleled example of true Christian service in a fallen world. Despite the allurements of power and position, of friends and family, and of every sort of distraction the world could offer, Wilberforce gave himself to his cause and became for us a model of selfless endurance against every sort of adversity. In later years he would be acknowledged as the greatest and most influential figure of his time and "the Washington of humanity."

In Kevin Belmonte's compelling narrative of the life and times of Wilberforce, we are challenged not only to remember the achievements of this illustrious man but also to recognize the call that his example still has upon us today. How often we're tempted to give up when the task is too hard. But the life and example of William Wilberforce take away our excuses, and the inspiring story in these pages gives courage and character a face we can recognize.

Sadly, Wilberforce has until recent decades been a figure all but lost to history. Our forefathers knew this man. His name was on the lips of America's founding fathers. In America's struggles with this very issue – the question of slavery and the tragedies that would befall the nation in the Civil War – it was the words and wisdom of Wilberforce that would ultimately prevail. This generation needs to be reminded of the heroic saga of William Wilberforce, and we have Kevin Belmonte to thank for bringing it so vigorously to the fore. Today, wherever people struggle for freedom from bondage and the tyranny of compromise, they will have this model and this example of compassion and tireless endurance.

It was, in fact, the determination, compassion, and wisdom exemplified by Wilberforce that prompted me to name our public policy institute in Washington, D.C., the Wilberforce Forum. But it was also this spirit that has motivated me for more than twenty-five years in my work at Prison Fellowship, bringing the love of God to those who are incarcerated in America's prisons, to their families, and to the victims of crime.

This volume, *William Wilberforce: A Hero for Humanity*, is an important and worthy achievement, not only profound but thoroughly enjoyable to read. It is a book that will help to spread the story of a remarkable man far and wide. I am grateful to Kevin Belmonte for his own perseverance and industry in getting it all, getting it right, and getting it out, for the benefit of readers everywhere. Wilberforce would be duly proud.

CHARLES W. COLSON
Chairman, Prison Fellowship
Ministries

PREFACE

On September 16, 1833, a special public meeting was held in New York City. Those in attendance had assembled at the Colored Presbyterian Church at the behest of the Officers of the Convention for the Improvement of the Free People of Color in the United States.

It was a singular event. For they were met together to consider how they ought to mark the passing of the British antislavery reformer William Wilberforce, who for nearly fifty years had been "the friend of Africa." For twenty years Wilberforce had led the fight to abolish the British slave trade – a victory achieved in 1807. Twenty-six years later and just days before his death in late July 1833, Wilberforce had learned that slavery itself would be abolished throughout Britain's colonies. News of this great human rights victory had just reached America's shores, as had the news of Wilberforce's passing.

And so sons and daughters of Africa met in New York to consider how they ought to pay tribute to Wilberforce's memory. During that September meeting several resolutions were unanimously adopted. A committee was also appointed to draft resolutions "expressive of the sentiments of regret felt by the people of color for the death of the Honorable William Wilberforce." It was their considered opinion that "the most extensive manifestations of feeling be recommended to the people of color throughout the United States."

The other resolutions adopted included a request that "colored freemen throughout the United States" be requested to wear a badge of mourning for thirty days. Pastors of the African-American churches in New York City were asked "to deliver discourses in the several Churches, as soon as practicable, descriptive of the life and virtues of the late William Wilberforce." Lastly a committee of five was appointed "to select a suitable person to deliver an Eulogy on the Life and Character of the distinguished Philanthropist whose death we so much lament." Soon afterward, this committee reported "that they had selected Mr. Benjamin F. Hughes, Principal of the Free School."

Hughes delivered his *Eulogium for William Wilberforce* on October 22, 1833. Marked by passages of great eloquence, the address was eventually published and widely distributed. It is now considered a classic work of African-American literature.

Perhaps no portion of Hughes' oration was more powerful than the one in which Hughes compared Wilberforce and Napoleon. "Napoleon," Hughes said, "and the band that preceded him in ambition's lawless strife have ceased to breathe ... the Corsican is no more; and with him sleep those vast designs, which convulsed the world in bloody contest for empire."

Hughes then posed an arresting question. Why is it, he wondered aloud, that "there is a charm that attracts the admiration of men to their destroyers; a propensity to applaud those very acts that bring misery on the human race; and on the other hand to pass by unheeded, the placid and even tenor of the real benefactors of their species?"

Hughes understood what the proper response to such a question should be. "There is a spectacle," he declared,

> more glorious and venerable than the transient blaze of a meteor; or the triumphant entry of a conqueror. It is the benign manifestation of those nobler feelings of our nature in behalf of the oppressed ... it is that species of love to man, desig-

nated philanthropy. It is not circumscribed within the narrow precincts of country, restricted to religion or party; – it is co-extensive with the world. Hence, of all men, it is to the Philanthropist that we are chiefly indebted; it is upon his disinterested deeds that we are to stare; – and his is the memory for which we should cherish the fondest recollections.

Hughes concluded by saying that for himself and for his fellow African-Americans, Wilberforce was a man of "unrivalled worth" – the "Hercules of Abolition."

To be sure, Wilberforce's labors as an abolitionist dominate the landscape of his legacy, but there are many other compelling and important facets of his life and character. Throughout his life he championed some seventy different philanthropic initiatives. He was an advocate of child labor laws and ardently supported the education of the blind and the deaf. He funded hospitals and schools with his own money and was a founder of organizations as diverse as the Royal Society for the Prevention of Cruelty to Animals (RSPCA) and the National Gallery (of Art). "Good causes," it has been said, "stuck to him like pins to a magnet."

Wedded to his numerous public and private philanthropies was a personality that captivated nearly everyone he met and won over many whom at one time or another opposed him. The philosopher and novelist Madame de Stael, who for many years had hosted the greatest minds of Europe in her Paris salon, considered Wilberforce "the best converser I have met with" and "the wittiest man in England." In an age where personal and partisan differences were often so sharp that duels were commonplace, he possessed a unique ability to come alongside philosophical opposites and work together with them. Edmund Burke thought Wilberforce's parliamentary eloquence was surpassed only by the greatest orators of ancient Greece. High praise from a man considered by many to be the leading orator of his day. Wilberforce was a man whose life and legacy had touched the lives of kings, presidents, and the downtrodden throughout the world – a fact as well known in the United States in his day as in the courts of Europe. In 1858 Abraham Lincoln, no less, had written that every schoolboy was familiar with Wilberforce's story. One prime minister, Lord Grenville, said during Wilberforce's lifetime: "Millions unborn will bless his memory."

Wilberforce's steadfast dedication to fostering cultural renewal and seeking social justice flowed from a Christian faith commitment as all-consuming and seminal as that which had transformed Pascal, whose writings he deeply admired and read for hours at a time. Where Martin Luther King Jr. had spoken in his timeless "I have a dream" speech of "a beautiful symphony of brotherhood" – Wilberforce had, 155 years before, written of a "concert of benevolence" in an abolition letter to President Thomas Jefferson. In words that Dr. King would have understood well Wilberforce had also written: "In the Scriptures no national crime is condemned so frequently, and few so strongly, as oppression and cruelty, and the not using our best endeavours to deliver our fellow-creatures from them."

William Wilberforce has been called "the greatest reformer in history." In the pages that follow, I have sought to chronicle the life of a man who was also one of the great souls of history. It has been a profoundly rewarding task.

KEVIN BELMONTE
Woodholme
January 2007

CHAPTER I

FOUNDATIONS

The Child is the father of the Man.
WILLIAM WORDSWORTH

I never saw anyone who touched life at so many points," a friend once said of William Wilberforce. So, fittingly, can commence the story of a man of whom it was also said, "Not one nation, but the whole human family participated in the benefit he conferred on his fellow men."

William Wilberforce was born in the English port city of Hull on August 24, 1759. His family was an ancient and respected one that could trace its ancestry back to the reign of King Henry II in the twelfth century.

The family patriarch was Wilberforce's paternal grandfather, also named William, and known as Alderman Wilberforce. Born in 1690, he had built a great fortune in the Baltic trade and inherited a considerable landed property from his mother. His holdings included a red-brick Jacobean mansion on High Street in Hull, land in three regions around Hull, and the estate of Markington near Harrowgate. The Markington estate contained tenant farms but no great country estate.

The merchant house run by Alderman Wilberforce imported hemp and timber from Latvia and Russia and iron ore from Sweden. In return, he exported Yorkshire products of all kinds, from Sheffield cutlery to ponies.

Aside from his business interests, Alderman Wilberforce was known for his intelligence, talent, and integrity. In 1722 he was elected mayor of Hull at the relatively young age of thirty-two. He was elected again in 1745.

He was also a forceful man who had seen much of life. He charmed his young grandson with tales of his travels and career. On one occasion he met the Duke of Marlborough, the hero of the Battle of Blenheim, in which Britain defeated France and Bavaria. Marlborough, then commander of the British army on the continent, invited Alderman Wilberforce to witness an approaching battle from a neighboring hill.

In 1745 the celebrated Jacobite rebellion against the English monarchy was led by Bonnie Prince Charlie, the heir of the only recently deposed Stuart royal line. Alderman Wilberforce displayed a good deal of military ardor and made sure that Hull was ready for any military threat. He raised volunteers and armed them with muskets. Ramparts built in the reign of Charles I – one hundred years before – were repaired and manned.

William Wilberforce, the Alderman's grandson and namesake, was the third child and only son in his family. Sadly, of the four children born to his parents, Robert and Elizabeth, only he and one of his three sisters – Sarah (called Sally) – survived to adulthood. Wilberforce recalled:

> The eldest [Elizabeth] died at about fourteen, when I was about eight.... She was at one of the great boarding schools of London.... The youngest, Ann, was I think one of the sweetest children that ever was born.... She was quite born, I know my mother thought, to be a comfort to her, for she lived with her all the time my sister ... Sarah was [away] for her education. [Ann] was only born just before my father's death, and she lived only about eight years.

In 1767 Wilberforce began attending the Hull Grammar School as a dayboy. Each day for two years he walked to school from the High Street mansion, carrying a satchel on his shoulder and eating his meals at home. On holidays he would visit his grandfather

The Wilberforce house in Hull, where William was born in 1759

at Ferriby, a pleasant village on the Humber River, seven miles away.

When Wilberforce began his schooling Alderman Wilberforce used his influence to secure the installation of Joseph Milner as the school's new headmaster. Milner, the son of a poor weaver, had been a pastor in North Ferriby and won the Chancellor's Medal while at Cambridge University. Milner was accompanied by his seventeen-year-old brother, Isaac, who served with him as a temporary assistant. At Cambridge, Isaac Milner would later achieve academic distinctions that far surpassed those of his brother, among them election to the prestigious Royal Society and service as the vice-chancellor of the university.

While he was attending the Hull Grammar School, Wilberforce impressed his teachers. "Even then," Isaac Milner recalled, "his elocution was so remarkable that we used to set him upon a table and make him read aloud as an example to the other boys." Despite being sickly, Wilberforce was also described as "a fine sharp lad" who actively participated in sports.

Wilberforce had weak eyesight, and throughout his life he was plagued by serious problems with his digestive system. Many years later he told an American friend, William Buell Sprague, that he had "great reason to be thankful that he had such a measure of health; for his life had been little else but a struggle with disease and debility."

Relatively little is known about Wilberforce's parents. His mother, Elizabeth, was described as "a woman of real excellence [and] highly cultivated talents." She was descended from the Oxfordshire family of Bird and had connections to many other notable families who themselves, like her, had strong ties to the Church of England. Among her younger relations was John Bird Sumner, Archbishop of Canterbury.

In later years Wilberforce would say that his parents were "decently religious" but that his mother, though "a very worthy woman, ... had no just conception of the spiritual nature and aim of Christianity." She was not, in short, what more evangelically minded Anglicans would call "a serious Christian" – one for whom an ardent faith was central to every facet of life.

Instead, Elizabeth Wilberforce was fond of the extravagant life of society enjoyed by many well-to-do, prominent families. The Wilberforces, well-established members of Hull's merchant class, engaged in lavish forms of entertainment. "The theatre, balls, great suppers and card parties were the delight of the principal families of the town," Wilberforce remembered.

His father, Robert, was a merchant who, like his ancestors for nearly a century before him, was involved in the Baltic trade. Born in 1728, he was managing partner in his father's countinghouse and probably attained this position in 1755 at the age of twenty-seven. Judging from the size of the inheritance he left to his son, he appears to have been a capable businessman.

Robert Wilberforce also possessed a strong sense of noblesse oblige. He was a generous supporter of the parish ministry of Dr. Richard Conyers, the rector of Helmsley, and built him a fine home. Visits to the Conyers family would have been the more frequent because Jane Conyers (the doctor's wife) was the elder sister of Hannah Wilberforce, Robert's sister-in-law. Hannah and Jane were Thorntons. Importantly, and as shall be seen later, their brother John was also to play a prominent role in William Wilberforce's life.

The picture that emerges from these years is one of father and son traveling together in the family coach through the Yorkshire countryside. It would have been an exciting time for a young boy, experiencing something of the wider world at his father's side, taking in the sights and sounds – perhaps hearing a story or two into the bargain, for the Wilberforces were a family of raconteurs. Yet these would prove to be halcyon days, all the more precious because they were so fleeting.

In May 1768 Wilberforce's father died. William was only eight years old. Shortly thereafter, news arrived from London that his elder sister, who was away at boarding school, had also died.

The shock of two deaths in such quick succession was devastating. Wilberforce's mother fell victim to "a most long and dangerous fever." Grief prolonged her slow recovery. Moreover, she was pregnant, which compounded the great concern the family felt for her. Some months later, she gave birth to her youngest daughter Ann.

For some time Elizabeth Wilberforce's life was despaired of. A wrenching, difficult decision had to be made: Wilberforce would be placed in the care of his father's elder brother, William, and his wife, Hannah.

One can only imagine how these upheavals affected Wilberforce, then described as a sensitive, affectionate child. His world had been rocked to its very core.

In later years Wilberforce could scarcely bring himself to speak of his father's death. He is only known to have spoken of his eldest sister's death once – to one of his sons many years later, in 1820.

In the wake of all that had happened, the choice to place Wilberforce in the care of his uncle and aunt proved a happy one. Childless themselves, they lavished love, time, and attention on him and made him their heir. He responded in kind. "My uncle and aunt," he later said, "I loved as if they had been my parents."

Wilberforce's uncle placed him at a school in the town of Putney. It was "a very indifferent school," Wilberforce remembered: "They taught writing, French, arithmetic, and Latin ... with Greek we did not much meddle. [The school] was frequented by the sons of merchants and they taught, therefore, every thing and nothing. Here I continued some time as a parlour boarder: I was sent at first amongst the lodgers, and I can remember even now the nauseous food with which we were supplied, and which I could not eat without sickness."

The unpleasantness of the Putney school aside, there were many happier reasons for this little newly knit family to have grown close. Uncle William and aunt Hannah were kind and affectionate, and they had a wide circle of friends to whom they introduced their nephew. Many of them had been converted under the ministry of the renowned evangelist George Whitefield.

The Wilberforces had embraced Whitefield's message and possessed a deep, abiding faith. Whitefield often visited them at their home, Lauriston House – a villa built in the Queen Anne style on five and a half acres on the south side of Wimbledon Common. Uncle William had purchased this home in 1766 and commissioned the Swiss-born artist Angelica Kauffman to paint the staircase walls and ceiling.

Wilberforce never met Whitefield, but he did meet another preacher with whom his uncle and aunt had grown close – John Newton.

Remembered now as the author of the great hymn "Amazing Grace," Newton was by any measure a fascinating man. His mother was religious and tried to raise him in the faith, but she died young. Newton's religious experience in the years that followed was tur-

The slave-trader-turned-minister, John Newton (1725–1807)

bulent. "I took up and laid aside a religious profession three or four times before I was sixteen years old," he remembered.

The son of an officer in the merchant navy, Newton went to sea at age eleven. Pressed into a king's ship and rated as a midshipman, he deserted, was flogged, and was demoted to the rank of a common seaman.

Newton left his ship and became the overseer of a slave depot on the Plantain Islands near Africa. He was then himself enslaved by a corrupt slave trader, and from 1746 to 1748 was forced to work on a lime plantation until rescued by his father.

These experiences brought him back to God but did not immediately make him the opponent of slavery he later became. He married his childhood sweetheart, soon after sailed as first mate on a slave ship, and in 1750 was placed in command of a slave ship. Newton ceased to be a slave ship captain for health reasons a few years later and felt a call to pastoral ministry. He was ordained a minister in the Church of England in 1764, and his first charge was the curacy of Olney in Buckinghamshire. Here he met and became the close friend of poet William Cowper.

Some have dismissed Newton as a hard man who exchanged the rigorous life of a slave-ship captain for an equally rigorous Calvinist faith. Though he worked hard, possessed a strong will and a faith of deep conviction, he was also capable of great tenderness. His love for his wife, Mary, verged on the idolatrous, and his letters to her were touching and beautiful. He had a deep and abiding love for the poor and wrote verse and hymns that compare favorably with Cowper's. All of these sides of his character were evident in his pastoral ministry. The story of his early life and struggles, related in his *Authentic Narrative*, was widely and avidly read during his lifetime.

William and Hannah Wilberforce appear to have met Newton in 1764 while he was in London awaiting ordination and compelled to stay in the city for several weeks. Speaking of this period, Newton remarked, "I have cause for wonder, praise, and humiliation, when I think what favor the Lord gave me in the eyes of his people, some of rank and eminence."

During the years Wilberforce stayed with his aunt and uncle, they visited Newton and his wife in Olney several times while on holiday. It was also Newton's practice to go regularly to the Wilberforce home to conduct what he called parlor preaching. In these sermons Newton would expound upon literary classics like *The Pilgrim's Progress* to the Wilberforces and their guests.

Newton endeared himself to all the Wilberforces, especially young William, who valued and loved him "as a parent when I was a child." Newton, himself childless, came in time to look upon the boy as a kind of son.

Another person to whom Wilberforce grew close during these years was his aunt Hannah's half brother, John Thornton. An evangelical like Hannah and William, he too had been converted through the ministry of Whitefield.

Widely known as one of the wealthiest men in Europe, Thornton adopted a "simple manner of life [which] left a large surplus out of his income, the chief part of which constantly flowed into the channel[s] of his beneficence."

Thornton utilized his considerable business operations as a means of furthering his philanthropies. He paid for Bibles to be printed and then used his company's ships to send them to their destinations. His friendship with Lord Dartmouth, another evangelical, prompted Thornton to help fund Eleazar Wheelock's mission to establish American-Indian schools in New Hampshire. He made generous contributions to this cause on many occasions. Dartmouth College historian L. B. Richardson has observed, "It is difficult to see how Wheelock could have carried the weight under which he labored in his later years without Thornton's help."

Thornton also made frequent, generous gifts of money to evangelical clergy. Perhaps the most significant instance of this kind of charity involved John Newton, who benefited immeasurably from Thornton's largesse. An examination of Newton's memoirs and letters presents a telling picture of their relationship. Both Newton and his wife, Mary, felt a deep sense of gratitude for Thornton's friendship and many kindnesses. Newton recalled that his wife "revered and regarded [Thornton] more than she did any person on earth, and she had reason. Few had nearer access to know and admire his character; and perhaps none were under greater, if equal, obligations to him than we."

Thornton valued Newton's pastoral and literary endeavors and supported him so that he could be free to pursue them. They met when Thornton, after reading Newton's *Authentic Narrative*, journeyed to the clergyman's residence at Olney and stated he was prepared to grant him an annual allowance of £200 – well over $50,000 in today's currency.

Thornton attached conditions to this stipend, requesting that Newton "be hospitable ... keep an open house [and] help the poor and needy." It was understood that should the occasion arise, Newton could prevail upon Thornton to increase his giving. Newton later estimated that throughout the course of his ministry at Olney he had received from Thornton upwards of £3,000 – nearly $800,000 today.

Thornton's philanthropies provide a window through which the character of his faith shines. One instance in particular affords a powerful example of this. While going through the day's correspondence one morning, Thornton opened a letter informing him of the wreck of a valuable ship and her cargo – a disaster that meant a considerable financial loss for him.

The news hit him hard and he became lost in serious reflection. After several moments, however, he resumed going through his correspondence, opening several letters requesting his aid or support. Remarkably, his mood began to lighten. He took out his checkbook and began to write out checks saying, "Let us try to do a little good while we still have the means to do so."

The picture of Thornton that emerges is one aptly summarized by his friend Thomas Scott. He was "plain, frugal, and self-denying in all matters of private expense; and yet liberal in supplying the want of others ... a combination ... which will seldom be found, except when true Christian principles possess and govern the heart."

John Thornton greatly influenced his young nephew. During Wilberforce's time with his aunt and uncle, Thornton once gave him a large gift of money. Wilberforce later said this incident assisted him in forming "what was undoubtedly a striking feature in his later character." The present, one "much exceeding the usual amount of a boy's possessions, intended to enforce the precept with which it was accompanied, that some should be given to the poor."

Thornton's celebrated liberality was honored by William Cowper in a fifty-line poem – part of which reads:

> *Thou hadst an industry in doing good,*
> *Restless as his, who toils and sweats for food....*
> *And if the genuine worth of gold depend*
> *On application to its noblest end,*
> *Thine had a value in the scales of Heaven,*
> *Surpassing all that mine or mint have given.*

A caring, thoughtful young man like Wilberforce could scarcely have failed to be influenced by John Thornton, uncle William, aunt Hannah, and John Newton. At a critical point during the troubled years of his childhood, Wilberforce was drawn into a web of relationships that provided him with much-needed love and support.

⌣

All of these relationships contributed to Wilberforce's embrace of the faith modeled for him by his mentors.

Evangelicals, however, whether within the Anglican fold or outside of it, were deeply suspect in the minds of many. Wilberforce's mother, now recovered, was among those who greatly distrusted "methodists," or, as she called them, "enthusiasts." They were regarded as people who had succumbed to "uncontrollable passions, a major social drawback in the upper classes of the day."

Elizabeth Wilberforce was not alone in her feelings. Many members of the clergy and upper classes feared that unless duly checked by reason, movements tainted by enthusiasm could cause disorder in church and society. She was anxious to get her son away from his aunt and uncle, Wilberforce said, "before I should imbibe what she considered was little less than poison, which indeed I at that time had done."

Many years later, Wilberforce said in a conversation with his son Robert: "It is impossible for you to have any idea of the hatred in which the methodists were then held.... I cannot better explain it to you than by saying that it is more like the account given in *Ivanhoe* of the persecutions against the Jews, than anything else I know."

Elizabeth traveled to London, got her son, and took him back to Hull. Hannah Wilberforce pleaded with her to change her mind, expressing sorrow that William be removed from the opportunities of a religious life. "You should not fear," replied Elizabeth caustically, "if it be a work of grace, you know it cannot fail."

The concerns of his mother were not the only issues that Wilberforce had to face. Alderman Wilberforce was also set against methodist teachings. He issued a severe ultimatum: "If Billy turns methodist he shall not have a sixpence of mine."

For Wilberforce, the pain of separation from his aunt and uncle was compounded by the fact that they were at odds with his mother and his grandfather. This was a trying situation for an adult, let alone a child of twelve.

He was filled with regret. The two years he had spent with William and Hannah had stirred parental sentiments within them, and he felt "the affection of a son" for them. "I deeply felt the parting," he said years later. "Indeed, I was almost heart-broken at the separation." Soon after his return home, he wrote to his uncle, "I can never forget you, as long as I live."

Once Elizabeth got her son safely back home in Hull, she sought to scrub his soul clean of methodism. However, it proved surprisingly tenacious.

"My religious impressions," Wilberforce remembered,

> continued for some time after my return to Hull, but no pains were spared ... to stifle them.... [N]o pious parent ever laboured more to impress a beloved child with sentiments of religion than [was done] to give me a taste for the world and its diversions.... At first all this was very distasteful to me, but by degrees I acquired a relish for it, and so the good seed

was gradually smothered, and I became as thoughtless as any amongst them.

Wilberforce said the years that followed were "a long period of what [Shakespeare] has so emphatically styled 'shapeless idleness'; the most valuable years of life wasted, and opportunities lost, which can never be recovered."

Soon after his return home he was enrolled in the grammar school of Pocklington under the supervision of the Reverend Kingsman Baskett, a man who had been a Fellow of St. John's College, Cambridge. Baskett was said to have been a man of easy, polished manners and an elegant, though not profound scholar.

During this stage of his education Wilberforce began to demonstrate that he too, like his grandfather and mother, had an active mind. He "greatly excelled all the other boys in his compositions," recalled the Reverend T. T. Walmsley, a former classmate, "though he seldom began them till the eleventh hour." For his own amusement Wilberforce committed English poetry to memory, and he went up to the university "a very fair scholar." James Beattie's long poem *The Minstrel* was at this time his favorite, and he learned it by heart during his morning walks.

In deference to his social station Wilberforce was given preferential treatment at Pocklington. He became fond of Rev. Baskett, despite being forced to attend Pocklington under circumstances he disliked. Some years later, in August 1795, he dined with Baskett and wrote that he was "pleased to see old scenes."

Wilberforce's natural gifts now began to make an impression on others. His agreeable nature and talent for singing made him a popular guest in the homes of the local gentry. He demonstrated a gift for writing quality compositions, though his early essays continued to reflect the methodist influence of his aunt and uncle.

During this time Wilberforce also spent a period of undetermined length under the guardianship of Joseph Sykes, who had several children and was the head of one of Hull's leading families.

That the Sykeses were celebrated among the wealthy set of Hull was underscored by their ownership of opulent homes, called "great houses." Lastly, perhaps most importantly, the Sykeses were not methodists.

Wilberforce developed a strong bond with the Sykes children, spending many holidays with the family and coming to think of them as his brothers and sisters. He grew especially close to their daughter Marianne, who when she grew up, married Wilberforce's great friend and cousin, Henry Thornton.

Wilberforce's stay with the Sykeses, like that with William and Hannah Wilberforce, indicates his great need for affection and a desire to express affection in return. The depth of his affection is clear in that he did not in the space of a few months get over the methodism he had learned from his aunt and uncle.

Wilberforce tried to cope with things as best as he could. He had been forcibly separated from his aunt and uncle and had been informed that all the religious ideas he had adopted were scandalous and hated. He found himself at odds with his mother and his grandfather concerning his faith. Friends of the family considered him "a little enthusiast." In many ways it must have been a deeply lonely and sad time.

It was, in all probability, a difficult time for Wilberforce's mother as well. She was not an irreligious woman. Nevertheless, she would not take her son even to highly formal Church of England services for fear it would stoke his methodism.

In retrospect, this shows how deeply seeds sown by William and Hannah Wilberforce had taken root in their nephew's heart. Elizabeth did love her son – he knew that, especially upon reflection as an adult. And he loved her, as deeply resentful as he may have been at times over what he had experienced during his teenage years.

What fed into the resentment was that his mother's love was manifested for the most part, if not completely, in aspirations for his future and her hopes to further the family dynasty. She did do things with him that he eventually came to enjoy, and perhaps appreciated, but the love his mother had for him was obscured by all these other things. She loved her son, but it was not a warm, embracing love; it was more a love at a distance. It was not the kind of love John Newton and Hannah Wilberforce would have demonstrated. They loved him for who he was. There was always a part of his mother's love that was focused only on the end product.

Despite his mother's disapproval, Wilberforce continued to correspond with his uncle William and aunt Hannah after she had removed him from their care. He also wrote letters to his friend Thomas Thompson of Hull, as described later by the Reverend John Scott.

> I have been favoured with the sight of several letters written by [Mr. Wilberforce at this time] which, amidst all the vivacity and playfulness belonging to his years and his character, discover a serious and feeling sense of religion, and even a distinct insight into the leading doctrines of Christianity. He alludes repeatedly to the preaching of [Joseph] Milner ... which he says he should rejoice again to attend ... but on the whole [he] is well content with all that may befall him, believing that it would work for his good.

By August 1772, two years after his mother had brought him back to Hull, Wilberforce was still in conflict with her. He was writing letters to his uncle and aunt, and he didn't stop doing so until 1774.

Perhaps she grudgingly accepted this, but one gets the picture of Wilberforce making excuses, going up into his room, and furtively writing letters. His letters to his aunt and uncle reveal a sincere and surprisingly mature faith, as well as the pain he felt at being separated from them. The postscript of one letter reveals how determined he was to maintain this correspondence: "I cannot write more because it is seen where the letter is to."

He told his aunt, "One of the greatest misfortunes I had whilst at Hull, was not being able to hear the blessed word of God, as my mama would not let me go to high church on a Sunday afternoon, but the Lord was everyday granting me some petition, and I trust I can say that I increased in the knowledge of God and Christ Jesus whom he sent, whom to know is life eternal."

Wilberforce later described the environment – the social diversions, the whirlwind of activities, and the trappings of wealth – that gradually diverted his attention from religious interests. "Hull was then one of the gayest places out of London. The theatre, balls, large supper and card parties, were the delight of the principal merchants and their families. They dined at two, and met at each other's houses for supper at six. Cards followed. I, being the son of one of the principal merchants of the place was invited to almost every party, and was made a great deal of."

In time the essays Wilberforce was writing at Pocklington began to shift away from his methodist leanings to a more conventional style, one devoid of the ardent faith he had once shown. Sometime in 1774, when he was fifteen, Wilberforce was asked to write an essay on the subject of patience. It reveals a decided gift for prose composition, yet it seems either he had resigned himself to parroting back the required style his instructor favored or that his faith had withered away like a plant deprived of water, good soil, and sunlight.

Where his essays had formerly voiced biblical principles, the essay on patience showed a stiff upper lip absent in his previous writings. He wrote,

> We must learn to bear whatever befalls us, so as on the one hand, not to be too much elevated or overjoyed by the smiles of prosperity, nor on the other too much depressed or cast down by the frowns of adversity.
>
> The stings of fortune, how severe soever they may seem to us, it is most likely we deserve; for we ought to learn to bear with patience, what we cannot possibly avoid. Life is a very

uncertain thing at best, therefore we ought not to rely upon any good fortune, since perhaps this moment we may enjoy the greatest worldly happiness; the next be plunged into the deepest abyss of unutterable misery.

Wilberforce, young as he was, had become rather fatalistic, reacting to all the loss in his life. The loss of faith, the loss of William and Hannah, the loss of Thornton, the loss of Newton, the loss of his father. What sounds like a fairly resigned, restrained essay is actually much more personal. It speaks to a greater source of hurt within him. He had experienced many upheavals. Important connections had been broken. The great joys and satisfaction that he had with Hannah and William – these joys were no more. His prose is indicative of a young man who has become sadly resigned to the way things have turned out.

It appears that Wilberforce's lapse from methodism took place in 1774. He wrote to his aunt for the last time on May 19 of that year. His essay on patience, though undated, was most likely written in the autumn of 1774. By the time he entered St. John's College, Cambridge, in 1776, this transformation had been complete for some time. He was now, as he later said, "as thoughtless as the rest of them."

CHAPTER 2

PRELUDE TO THE TASK

O gentlemen! the time of life is short;
To spend that shortness basely were too long.

WILLIAM SHAKESPEARE

Wilberforce's family decided he would attend St. John's College, Cambridge, because of its ties to the Pocklington School. The master of Pocklington, Rev. Baskett, had formerly been a Fellow there. Elizabeth Wilberforce, in placing her son at Pocklington, had selected what was then an expensive school – but then she felt it was a fit training ground for her son. Rev. Baskett was not a profound scholar, but he was safe, cultured, and the kind of person who could prepare her son for his entry into society. If St. John's was good enough for Rev. Baskett, it was good enough for William.

By 1776 Wilberforce had changed markedly from the boy he had been five years before, when he left the care of his uncle William and aunt Hannah. As one biographer has observed:

He had grown up to be a very charming young man. He was small, [a] little over five feet ... and so slight that he inspired such whimsical descriptions as "all Soul and no body." None of his features were handsome, but they had a liveliness which was attractive. His movements were very fast and he was seldom still. His conversation followed the same pattern. He would pick up an idea very quickly, play with it, and turn to another only to abandon it in its turn.

All this was done with a speed and pleasure which entranced his listeners. He took an obvious and innocent joy in meeting people, in talking to them and exchanging ideas.... Pocklington, while fatal to his Methodism, had put a polish on his manners.

His mind was so quick that his contemporaries found it difficult to gauge his intellectual powers. He was facile and fast to grasp a point but too interested in other things to worry at it for long. He could keep up a reasonable standard with little effort; it was to be many years before it could be seen what he might achieve when he immersed himself in a subject.... All methodist seriousness forgotten, he abandoned himself to a life of pleasure for which his wealth, gaiety and charm made him perfectly equipped.

The young William Wilberforce

The first night that Wilberforce spent at Cambridge he had supper with his tutor, William Arnald, who introduced him to two undergraduates Wilberforce later described as "two of the most gambling, vicious characters, perhaps, in all England." By the time he went up to Cambridge, in October 1776, he could already play cards well. But he may well have picked up some skills from these early friends. When he later played faro in the great gaming clubs of London, he won a good deal of the time.

Wilberforce's tutor, Arnald, had enjoyed something of a meteoric rise in his early academic career. He may have been a more profound scholar than Rev. Baskett, but he was not a very moral person. He made no attempt to guide Wilberforce. Far from it. He introduced Wilberforce to his gambling friends, he didn't encourage good study habits, and he seemed to relish the academic life only for its social aspects. Arnald may once have been committed to scholarship, but it doesn't appear that commitment held once he achieved the level of success where he found his comfort. Tragically, in 1782, not long after Arnald was appointed a tutor in natural science to the Prince of Wales, he went insane.

Wilberforce's academic career did not begin auspiciously. Within a short time of his arrival at St. John's it became clear that he was devoting a significant amount of time to enjoying himself and precious little to his studies. After a while, however, he forsook the company of the young men Arnald had introduced to him. They were clearly beyond his pale, and the breaking of his friendship with them meant, in all likelihood, that he would keep more of his money anyway. He could also receive the broader acquaintance with ideas and culture that his mother and grandfather wished him to obtain.

Wilberforce still spent much of his time playing cards, singing, drinking, attending music performances, and hosting dinners for other students in his room. He was, however, more irresponsible than immoral – and typical enough for his day. His priorities weren't set, and he was attempting to find his way. Insofar as he knew where he was headed, his more rakish gambling friends weren't a part of the picture. Politics weren't yet on his horizon.

For all his indolence, Wilberforce's friendliness, animation, and hospitality made him a popular man among his classmates. A fellow student, Thomas Gisborne, remembered that during their undergraduate days Wilberforce had few peers when it came to providing entertainment. Singing, dancing, and going to pubs were the kind of activities in which he indulged, since he did so often just after leaving Cambridge, and it is unlikely he would have developed wholly new habits upon entering political life in 1780.

Early in his political life Wilberforce was fond of attending performances of the ancient music, going to the opera, attending balls, plays, and horse races. Within a few years, he would often visit the pleasure gardens of Vauxhall or the rotunda at Ranelagh – "the enchanted palace of a genie," novelist Tobias Smollett had written, "crowded with the great, the rich, the happy and the fair." Wilberforce played cards and gambled – primarily for drinking and chat. He was never a compulsive gamester and later abandoned hard play at high stakes after a night when he won a large sum and noticed the annoyance of the losers, who, as those yet to inherit their fortunes or as younger sons, could not really afford to play.

An incident related by George Selwyn – the well-known wit and member of the infamous Hellfire Club – describes what Wilberforce was like when out on the town. One night in the early 1780s Selwyn was leaving the House of Commons when he passed a roomful of young men "who made me, from their life and spirit, wish for one night to be twenty. There was a table full of them drinking – young Pitt, Lord Euston, Barkley, North, etc. etc. staging and laughing.... Some of them sang very good catches: one Wilberforce, a Member of Parliament sang the best."

Wilberforce was adept at turning a bon mot. He had a gift for improvisation, and one of the forms it took was his ability to compose puns, or doggerel poetry. One night Wilberforce, his cousin

Bob Smith, and several other bachelors were dining together. Someone began to sing the praise of a pretty girl, Barbara St. John, the unmarried sister of Lord St. John of Bletso, one of Wilberforce's college friends. Without missing a beat, Wilberforce spun a doggerel ending in an outrageous pun:

> *And if you continue to torture poor us*
> *You are no longer Barbara but barbarous.*

The host of the evening, a bachelor, stood and declared: "That is the mother of my children." Many years later, Wilberforce's son Samuel – who later served as chaplain to Prince Albert and bishop of Oxford – showed he had inherited his father's gift for poetic improvisation when he spun the following poem on the spur of the moment:

> *If I were a cassowary*
> *On the plains of Timbuctoo,*
> *I would eat a missionary,*
> *Cassock, band, and hymn-book too.*

Another story concerning Wilberforce's life at this time has come down from Thomas Babington Macaulay. Macaulay's journal entry for May 16, 1850 (several years after Wilberforce's death), records a conversation when Samuel Wilberforce was one of six guests at breakfast at Macaulay's London house: "I was surprised at the Bishop's telling us that his father when young used to drink tea every evening in a brothel – 'Not,' said his lordship, 'from any licentious purpose – But it was the mode among young men.' I should have kept the secret from my son, if I had been Wilberforce senior, and from the public if I had been Wilberforce junior."

Wilberforce was also fond of throwing parties. Thomas Gisborne remembered that Wilberforce's room swarmed with idle students from the time he arose, which was usually very late, until he went to bed – which was also very late.

One of the featured attractions of Wilberforce's room was the table he set, Gisborne recalled: "There was always a great Yorkshire pie in his rooms, and all were welcome to partake of it. My rooms and his were back to back, and often when I was raking out my fire at ten o'clock, I heard his melodious voice calling aloud to me to come and sit with him before I went to bed. It was a dangerous thing to do, for his amusing conversation was sure to keep me up so late, that I was behind-hand the next morning."

Wilberforce had access to money through his mother, who wanted him to get ahead socially. His parties were attended by friends grateful for free meals, flowing wine, and sparkling conversation. He provided all in abundance. His reputation as someone always up for a good time grew, and he made it a point never to disappoint anyone expecting fun.

Other members of Wilberforce's set included William Cookson, uncle of the poet William Wordsworth; Gerard Edwards, a man who later had a hand in Wilberforce's taking up the abolition of the slave trade; Charles Long, later a member of Parliament along with Wilberforce; and Edward Christian, brother of Fletcher Christian, the leader of the mutiny on the *Bounty*. Wilberforce was continuing to connect with people who would become well known (or who were already well known) – a constantly recurring theme throughout his life, given links already established with George Whitefield, John Newton, and John Thornton.

Though he often neglected his studies, Wilberforce had a gift for classical languages and literature. He applied himself to these studies – not from any real sense of industry – but rather from a "natural love of classical learning, and [the knowledge] that it was necessary for a man who was to be publicly examined to prevent his being disgraced." In short, he was afraid of looking silly in front of others when oral exams were given.

Still, Wilberforce's tutor, Arnald, did nothing to discourage his student from squandering his time. "[My] tutor, who ought to have repressed this disposition," Wilberforce recalled, "if not by his authority, at least by his advice, rather encouraged it: he never urged me to attend lectures and I never did."

In 1822 Wilberforce remonstrated with the Reverend Dr. Frewen, an old friend who had been an instructor at Cambridge during Wilberforce's years there. "I can never review," he told Frewen, "but with humiliation and shame, the course I ran at college, and during the three or four first years of my parliamentary life which immediately succeeded it." This was a note of remorse sounded again and again throughout Wilberforce's later writings. Yet he did not consider himself wholly to blame. As he explained:

> It is only fair to state, that at least as much pains had been taken by my nearest relatives and guardians to make me dissipated and vain – and, though they did not mean it, vicious also – as are commonly used to counteract these dispositions.... I add that even at college most of those very men who ought to have used both authority and influence (and of the latter at least I was susceptible) to root out these propensities, and to implant better – rather confirmed than abated them.

Why hadn't any of his friends, instructors, or tutors taken him aside and told him he was on a dangerous path? He put this question to Frewen:

> Would not the golden rule have prompted you to use towards me the language of a friend, if not of a father? (My natural father I lost when eight years old, and my grandfather and uncle soon after I went to Cambridge.) Ought you not to have urged me to ... consider what must be the issue of the course of life I was pursuing, and of the choice I was making of associates and friends?

Wilberforce came next to the heart of the matter, wondering what he would have been like had he not eventually forsaken the dangerous path he had been on.

Though while my youthful spirits should remain I might continue an entertaining companion, [why did you not tell me] that I should ere long bitterly lament that I had suffered the years and circumstances ... for acquiring useful knowledge ... for cultivating and strengthening the intellectual powers, to pass away wholly unimproved?

Ought you not to have reminded me of the great account I had to render of the talents committed to my stewardship, and [of] all the uncommon blessings which had been lavished on me ... (I allude ... to my having a handsome fortune, my being born in the middle rank of life, and my having, I hope, a fair proportion of natural talent.) ...

You did not spend night after night at cards with me, but did you suggest to me the fate of the unprofitable servant? All this went on, with grief and shame I say it, till by degrees I came to myself; for to no one can the phrase be more justly applicable. This began in the summer and autumn of 1785.

Wilberforce's neglect of his studies bothered him more than anything else about his years at Cambridge. "I was a good [classicist]," he later recalled, "and acquitted myself well in college examinations; but mathematics, which my mind greatly needed, I almost entirely neglected.... Whilst my companions were reading hard and attending lectures ... [my] tutors would often say within my hearing that '*they* were mere saps, but that I did all by talent.' This was poison to a mind constituted like mine."

Wilberforce had changed from a boy who had largely been a sensitive, thoughtful youth. On his own for the first time, he was carving out a life for himself among young men of his own age and trying things for the first time. Instead of getting or seeking good advice and counsel, he was using his wealth to grease the skids toward social prominence. There was a real possibility of his taking the wrong fork in the road and living a spendthrift life.

One aspect of Wilberforce's years at Cambridge that he thoroughly enjoyed – and for which he retained a love throughout his life – was walking and riding tours through the countryside, particularly England's celebrated Lake District. His love of the country probably developed while he was staying with his aunt and uncle, because their Wimbledon home was in what was then a beautiful rural setting. They took him for long carriage rides through places that would catch the eye. They traveled to hear John Newton preach in Olney, a region surrounded by pastoral scenes that had for years enchanted and inspired the poet William Cowper.

In time Cowper became Wilberforce's favorite poet, and Wilberforce would later take special pains to retrace Cowper's steps and visit places that had captivated him. Visits to John Thornton in the then idyllic village of Clapham, with its rolling common, fed his growing love of nature. When, starting in his Cambridge years, he was able to command his own time, he indulged this love. For the rest of his life, whenever he could, he went away into the country,

Wilberforce's favorite poet, William Cowper (1731–1800)

The village of Clapham, where Wilberforce lived from 1792 to 1808

taking his family or going by himself. He rented homes or secured lodgings for long periods of time. Rest, renewal, and exercise amid natural beauty – all of these were a tonic to him.

This was a little-known facet of Wilberforce's personality while at Cambridge. Known as someone who was very gifted socially, who hosted parties, and was constantly seeking entertaining company, Wilberforce sometimes needed to escape the social pressures. The sensitive side of his nature had never wholly deserted him. He longed for and needed time periodically to get away and reflect.

Wilberforce was never happier than when traversing hills, mountains, valleys, or walking along sea cliffs and beaches. He later told his friend Lady Olivia Sparrow: "It is not mere imagination that ... a country of lakes and rocks and mountains ... appears to call forth all the affections into augmented animation.... When I was a very young man ... I was always in danger of falling in love when I was an inhabitant of romantic countries."

Wilberforce was a vigorous tourist. A diary he kept during a tour of the Lake District in the summer of 1779 reveals that, despite recurring health problems (occasionally troublesome eyesight and digestive ailments), he was quite capable of strenuous physical activity. Many days were spent mountaineering or riding for long distances (including a remarkable one-day ride of forty-three miles).

Toward the end of his college days, especially during the winter of 1779–80, Wilberforce also developed an ardent interest in politics. His grandfather, Alderman Wilberforce, supplied a precedent of interest and involvement – as did his cousin Abel Smith – a member of Parliament.

These precedents were important. Yet it appears to have been an acquaintance formed with William Pitt, son of the Earl of Chatham, that was the key to Wilberforce's decision to enter political life.

Chatham, known as "the Great Commoner," had spoken out for many years against the disastrous war with America. Indeed, the younger Pitt had carried his father out of the House of Commons when his father collapsed during his last speech condemning the war. The war, its politics, and Chatham's role opposing it were part of the dominant scene of politics in England at this time. In meeting Pitt, Wilberforce had secured an entrée into a new and exciting life. Pitt was being groomed for greatness, and he moved in the highest echelons of British society. Through him, Wilberforce was too.

It is not known just how Wilberforce and Pitt first met. As an old man, Wilberforce told his young friend John Harford: "I was acquainted with Mr. Pitt at Cambridge, but we were not at that time [close]. He, indeed, lived in a higher set than myself; but in the winter after we had each left college I often met him in the gallery of the House of Commons, which we were both fond of attending." Wilberforce and Pitt soon discovered they had much in common.

William Pitt (1759–1806), the youngest Prime Minister in British history

The natural choice for his career would have been to enter the family business as a merchant. But he clearly recognized this was not for him. He had nothing of a meticulous, disciplined, or focused nature – qualities a merchant needed to be successful. He had not applied himself to mathematics while in college. Moreover, his cousin Abel Smith (son of the member of Parliament) had ably managed the family business while he was at Cambridge. Wilberforce saw no reason to change what was for him a very convenient arrangement. He was receiving a steady and growing income and had to take no trouble to get it. He had the funds to make a run for political office.

Wilberforce had been left, by the death of Alderman Wilberforce and his uncle William, "the master of an independent fortune." He also had Lauriston House (the Wimbledon home of his aunt and uncle) at his disposal. The size of his fortune was large enough for him to become a "sleeping partner" in the family firm. He could become the kind of person his mother was – a person of standing – and he knew now that he wished to make a name for himself.

Politics was far more interesting than the family business and was a logical career choice for someone with Wilberforce's personality, gifts, and wealth. For several years now he had been forming close friendships and spending long nights with young men who had already settled upon careers in politics. He had begun to sense that he belonged in such a setting. He enjoyed going to the House of Commons, sitting in the Visitor's (or Stranger's) Gallery, and listening with fascination to the great debates on the American War. He was impressed by the spectacle of seeing great men like Lord North, Charles Fox, and Edmund Burke debate issues related to the war and other important matters of the day.

He began to desire a place in their company.

Besides wealth, he had many natural talents that lent themselves to political life. He had quick intelligence, charm, and eloquence as a speaker. He had a growing list of powerful connections – many of them friends who could guide him. That he had made so many friends was a hopeful sign indeed that, even as he learned to move easily in the highest circles in his hometown, he was becoming more and more adept at moving in the highest social circles London boasted.

Wilberforce had overcome many difficult obstacles associated with his early years, and his confidence in his abilities was growing. When he compared himself to other friends set on careers in politics, he had as much reason to think that he could do as well as they. If he, and they, were successful in winning election to Parliament, they could go on together. It was a very pleasant prospect.

Pitt, meanwhile, like his father, was vehemently opposed to the war with America. As Wilberforce's friendship with Pitt deepened, his opposition to the war did as well. Economically, it had hit Britain hard, perhaps even hurting the trade in which the Wilberforce family engaged. A general worsening of economic conditions would not have been lost on a merchant's son, however uninterested he might have been in taking up the family business. If he entered politics, Wilberforce could stand alongside Pitt and do what he could to extricate Britain from the American conflict. To the extent that he might have shared such thoughts with Pitt, he would have received encouragement. He very likely did, because he and Pitt grew increasingly close throughout the winter of 1779–80.

Determined to make a run for Parliament, Wilberforce now began an active canvass of the voters of Hull, his hometown. In later years, he vividly recalled this first campaign, which showed that at this time politics was not a calling for the faint of heart.

"When I first canvassed the town," he remembered, "there lived at Hull a fine athletic fellow ... a butcher, named ... Johnny Bell. I rather shrunk from shaking hands with him, saying to one of my staunch supporters, that I thought it going rather too low for votes. 'O sir,' was his reply, 'he is a fine fellow if you come to bruising.'" Wilberforce shook his hand.

One day someone threw a rock at Wilberforce as he campaigned. It missed him, but the day following the election, Bell came to Wilberforce privately and said, "I have found out who threw the stone at you, and I'll kill him to-night." The threat was seriously intended, Wilberforce recalled, "and I was forced to repress his zeal by suggesting, that it would be too severe a punishment for what had proved, after all, a harmless attempt: 'you must only frighten him.'"

After a successful canvass in Hull, Wilberforce traveled to London, where about three hundred Hull freemen resided in the vicinity of the river Thames. There they pursued business interests much like those of Wilberforce's family. Hull was one of England's most important ports, and men from Hull conducted business in London, Britain's major port. They would then return home when elections were held. Wilberforce entertained them at suppers in the neighborhood pubs of Wapping, making speeches that helped him gain confidence in public speaking.

Within days of Wilberforce's twenty-first birthday the Hull election was held. He received nearly every vote.

His wealth was a major contribution to his triumph at the polls. Then, as now, large financial reserves were indispensable to achieving political victory. In Wilberforce's day, eligible voters expected to be rewarded for their support. The formula for electoral success was essentially, "Line their pockets, and their hearts and minds will follow."

English parliamentary elections at this time were marked by corruption. Nomination boroughs and seats were bought and sold like articles of commerce or leased like farms. In 1768 Benjamin Franklin, who was in England, wrote to a friend, "Four thousand pounds is now the market price for a borough. In short, this whole venal nation is now at market, will be sold for about two millions, and might be bought out of the hands of the present bidder if he were offered half a million more by the very devil himself." In short, bribery was the rule of the day. It was encouraged by the crown, the ministry, the nobility, and landholders.

In the early nineteenth century, money was often piled upon the table of a committee room to which electors were conducted, that they might count out their bribe, and say afterward nobody had paid them anything. Another common practice was called *cooping*. One party would lay hold of a certain freeman or freeholder loyal to another party and carry him off to a pub or tavern in the country. There they would keep, or coop him in pubs and other amusements until they could triumphantly take him to the polling booth – after the close of the poll.

Wilberforce knew of such practices, though he did not employ all of them. His charm and purse, supplemented by an ox roast for the whole town on his twenty-first birthday, enabled him to beat both his opponents. When all was said and done, he had spent £9,000 (nearly $2.4 million in today's currency).

Of course, qualities other than wealth and charm made Wilberforce an attractive political candidate – there was the prestige afforded by his family connections. Nonetheless, he essentially paid for the privilege of joining the House of Commons.

William Pitt came into Parliament in November, a few months after Wilberforce, and their friendship quickly grew close. They spent a great deal of time together in a club that was chiefly composed of well-born young men who had left college about the same time and who held the same political opinions.

This group included Richard "Pepper" Arden (later Lord Alvanley), Henry Bankes, Lord Chatham (Pitt's elder brother), Edward Eliot, Lord Euston, William (later Lord) Grenville, and John Pratt (later Lord Camden). Each of these men made his mark in British political life.

Given this, it is not difficult to understand why Wilberforce said of himself at this time: "Emulation, and a desire of distinction, were my governing motives; [I was] ardent after the applause of my fellow-creatures." Many of these men were sons of privilege, whose families were well-established dynasties. Wilberforce had a sizable fortune, but modest hereditary standing – and he was starting much further back in the pack. He had much to do to catch up and keep up. He had truly become the ambitious grandson of Alderman Wilberforce.

Lord Grenville later became prime minister. Lord Camden served in many prestigious posts: a member of the Admiralty and Treasury Boards, Lord Lieutenant of Ireland, secretary of state for war and the colonies. Lord Alvanley served as solicitor-general. Edward Eliot was a member of the Treasury Board. Lord Euston later became Pitt's fellow parliamentary colleague for Cambridge University. Henry Bankes was a member of Parliament for most of his life. Lord Chatham served as First Lord of the Admiralty.

Pitt himself was a natural leader for this group. He would not have imposed himself on the others as such, but his gifts, personality, and views would have been easy to get behind. Wilberforce always admired Pitt's intellect, his capacity for logical argument, and his eloquence – which was reinforced by an ability to make apt allusions to literature and poetry. Pitt was also distinguished by his wit, integrity, and political independence.

Wilberforce did not have Pitt's highly disciplined intellect or his logician's gift for argument during speeches, but he was like Pitt in nearly every other respect.

This explains why the two got on so well together and why their respect was mutual. Pitt once said, "Of all the men I ever knew, Wilberforce has the greatest natural eloquence." Pitt was more of a logician in argument, but Wilberforce could infuse his thoughts with a passion that often swayed the House of Commons. From the first it was also true that Wilberforce, like Pitt, was an independent man. Like Pitt he had entered Parliament as an opponent of the war with America and of Lord North's administration.

Wilberforce had settled upon politics as a calling later than Pitt. But he proved himself a good student and in Pitt (who had been trained for a political career by the Earl of Chatham all his life) he had the best of guides and friends. From his very first speech, Pitt had revealed himself his father's son – speaking with authority and erudition. He did not court public applause, but he spoke in a manner calculated to shape public and political opinion.

In contrast, Wilberforce got up to speed as a parliamentary speaker gradually. Pitt already knew how the Commons functioned and what it required in a speaker. Wilberforce spoke little in the first months he was there but listened a great deal. He knew he could speak well. Watching Pitt and his other more established colleagues, he was learning how to speak effectively.

"Attend to business," Wilberforce later said, "and do not seek occasions of display; if you have a turn for speaking, the proper time will come. Let speaking take care of itself. I never go out of the way to speak, but make myself acquainted with the business, and then if the debate passes my door I step out and join it."

As much as Wilberforce was in some ways the learner and Pitt seemingly a seasoned veteran of politics, Wilberforce was from the very start determined to be independent, to vote and to speak as his conscience dictated. Not even to friendship with Pitt would he sacrifice his independence. "I well remember," he said, "the pain I felt in being obliged to vote against Pitt, the second time he spoke in Parliament."

Such demonstrations of independence did no harm whatsoever to their friendship. Mutual respect grew. Wilberforce, Pitt, and their friends generally dined together when the House of Commons was in session, and most often they had supper together.

One night, they spent "an evening in memory of Shakespeare" at the Boar's Head tavern in East Cheap. "Many professed wits were present," Wilberforce recalled, "but Pitt was the most amusing of the party, and the readiest and most apt in the required allusions." Henry Bankes often entertained them at his house in London, and Wilberforce received them at his villa in Wimbledon. Both Wilberforce and Bankes were already in possession of their fortunes. The rest were chiefly younger sons, or eldest sons who had yet to inherit theirs.

Pitt, who delighted in the country air, shared lodgings with Wilberforce for months after the House of Commons was in recess. Both men enjoyed getting away to spend time at Lauriston House, Wilberforce's country home in Wimbledon. "Hundreds of times," Wilberforce recalled, "I roused him out of bed in the morning and conversed with him." In fact "I was, at this time, the depository of [Pitt's] most confidential thoughts."

⌒

Wilberforce's landed property in Yorkshire contained no country mansion, and he was left at liberty to choose his place of residence when released from parliamentary attendance. His passion for the beauties of scenery and the retirement of the country was unabated. For seven years he rented a handsome cottage, Ray-rigg, on the banks of Lake Windermere. He went there in this and succeeding summers as soon as the parliamentary recess commenced, with a large assortment of books – classics, legal statutes, and history.

His studious intentions were frustrated, however. His friend St. Andrew St. John "was with me for months together during this summer," he recalled. "Occasionally, too, my mother and my sister, and different college friends joined our party. Boating, riding, and continual parties at my own house, and Sir Michael le Fleming's, fully occupied my time until I returned to London in the following autumn." Le Fleming was known as the "brilliant baronet" – James Boswell described his remarkable social and literary gifts in *The Life of Samuel Johnson*.

Wilberforce took part more often in general business during the next parliamentary session. He assisted in the general onslaught on Lord North's policy as to the war with America.

On February 22, 1782, he gave a speech against Lord North's administration that was greatly praised. Wilberforce "declared that while the present ministry existed, there were no prospects of either peace or happiness" to Britain. This sounded a note in concert with Pitt, who believed that economic and "collateral difficulties" had been a source of great discontent and political unrest among Britons, putting "the people out of temper little by little." At last it had "provoked them to 'turn their eyes inward upon themselves.'"

Wilberforce's belief that "there were no prospects of either peace or happiness" led him to censure North and his ministers for "their ... conduct, respecting the American War.... Their career hitherto," he said, "had rather resembled the career of furious madmen more than the vigorous and prudent exertions of able statesmen."

Wilberforce's use of the phrase "furious madmen" shows that he was not above the use of invective. He was strongly opposed to the war with America, but he did not really think that North was the personification of evil. Less than a year before, Wilberforce had written of North to his friend B. B. Thompson of Hull:

> The papers will have informed you how Mr. William Pitt, second son of the late Lord Chatham, has distinguished himself; he comes out as his father did a ready-made orator, and I doubt not but that I shall one day or other see him the first man in the country. His famous speech, however, delivered the other night, did not convince me, and I [voted] with [Lord North], the old fat fellow – by the way he grows every day fatter, so where he will end I know not.

Wilberforce, then, had once sided with North and not Pitt. Wilberforce certainly opposed North's policy on the war, but his use of invective stemmed not from the belief that North was mad, but from a wish to discredit an administration he did not support. Wilberforce was starting to show that he could devastate opponents with his tongue – even more experienced and powerful politicians like North.

Wilberforce had a gift for mimicry and satire. He could also captivate listeners like the Prince of Wales when he sang, and the same voice that garnered admiration could also imitate to perfection North's rhetorical style. He may well have mocked and mimicked North in speeches – for he did so often enough outside the Commons as to receive a stern rebuke from the elderly former Lord Chancellor, Lord Camden, for doing so.

Wilberforce's biographer sons wrote that their father "could often set the table in a roar" by his perfect imitation of North. "When invited by my friends to witness my powers of imitation," Wilberforce recalled, "[Lord Camden] at once refused, saying slightingly for me to hear it, 'It is but a vulgar accomplishment.'"

"Yes, but it is not imitating the mere manner; Wilberforce says the very thing Lord North would say."

"Oh," was his reply, "every one does that."

Wilberforce was chastened, surprisingly, for a young politician rather full of himself. Thereafter he often stole away from merriment and light amusements to discuss politics, men, and affairs with the veteran statesman – and the two in time grew close.

⌐

Wilberforce concluded his February 22 speech by saying that he dreaded any plans of North's administration "to pursue the ruinous war in the former cruel, bloody, impracticable manner." Here he was on firmer ground, where there was more general agreement. Those opposed to the war were all virtually in agreement that it was ruinous, cruel, and impracticable, particularly the first and last. Given this, it is easy to understand why – a little more than a year later – Wilberforce would be greeted heartily by Benjamin Franklin as "a rising member of the English parliament, who had opposed the war with America."

After several close divisions in Parliament, the onslaught on North's administration in which Wilberforce had taken part led to North's resignation and the formation of the Rockingham administration on March 20, 1782. Wilberforce's speech on February 22 was so well regarded that the new administration tried to win his support. He was invited, along with Pitt and several others, to attend a meeting with Charles Fox and Lord Shelburne, who were forming a new administration under Lord Rockingham. Alderman Wilberforce's grandson was going places, and his star was clearly on the rise.

Wilberforce's circle of friends now included many members of the Rockingham ministry, and he attended dinners hosted by Charles Fox, the foreign secretary. "In 1782," he recalled, "I first knew Fox well; ... he [gave] us dinners twice or thrice [and was] very pleasant and unaffected."

At the same time Wilberforce was courted by other members of the new administration, among them the secretary of state for the Home Office, Thomas Townshend. Those in the know now whispered that Wilberforce was in line for a junior government post or a peerage.

Rockingham himself treated Wilberforce with great civility, and the two visited together in Rockingham's home. So prevalent at this time was the idea that Wilberforce was to be included in the new ministry and raised to a peerage, that he received various applications for the supply of his robes (the attire worn by a peer) upon that occasion.

Lord Rockingham died in July 1782, however, and Wilberforce's hopes for office died as well. King George III offered the premiership to Lord Shelburne. Fox, who had fallen out with Shelburne, resigned with most of his group. Pitt became chancellor of the exchequer and the leader of the House of Commons.

In all likelihood Pitt could have helped him if Wilberforce had asked. But in keeping with his desire to remain politically independent, he had decided that he would never ask Pitt for such a favor. Very likely, too, was the thought that since Rockingham had taken such notice of him, the time would come in the future when another prime minister would. Rockingham's attentions had bolstered his confidence. He may well have said to himself that, welcome as Pitt's possible intercession might have been, he didn't need it. He could make it on his own.

Wilberforce's optimism, if it took this form, would not have been misplaced. In 1780 he had been a political neophyte. Now, two years later, he warranted the serious attention of those who could tap him for a post in the government or a peerage. That he could have come so far so fast meant he was essentially moving up several rungs on the political ladder. At twenty-three he knew he was someone those in power wished to keep an eye on.

Pitt, in contrast, had been unique. He had been groomed for the premiership from boyhood. But Pitt realized Wilberforce was

special too. Wilberforce didn't have the advantages of early training and education, but he had a considerable amount of natural talent and a strong commitment to a common set of political ideals.

Wilberforce did not pledge unqualified support to the Shelburne ministry but was among the more visible of Pitt's general
supporters. In the spring of 1782, he and Pitt set off for Brighton
to spend the Easter holidays together. Being driven from there on
the very night of their arrival by bad weather, they proceeded to
the city of Bath (the famous spa and fashionable resort) for the
rest of the vacation. There they found quarters and entertained
lawyers living in the region. There was, Wilberforce recalled, an
"abundance of ... dinners and jollity."

Wilberforce's Wimbledon villa, Lauriston House, had eight or
nine bedrooms. Here Pitt, to whom it was a luxury to sleep in
country air, also frequently resided. He often rode down late at
night to occupy his rooms, even though Wilberforce may have
been in town. In one spring Pitt resided there for four months.

Those who saw Pitt only in public did not know that his rather
stiff, ordinary manner gave way in the company of close friends.
In unguarded hours he freely indulged in high jinks in the garden at Wimbledon. One night, according to Wilberforce, Pitt had
taken a hat Dudley Ryder had worn to an opera performance
(without Ryder knowing it) and torn it into pieces. Pitt rose early
the next morning and meticulously planted each piece in one of
Wilberforce's flowerbeds. Ryder discovered the remains of his hat
the next day while strolling in the garden.

At other times Wilberforce, Pitt, and Edward Eliot (Pitt's future
brother-in-law) went fishing. They often lounged in the garden
at Wimbledon if the day was hot. At night, when it was cooler,
they might indulge in "foining" (that is, verbal banter, or physical horseplay – such as fencing with wooden sticks). Pitt, a friend
once told Lord Shelburne, "passes, as usual, most of his time with
his young Friends in a Society sometimes very lively – Some little
excess happen'd lately at Wimbledon.... In the Evening some of

the Neighbours were alarmed with noises at their doors, but Nobody, I believe, had made any ill-natured reflection upon a mere
frolic – It has only been pleasantly remarked, that the Rioters were
headed by [Pitt]."

In this way, and through close dealings on more serious political matters, Wilberforce's friendship with Pitt matured.

In other ways too this was a critical period of Wilberforce's
life. He moved in circles where a man possessing a large fortune
could easily have frittered it away. He possessed money, a luxurious home, and obvious social gifts. Everybody wanted to be his
friend. But he needed to be careful. As enticing as such attention
and pursuits could be, there was always a danger that he could
find himself, all too quickly, the odd person out. There were shallow elements of the society in which he moved; elements that
could prove vicious.

Wilberforce himself had become shallow in some ways, and
at times vicious. Driven by ambition and urged on by friends,
he could devastate opponents in parliamentary debate. Like his
grandfather, who had once threatened him with disinheritance,
Wilberforce himself was now a forceful person – someone you
didn't want to tangle with in the well of the House of Commons.

On the other hand, Wilberforce's friends found him as good as
gold. His gift for hospitality endeared friends like Pitt to him and
put them at ease. New acquaintances – powerful and potentially
helpful (in terms of social advancement) – discovered this too.

Wilberforce's gifts as a singer also drew attention during these
years. He often was asked to sing at parties, where he was always
a favorite guest. "Wilberforce," said a friend after a soirée at Devon-
shire House hosted by the Prince of Wales in 1782, "we must have
you again; the Prince says he will come at any time to hear you
sing."

For the first time Wilberforce had found acceptance on his own
terms with friends he admired. He was intensely loyal to them and
felt genuine affection for them. His loyalty and naturally irritable

temper also meant that if you crossed Wilberforce's friends, you crossed him.

Notwithstanding the seductions of society and fashion, Wilberforce was also faced with the more serious temptations of ambition. With talents and eloquence surpassed by few, he entered public life with the best personal connections, especially his friendship with Pitt. All of these things were at his disposal. If he had decided to see how far his star could rise, to pursue headlong the distinction that he said was at this time his "darling object," the temptation was to become a complete political animal. He didn't do this ultimately, but it certainly was a carrot that dangled in front of him.

It is interesting that, despite occasional shallowness and combativeness, Wilberforce was in one respect safe from the fascinations of ambition. In 1783 he and his friends formed a club called the Independents. It consisted of about forty members of the House of Commons, most of them opponents of the Fox-North coalition ministry. They had decided to renounce the political spoils system of the day, refusing to be bought off by the offer of plum appointments or sinecures – positions that required little or no work – or to be raised to the nobility. These prospects would have been very appealing to young men like Wilberforce who had been born to the middle class, because they were powerful ways to buy and retain political loyalty.

Nearly all of Wilberforce's fellow Independents failed to keep their resolution. Within a few years, the strength of their views had faded to the point that Wilberforce and Henry Bankes alone of all the party retained their vow. Wilberforce himself was the only county member of Parliament who was not raised to the peerage. The temptation to renounce his vow came very close indeed. Bob Smith, his cousin and close friend, was ennobled by Pitt as Lord Carrington.

The truth is that after Pitt became prime minister (in late December 1783) Wilberforce only had to ask to be granted a peerage.

Many years later he explained this to his friend Samuel Roberts. He told Roberts that more than half of the House of Lords by 1811 had been created or gifted with their titles (excluding all hereditary descent) since he came into Parliament in 1780. Furthermore, he added, "My [friendship] with Mr. Pitt for so many years may be supposed to have rendered it not difficult for me to obtain such an elevation."

The pamphleteer William Cobbett had once said it was pride that kept Wilberforce from accepting a peerage. Wilberforce candidly told Roberts: "I will not deny all force to the remark; but ... pride would never have had the effect of preventing my accepting a seat in the House of Lords – they were principles of a very different and far higher order which produced that operation." In the early 1780s there was within Wilberforce, despite his youth and acceptance of the prevalent political climate, a capacity for principled resolve.

Perhaps most importantly, as Wilberforce said on another occasion, "[Pitt] knew I should not ask anything of him." To a powerful politician from whom nearly everyone wanted something, this must have been and was most welcome. It was one important reason Wilberforce and Pitt had such a close friendship – one rooted in trust. Wilberforce said Pitt "reposed so much confidence in me as to be persuaded that I should never use any information I might obtain from him for any unfair purpose, he talked freely before me of men and things, of actual, meditated or questionable appointments and plans, projects [and] speculations."

From Wilberforce's perspective, he gained something from Pitt far more important than information he could use to his own advantage – a true friend. For a young man who had known many sad partings in his youth and several strained or severed relationships, such a friendship meant a great deal.

It meant a great deal to Pitt too. In the autumn of 1783, when Pitt planned a tour of France after the dissolution of Lord Shelburne's cabinet, he wanted to travel with Edward Eliot and Wilberforce.

On September 11 the three friends met at Canterbury. On the following day they embarked at Dover and, in spite of a heavy sea, crossed to Calais. From there they proceeded straight to Rheims, to find, as Pitt said, "some charitable persons who will let us practise our French upon them."

They stayed in Rheims for about a month before going to Paris, becoming acquainted with the nobles who resided in the neighborhood. From the archbishop of Rheims, they received gracious hospitality and the run of his estate. On October 16 the archbishop introduced them at the French court. They were soon on a familiar footing with the king and queen.

On the morning of October 17 Pitt went stag hunting while Wilberforce and Eliot departed in a chaise to see Louis XVI. The king, Wilberforce wrote in his diary later that day, was a "clumsy, strange figure in immense boots."

Three days later they all dined at the Marquis de Lafayette's. He was, Wilberforce wrote, a "pleasing enthusiastical man [and] his wife a sweet woman." Benjamin Franklin and his grandson, fourteen-year-old Benjamin Bache, also attended the dinner.

Wilberforce received with interest the hearty greetings that Franklin extended to him as a rising member of the English Parliament who had opposed the war with America. Franklin knew the part Wilberforce had played in bringing down Lord North's government and was aware of Wilberforce's speech against the American War on February 22, 1782. Later Wilberforce's fellow member of Parliament for Hull, David Hartley, would sign – along with Franklin, John Jay, and John Adams – the Treaty of Paris, ending the war with Britain.

In another respect, Wilberforce's meeting with Franklin was deeply important. Symbolically it prefigured the commitment of both men, several years later, to abolitionism. One of America's greatest champions of liberty had met the young member of Parliament who would later become one of Britain's greatest champions of liberty. Franklin was near the close of his career; Wilberforce's had just begun.

Wilberforce took up the abolition of the British slave trade in 1787. In April of the same year Franklin agreed to serve as the new president of the Pennsylvania Abolition Society. Franklin had decided to make the antislavery cause the final one he would undertake. Three years later, on February 12, 1790, the American House of Representatives received a petition from the Pennsylvania Abolition Society, urging Congress to "take such measures in their wisdom, as the powers with which they are invested will authorize, for promoting the abolition of slavery, and discouraging every species of traffic in slaves." It was signed by Franklin.

Franklin was virtually alone among America's foremost founding fathers in daring to break what has been well described as "the silence" of the founders on the subject of slavery. His moral courage was demonstrated at the end of his life; Wilberforce's moral courage as an abolitionist would be demonstrated for the rest of his.

While in Paris in the autumn of 1783 Wilberforce also took note of the singular position occupied by the Marquis de Lafayette, who seemed, in the very presence of the monarch, to be the representative of democracy. Lafayette's home was ordered upon the English model. Amidst the gaiety and ease of the royal court at Fontainebleau, he assumed an air of republican austerity. When the fine ladies of the court attempted to drag him to the card table, he shrugged his shoulders with an affected contempt for the customs and amusements of the old regime.

Not long afterward, a special messenger recalled Pitt to London and cut short the tour. After a six-week absence, Wilberforce returned to England with his friends on October 24, "better pleased with [my] own country than before [I] left it." Writing to Henry Bankes, he described their tour. "At Fontainebleau we dined and supped with ministers, and every night we spent with the Queen, who is a monarch of most engaging manners and appearance. The King is so strange a being of the hog kind, that it is worth going a hundred miles for a sight of him, especially ... boar hunting.... They are certainly, we have every reason to say, a most obliging people; and we all returned charmed with our reception."

Wilberforce, Eliot, and Pitt had returned not a moment too soon. Less than two months later, on December 19, 1783, the administration of the Fox-North coalition ended. Pitt became prime minister at the age of twenty-four.

This set in motion a whirlwind of political maneuvering, for Pitt's fledgling government was seen as "a mince-pie administration" and needed shoring up. A general election was decided upon in hopes that enough new members would be returned to strengthen Pitt's mandate to govern.

⌒

And so it was, in late March 1784, that Wilberforce went down to Yorkshire to attend a county meeting. Though he had not told anyone else, he was going to try to become one of Yorkshire's representatives in Parliament. To anyone else it would have appeared a mad scheme, for Wilberforce had few important political connections to facilitate this plan.

It was certainly bold and extremely ambitious. The county meeting was attended by the Duke of Norfolk, Lord Carlisle, Lord George Cavendish, and many other men of rank and influence, who arrived in splendidly arrayed coaches. Yorkshire was the largest and most powerful constituency in England, the seat that all commoners really desired.

The meeting took place in the Castle Yard on March 25. Despite its being a cold and stormy day, with intermittent hail, the meeting lasted from the late morning until four in the afternoon. Every speaker obtained a hearing.

When the meeting started, the two parties who opposed Charles Fox (Pitt's political rival) were divided, but Wilberforce sought to unite them by his speech. He had considered the subject well and later recalled, "I have scarcely ever spoken better." His speech was so impressive, in fact, that it was immediately suggested he should become one of the two members of Parliament for Yorkshire.

One observer who heard Wilberforce's speech was James Boswell (just returning from Edinburgh to stay with the ailing Samuel Johnson): "I saw what seemed a mere shrimp mount upon the table," Boswell wrote, "but as I listened, he grew, and grew, until the shrimp became a whale."

Wilberforce was immensely pleased with this turn of events. When a count was taken to determine the amount of political support he could depend on, the result was such that he was put in nomination and elected by a very large majority.

During this time Wilberforce received daily letters from Pitt, who took a deep interest in the result of the Yorkshire elections. In fact, Wilberforce's victory was complete and so decisive that Pittite candidates throughout the nation traced their success to Wilberforce's lead. "My dear Wilberforce," Pitt wrote from 10 Downing Street on April 8, "I can never enough congratulate you on such glorious success. I am going to dine at Wimbledon today, to mix my joy with Mrs. Dixon's, who has all the trophies of victory, such as handbills, ballads, &c. to adorn your [house]."

Wilberforce, flushed with success, began to indulge himself in the heady world of London society. He belonged to no less than five clubs, including Brookes' (with its reputation for heavy gambling), of which he had been a member since he was twenty. Looking back on this period, he remembered:

> The first day I went to Brookes' ... I [did so] knowing scarcely anybody. Through mere shyness I played a little at the faro table, where George Selwyn, of fashionable notoriety, presided, keeping the bank. An acquaintance of mine, who saw me at

play, and was aware of my inexperience, exclaimed, in a tone akin to pity, as though he viewed me as victim dressed out for sacrifice, "What, Wilberforce! is that you?" Selwyn seemed quite disconcerted by this interference, and, patting me on the back, said, "Don't interrupt him – he could not be better employed."

Political luminaries such as Pitt, Fox and the playwright/ politician Richard Sheridan frequented these clubs. In addition to enjoying their company, Wilberforce experienced the luxury of these places. Clubrooms were very handsome and splendidly furnished. Members met there on the easiest terms of society. One could play cards, gamble, or talk, according to their desire. Two lavish dinners were provided daily. It was, Wilberforce later said, an "altogether ... profligate place."

Among the other clubs to which Wilberforce belonged were White's and Boodle's (a club where, on one occasion, Wilberforce won twenty-five guineas from the Duke of Norfolk). Life was indeed sweet, so far as he was concerned. But a life-altering change was in the offing, one that would prove so radical that, after having come through it, it took his name off the lists of all five clubs he belonged to – in one day.

CHAPTER 3

THE GREAT CHANGE

Acquaint thyself with God....
Admitted once to his embrace,
Thou shalt perceive that thou wast blind before.
WILLIAM COWPER

Many consider the abolition of the slave trade to be the greatest moment in Wilberforce's life. The distinguished historian G. M. Trevelyan called this achievement "one of the turning events in the history of the world." From Wilberforce's perspective, however, the supreme event of his life was his Great Change, or embrace of Christianity. He believed that "God's good providence had checked and turned him through a miracle of mercy." This transformation redirected the course of his life, and without it he would not have become the reformer he was.

Wilberforce was intensely aware of this. "The first years that I was in Parliament I did nothing – nothing I mean to any good purpose – my own distinction was my darling object." How strongly his drive for distinction ran was revealed in 1784 when he staged his unprecedented defeat of the Whig political machine in Yorkshire, becoming that county's member of Parliament. The Whigs were a party dominated by aristocrats who owned great estates, and for many years they had determined who was elected to the two seats representing Yorkshire in the House of Commons.

Ambition made Wilberforce willing to challenge this powerful and entrenched political interest. His natural gifts and quickly maturing skills as a politician were instrumental to his victory.

Wilberforce was also the son of a Hull merchant. That he should seek and win election to Parliament as MP for the county of Yorkshire was, he recalled, "very contrary to the aristocratic notions of the great families of the county." Wilberforce had few political connections among men of rank and influence in the county – men such as the Duke of Norfolk, Lord Carlisle, and Lord George Cavendish. To all appearances, his candidacy was something of a fool's errand. Not even Pitt, his closest friend, had suggested this. "It was a very bold idea," Wilberforce later admitted, "but I was then very ambitious."

The means Wilberforce took to achieve victory in the election of 1784 were not ones he would have used after his religious change. By his own admission, he had used morally questionable methods of gaining support. While on the hustings on that cold, hailing day in March, Wilberforce was handed an express letter from Pitt. Briefly reading it, he learned of Pitt's desire that he "tear the enemy to pieces." He did so, vigorously attacking the coalition ministry of Charles Fox and Lord North. He described it as an "unnatural conjunction," marked by violence and corruption.

Early in the first parliamentary session of 1784, Wilberforce had used one of his most potent oratorical weapons, a gift for devastating sarcasm, to attack Fox with great bitterness. He had done this so often and so caustically that Fox hated him for a time. Even Pitt felt it necessary to rebuke Wilberforce for launching such virulent personal attacks.

Wilberforce also had deep pockets, and though he did not have to use his own money in the Yorkshire election, he had liberally used part of his considerable fortune to secure his election as MP for Hull four years earlier. He sponsored lavish events and observed the long-established custom of financially rewarding resident and nonresident voters who would give him their support. In short, he was quite willing to savage his political opponents and bribe voters.

⌒

Wilberforce's Great Change, it should be said, was no sudden flash of spiritual insight. Rather, it took place gradually over an extended period that lasted from October 1784 through Easter 1786. He was, afterward, somewhat suspicious of claims of sudden conversion, for besides his own spiritual transformation, that of others he respected had been gradual. The most notable of these was John Newton, who had undergone a transformation even longer than Wilberforce's and had wrestled with many doubts and questions in the process.

That Wilberforce viewed the Great Change as a gradual process was underscored by his use of a rustic metaphor in a letter written many years later to his son Samuel. "I am anxious to see decisive marks of your having begun to undergo the great change," he wrote. "I come again and again to look to see if it really be begun, just as a gardener walks up again and again to examine his fruit trees and see if his peaches are set; if they are swelling and becoming larger, finally if they are becoming ripe and rosy."

Wilberforce's Great Change was the result of an incredible chain of events – he himself believed as much – but it was also a highly unlikely chain of events. He wrote at some length about this transformation and also dictated detailed accounts to friends and family members.

The story began simply enough. Planning to embark on a continental tour with his mother, sister, and other members of his extended family, Wilberforce found himself wishing for an intelligent and agreeable friend to accompany him. He asked Dr. William Burgh of York, a man of letters and advocate of parliamentary reform whom he had known for some years. Burgh was warm and generous; he was knowledgeable, cheerful, and lively – all qualities that would have "rendered him a delightful companion." Burgh was, however, rather reserved when it came to religious topics. "Had he been my fellow-traveler," Wilberforce later said,

"I should never have benefited by him in the most important of all concerns; indeed I am persuaded that neither of us should ever have touched on the subject of religion except in the most superficial and cursory way."

As it happened, Burgh was unable to go. Shortly after he learned of this, however, Wilberforce met his former tutor Isaac Milner at the Scarborough races. Glad to have fallen in with an old friend, he impetuously asked Milner to take Burgh's place.

Nine years older than Wilberforce, Milner was an imposing figure – possessing great physical strength and gifts. In appearance and manner, he reminded many who knew him of Samuel Johnson. He had a stentorian voice, a love of truth and debate – and great intellectual curiosity. In other ways, Milner resembled Johnson – in "the warmth of his affection and the tenderness of his sympathy." His letters revealed what many had come to know in person: "the constancy of his friendships."

Milner had been apprenticed to a weaver as a boy, but through hard work and great determination, he had gone on to earn much acclaim at Cambridge University. He eventually served as president of Queen's College and as a member of the prestigious Board of Longitude.

Wilberforce admired Milner's talents and achievements. He enjoyed his cheerfulness, good nature, and powers of entertainment. This was important, for during the long journey the two would travel together in Wilberforce's carriage, while the ladies traveled with their maids in a coach.

Ironically, Wilberforce learned long afterward that his grandfather, Alderman Wilberforce, had actually once intended that he finish his education by going abroad with Milner as a tutor. This was after Wilberforce's removal from the guardianship of his aunt and uncle in the early 1770s. The Alderman had no stomach for evangelicals, or methodists – as they were often called. "Billy shall travel with Milner as soon as he is of age; but if [he] turns methodist he shall not have a sixpence of mine."

Isaac Milner (1750–1820), the brilliant Cambridge don who could compellingly set forth "the intellectual heart of Christianity"

Later Wilberforce described this encounter with Milner. He wrote of "the singular accident (as it seemed to me) of my asking Milner to go abroad with me in 1784. How much it depended on contingencies! – His coming to Hull with his brother – being known to my grandfather – [his] distinguishing himself [at Cambridge], &c. If he had been as ill as he was afterwards, or if I had known his [religious] character we should not have gone together."

When Wilberforce invited Milner to come with him to Europe, his motives were then much the same as his grandfather's. He was not influenced to select Milner because he had religion more at heart than the bulk of Cambridge society. On the contrary, Milner "was very much a man of the world in his manners, and was lively and dashing in his conversation."

Wilberforce himself was at this time a religious skeptic and had rented a pew at Theophilus Lindsey's Unitarian Chapel on Essex Street in London. Lindsey's teachings, the basis of modern Unitarianism, were widely influential. Thomas Jefferson and John Adams were among the many prominent persons of Wilberforce's day influenced by them. Lindsey and his parishioners worshiped a God best defined as a benign Providence who would judge their actions. They rejected the orthodox belief in Christ's divinity, the Christian doctrine of his atonement, and the authority of Scripture.

Wilberforce's party set out for the continent in October 1784. In the early stages of the journey he was very much the conventional tourist. He indulged his great love of nature and society, writing at length about the many scenes that captured his fancy. Crossing France to Lyons, the party embarked upon the Rhône and sailed down to Avignon. Traveling through Marseilles and Toulon, they reached Nice on November 30. They were soon settled "in a house separated from the Mediterranean only by a grove of orange trees." They found themselves surrounded by many members of the British nobility, including the Duke of Gloucester and the Duchess of Ancaster.

Wilberforce vividly recalled these days. There were nightly card parties, a great deal of gambling, assemblies, balls, and dinners – several of which Wilberforce hosted.

Even as they do today, the idle rich of that era indulged in curious fads. Lord North's son Frederick, who had a nervous temperament, was one of many who placed great faith in treatments given by so-called animal magnetizers. Wilberforce and Milner allowed the chief practitioner of this art, M. Taulay, to try his skill on them. As Wilberforce wrote, however, "neither of us felt anything, owing, perhaps, to our incredulity. North, on the contrary, would fall down upon entering a room where they practised on him.... He even maintained to me that they could affect the [bodily] frame though in another room, or at a distance, and you were ignorant of their proceedings."

Wilberforce's party stayed at Nice until February 3. During the last three weeks of their stay, he dined frequently in the open air and rode out often with Milner. Amid the cycle of assemblies, dinners, and sightseeing, Wilberforce learned more about his traveling companion.

It turned out that although Milner's religious principles were in theory those of his later life, they had at this time little practical effect upon his conduct. He had no apparent vices but was no more attentive than others to religion. He appeared in all respects like an ordinary man of the world, mixing, like Wilberforce, in all companies and joining, as readily as others did, in the prevalent Sunday parties.

When Wilberforce had extended his invitation to Milner, he was unaware that Milner had any deeper principles. He did not learn that this was so until the two dined together in Scarborough before leaving England. The conversation turned to an evangelical, the Reverend James Stillingfleet, the rector of Hotham. Wilberforce spoke of him as "a good man, but one who carried things too far." "Not a bit too far," Milner replied.

"This declaration greatly surprised me," Wilberforce recalled, "and it was agreed that at some future time we would talk the matter over. Had I known at first what his opinions were, it would have decided me against [t]aking him [abroad].... Yet ... a gracious hand leads us in ways that we know not, and blesses us not only without, but even against, our plans and inclinations."

Wilberforce himself proved to be the catalyst for this discovery. He recalled, "Milner was a sincere believer, and when I let loose, as I sometimes did, my skeptical opinions, or treated with ridicule the principles of vital religion, he combated my objections, and would say, 'Wilberforce, I don't pretend to be a match for you in this sort of running fire; but if you really wish to discuss these topics in a serious and argumentative manner, I shall be most happy to enter on them with you.'"

Wilberforce's tendency to condemn evangelical beliefs had probably been increased by his attendance at Lindsey's chapel. He said he went there "not from any preference for [Lindsey's] peculiar doctrines, for in this, except on some great festivals, his preaching differed little from that which was then common amongst the London clergy, but because he seemed more earnest and practical than others."

Moreover, Wilberforce's recollections now of the years spent with his aunt and uncle

> had left in my mind a prejudice against their kind of religion as enthusiastic and carrying matters to excess. It was with no small surprise I found [Milner's] principles and views were the same with those of the clergymen who were called methodistical. This led to renewed discussions, and Milner (never backward in avowing his opinions, or entering into religious conversation) justified his principles by referring to the word of God.

Before leaving Nice, Wilberforce noticed a book his cousin Bessy Smith had left lying on a table in their quarters. It was Philip Doddridge's *Rise and Progress of Religion in the Soul.* He picked it up and asked Milner what he thought of it. "It is one of the best books ever written," Milner replied. "Let us take it with us and read it on our journey."

The reading of Doddridge's book proved to be a pivotal point in the long process of Wilberforce's Great Change. As he later wrote to his son Samuel: "I understand you are reading Doddridge's *Rise and Progress.* You cannot read a better book. I hope it was one of the means of turning my heart to God. Certainly, there are few books which have been so extensively useful." To his son Robert he wrote in 1822: "I happened to meet with [Doddridge's *Rise and Progress*] by ... Providential arrangement at a very critical period of my life ... [I]t was ... of singular benefit to me."

Philip Doddridge (1701–51), the author of The Rise and Progress of Religion in the Soul, *a book instrumental in Wilberforce's self-described "great change," or embrace of Christianity*

Doddridge's book has been described as "a reasoned, elegant exposition [of Christianity] suited more to parlors than to market crosses or hillsides." Doddridge was a man of broad sympathies and charm, whose published writings were popular in polite society. One of his surviving friends told Wilberforce's friend Hannah More that he never knew a man of so cheerful a temper as Doddridge.

This was an ideal book for Wilberforce, who had been raised in polite society and whose temperament was ill suited to anything that might have been written in an austere, pedantic tone. It was a literary complement to Milner's engaging personality and his ability to explain the Christian faith in a winsome manner.

Wilberforce always placed great emphasis on the instruction he derived from Milner, for in addition to "very extraordinary natural and acquired powers," the Cambridge don had "a clear grasp of the intellectual heart of Christianity." As a former university student recalled, Milner had "the ability of bringing abstruse subjects within the reach of ordinary and youthful comprehension." This guided tour of Doddridge's book had a profound impact on Wilberforce – so much so, that he decided to examine the Scriptures himself to see if things were stated there in the same manner.

⌐

While on the Riviera in late January 1785, Wilberforce received a summons from Pitt to return for an important motion on parliamentary reform. He and Milner interrupted their stay and set out for England with great speed. The ladies of their party were to remain in Europe.

A journey across France at this time of year was hazardous. Leaving Nice, they traveled from Antibes through eighteen days of snow. On the hills of Burgundy, while climbing a frozen road, the weight of their carriage overpowered the horses. It was about to run over a precipice when Milner, who was walking behind the carriage, perceived the danger. He took hold of the carriage and, using his great strength, held it until the horses secured a more stable footing.

Pitt's motion for parliamentary reform was set for March 23, when, according to Wilberforce's diary, it was put off. Wilberforce and Pitt seized this opportunity to perfect its details over the next month. They spent whole days together. Upon going to London on April 18 for the crucial debate, however, they were, as Wilberforce wrote, "terribly disappointed and beat."

During the remainder of the parliamentary session, Wilberforce attended the House constantly and took part in the debates. He dined two or three times a week with Pitt, and together they joined in festivities at Wimbledon and Richmond with their friend Henry Dundas. Wilberforce often sat up all night singing.

The parliamentary session had been expected to end in May 1785 but did not conclude until the end of June. Early in July Wilberforce and Milner rejoined the ladies of their party in Genoa, Italy. "We went thither by way of Switzerland," he recalled, "and I have never since ceased to recur with peculiar delight to its enchanting scenery, especially to that of Interlaken, which is a vast garden of the loveliest fertility and beauty stretched out at the base of the giant Alps."

Almost immediately Milner and Wilberforce resumed the subject of religion. His budding evangelical convictions were confirmed and deepened. They read parts of the New Testament together in Greek. Wilberforce pressed on Milner his various doubts, objections, and difficulties. The final result of these discussions, Wilberforce said, "was a settled conviction in my mind ... of the truth of Christianity."

Wilberforce's Great Change was proving different from standard notions of the evangelical experience today – where the heart, not the intellect, is typically affected. For Wilberforce, this was not unusual. Throughout his life, he would not declare his acceptance of religious teachings that he had not thoroughly examined. As an undergraduate at St. John's College he had refused, when unexpectedly required, to declare his assent to the Articles of the Church of England. This delayed the awarding of his degree for several years.

Wilberforce later stated that Milner's sentiments "long remained merely as opinions assented to by my understanding, but not influencing my heart. At length I began to be impressed with a sense of their importance. Milner, though full of levity on all other subjects, never spoke on this but with the utmost seriousness.... All he said tended to increase my attention to religion."

Returning home in October 1785, Wilberforce began to wrestle with the implications of embracing Christianity. On October 25 he wrote, "[I] began three or four days ago to get up very early. In the solitude and self-conversation of the morning had thoughts, which I trust will come to something." He also recalled: "The deep guilt and black ingratitude of my past life forced itself upon me in the strongest colours, and I condemned myself for having wasted my precious time, and opportunities, and talents."

Reflections like these led Wilberforce to deep and earnest prayer. He was brought under strong conviction of sin and looked back on his past life with genuine remorse. "My anguish of soul for some months was indescribable," he recalled, "nor do I suppose it has often been exceeded."

In a letter written to a friend years later, Wilberforce described this time in his life:

I can with truth speak to you the language of encouragement. I should be sorry for your (mental) sufferings, were it not for the indication they afford me that you are in the right road. I myself have travelled it.... When I was first awakened to a sense ... of the importance of Divine things, the distress I felt was deep and poignant indeed. I wondered, also, to find that my feelings too little corresponded with the convictions of my understanding.

But looking into the writings of many great and good men I found that their feelings and complaints had been exactly similar to my own.... [I felt a] strange torpor and coldness which ill accord[ed] with the mercies I [had] received, and the sense of obligation of which I [was] conscious. This [led] me to prayer and self-abasement – to penitential sorrow – to humble but earnest supplication for the promised aids of the Holy Spirit, for the sake of that Saviour who died upon the Cross to atone for our transgressions, in order to soften, to animate, to warm my dull heart.

Wilberforce's spiritual crisis bore the mark of a classic Christian conversion. In language that recalls *The Confessions of St. Augustine*, he wrote: "I must awake to my dangerous state, and never be at rest till I have made my peace with God." His was the restlessness of a heart that had yet to find its rest in God.

A depiction of Wilberforce's December 1785 interview with John Newton, from American writer Mary Collier's 1855 biography of Wilberforce

Almost the first person in whom Wilberforce confided was John Newton, whom he had so often heard preach when living with his uncle and aunt. "I had no other religious acquaintances," he wrote.

This decision was not easily made. Wilberforce remembered the painful religious period of his youth, when he had revered Newton "as a parent." If word got out that he had renewed this friendship, he could become a pariah in his political and social circles. Diary entries began to trace the fluctuations of his mind about this.

In seeking out Newton, Wilberforce was seeking to regain his spiritual footing. Still, he was wary. Rather than openly communicate his intentions, he delivered a sealed letter to Newton at his church.

"There is," he wrote,

> no need for an apology for intruding on you when the errand
> is religion. I wish to have some serious conversation with you,
> and will take the liberty of calling on you for that purpose, in
> half an hour; when, if you cannot receive me, you will have
> the goodness to let me have a letter put into my hands at the
> door, naming a time and a place for our meeting, the earlier
> the more agreeable to me.
>
> I have had ten thousand doubts within myself, whether
> or not I should discover myself to you; but every argument
> against doing it has its foundation in pride. I am sure you will
> hold yourself bound to let no one living know of this applica-
> tion, or of my visit, till I release you from the obligation....
> P.S. Remember that I must be secret, and that the gallery of the
> House [of Commons] is now so universally attended, that the
> face of a Member of Parliament is pretty well known.

A date was set for Newton and Wilberforce to meet. Once, then
twice, Wilberforce walked around Charles Square, which bordered
Newton's home. Knocking on the door at last, the two retired to
Newton's study and had a lengthy conversation.

Wilberforce was greatly moved. Newton confided to him that
for many years he had believed God would sometime bring about
the renewal of Wilberforce's religious convictions. "When I came
away," Wilberforce wrote in his diary, "my mind was in a calm,
tranquil state, more humbled, looking more devoutly up to God."

Wilberforce's decision to confide in Newton could not have
been better made – nor could he have received better advice. He
remembered: "Mr. Newton, in the interviews I had with him,
advised me to avoid at present making many religious acquaintances ... to keep up my connection with Pitt, and to continue in
Parliament."

Wilberforce had need of such counsel, for he had been urged
by at least one friend to retire from Parliament. Long years later,
the Reverend Thomas Scott – in whom Wilberforce also confided –

recalled: "I withstood with all my energy [the] counsel [that] Mr. Wilberforce ... retire from public life." Scott saw only too clearly why this could have proved disastrous. "Had that counsel been followed," he wrote, "the slave trade might have been continued to future generations."

⌐

Strange reports now began to circulate. Wilberforce was said to be out of his mind and "melancholy mad." These reports were conveyed to his mother and relations in Yorkshire and for some time made them very uneasy. But he went to visit them and took particular pains to be cheerful, pleasant, and kind. "My natural disposition was irritable," he recalled, "and it had often cost them much pain. They were exceedingly struck by my altered deportment – they found me so much more kind and patient – so much more forbearing and considerate than formerly that one of them remarked, if such were the effects of becoming 'melancholy mad,' it would be well if many of our acquaintance would take the infection."

Just prior to visiting Newton, Wilberforce had written to Pitt, frankly telling him of the Great Change that had taken place in his views. He alluded to the effects this change would probably produce upon his public conduct. "I told [Pitt] that although I should ever feel the greatest regard and affection for him, and had every reason to believe that I should in general be able to support his measures, I could no longer act as a party man."

Pitt's reply was everything Wilberforce could have wished for, and a testament to what one writer has called their "brotherly intimacy." Nothing, the prime minister said, could ever alter their friendship. He hoped Wilberforce would always act as he thought right.

Wilberforce had said that perhaps it would be as well not to enter into any discussion upon the topics of his letter. Pitt replied, "Why should we not discuss them?" He thought Wilberforce was in low spirits, and proposed to come to Wimbledon and spend the next day with him at Lauriston House.

Pitt came, and the two had a great deal of conversation. At first Pitt tried to reason Wilberforce out of his convictions, but he found himself unable to question their justness, or the propriety of Wilberforce's resolutions, on the supposition that Christianity is true. Pitt "was at that time inclined to be skeptical," Wilberforce recalled. "The fact is he was so absorbed by politics that he had not allowed himself time for due reflection on religious subjects."

Lord Rosebery, the late-Victorian prime minister who was both a relation and biographer of Pitt, wrote: "Surely a memorable episode, this heart-searching of the young saint and the young minister. They went their different ways, each following their high ideal in the way that seemed best to him. And so it went on to the end, Wilberforce ever hoping to renew the sacred conversation."

Wilberforce's friendship with Pitt was unique. Pitt had a reserve that persisted even in long, private friendships with others. It melted only in the company of Wilberforce and Pitt's brother-in-law, Edward Eliot, to whom he habitually opened his heart. Pitt's enduring regard for Wilberforce would survive disagreements in public life and a widening diversity of religious views. For his part, Wilberforce longed to draw Pitt into sympathy with his newfound convictions. It was his regard for Pitt that led him to explain himself so fully.

⌒

The complementary advice that Wilberforce received from Newton, Scott, and Pitt had profound implications. His quandary over whether he ought to withdraw from public life has been described as the "Eusebian temptation," the belief that one could best serve God in sacred rather than secular activities. In Wilberforce's case, he contemplated leaving politics to pursue Holy Orders or some other sphere of Christian service. Pitt sought to dissuade him, stating forcefully, "Surely the principles as well as the practice of

Christianity are simple, and lead not to meditation only but to action."

This was an important and powerful statement. On the one hand, it was tactful. Pitt did not criticize Wilberforce for adopting views that had prompted many to call him melancholy mad. He treated Wilberforce with respect. On the other hand, he appealed to Wilberforce on Christian terms, posing the query, "If a Christian may act in the several relations of life, must he seclude himself from them all to become so?" To Wilberforce, a man wrestling with the implications of his Great Change, it would have been hard to dismiss such a question as being unreasonable.

On a relational level, it was gratifying and comforting for Wilberforce to have received a letter that so ardently affirmed Pitt's friendship. Wilberforce confided to his diary: "[I received] Pitt's answer [and was] much affected by it.... [It] was full of kindness."

A letter to his sister Sarah – written shortly after his meetings with Newton and Pitt – affords a window on Wilberforce's thinking at this time.

> What my heart most impels me now to say to you is "Search the Scriptures," and with all that earnestness and constancy which that book claims, in which "are the words of eternal life." Never read it without praying to God that he will open your eyes to understand it; for the power of comprehending it comes from him, and him only....
>
> There is no opinion so fatal as that which is commonly received in these liberal days, that a person is in a safe state with respect to a future world, if he acts tolerably up to his knowledge and convictions, though he may not have taken much pains about acquiring this knowledge or fixing these convictions.

Throughout his life it was Wilberforce's habit to commend to others practices he had found beneficial. Thus he was advising his sister to do what he himself had come to do. He now spent several hours daily in earnest study of the Scriptures. He also set aside time for self-examination and reflection, that he might better perform "the duties of life." He believed that if he did not, "the most pressing claims will carry [my heart], not the strongest." In his diary he cited Sir Francis Bacon, whose *Essays* he read avidly all his life and from which he derived much guidance: "It is a sad fate for a man to die too well known to everybody else, and still unknown to himself."

Throughout the winter of 1785–86 Wilberforce took lodgings near Newton's church, St. Mary Woolnoth, to be within reach of Newton's pastoral counsel. At other times, Newton would come to Lauriston House in Wimbledon.

On January 12 Wilberforce and Newton were walking on Wimbledon Common when they unexpectedly met Wilberforce's cousin William Thornton, who had recently taken the name and arms of Astell. Wilberforce wrote in his diary: "Thornton-Astell surprised us together on the common in the evening. [I] expect to hear myself now universally given out to be a methodist: may God grant it may be said with truth."

To his mother, who had been alarmed by this kind of rumor, Wilberforce explained his sentiments. "It is not, believe me, to my own imagination, or to any system formed in my closet, that I look for my principles; it is to the very source to which you refer me, the Scriptures."

Wilberforce conceded that if he did this he would be subject to charges of excess and singularity. He urged his mother, however, to consider that his principles were derived from "our great Master's own words; 'Thou shalt love the Lord thy God with all thy heart, with all thy mind, and with all thy strength; and thy neighbour as thyself.'" If one were then led to ask what kind of conduct flowed from this premise, one ought to consider the question that followed, "Who is my neighbour?" Wilberforce stated that he took his cue from the parable of the good Samaritan. He concluded: "It is evident we are to consider our peculiar situations, and in these to do all the good we can."

Wilberforce addressed his mother's fear that he meant to cloister himself in town or occupy a hermitage in the country. "Some are thrown into public, some have their lot in private life," he asserted, "these different states have their corresponding duties.... [It] would merit no better name than desertion ... if I were thus to fly from the post where Providence has placed me." Closing his letter, he wrote:

> When I consider the particulars of my duty I blush at the review; but my shame is not occasioned by my thinking that I am too studiously diligent in the business of life.... On the contrary, I then feel that I am serving God best when from proper motives I am most actively engaged in it. What humbles me is the sense that I forego so many opportunities of doing good; and it is my constant prayer, that God will enable me to serve him more steadily, and my fellow-creatures more assiduously.

"This," Wilberforce's sons wrote, was "not the heated tone of enthusiasm, but the sober reality of a reasonable faith. It was ... a gradual work [to which] he looked forward."

Writing to a college friend in June 1795, Wilberforce described his Great Change in terms that are at once eloquent and philosophical:

> It is scarce too strong to say, that I seem to myself to have awakened about nine or ten years ago from a dream, to have recovered, as it were, the use of my reason after a delirium. In fact till then I wanted first principles; those principles at least which alone deserve the character of wisdom, or bear the impress of truth.
>
> Emulation, and a desire of distinction, were my governing motives; and ardent after the applause of my fellow-creatures, I quite forgot that I was an accountable being; that I was

hereafter to appear at the bar of God; that if Christianity were not a fable, it was infinitely important to study its precepts, and when known to obey them; that there was at least such a probability of its not being a fable, as to render it in the highest degree incumbent on me to examine into its authenticity diligently, anxiously, and without prejudice....

I am not now what I ought to be; yet I trust ... through the help of that gracious Being who has promised to assist our weak endeavours, to become more worthy of the name of Christian.

"Watch and pray," Wilberforce had written to his sister, "read the word of God, imploring that true wisdom which may enable you to comprehend and fix it in your heart, that it may gradually produce its effect under the operation of the Holy Spirit, in renewing the mind and purifying the conduct. This it will do more and more the longer we live under its influence."

It was, he asserted, to the honor of the Christian faith that those who began this course "in extremes, enthusiastic perhaps, or rigidly severe, will often by degrees lose these types of imperfections." He maintained that over time these imperfections would disperse like clouds and vapors in "some of our Westmoreland evenings, when ... towards [their] close the sun beams forth with unsullied lustre, and descends below the horizon in the full display of all his glories."

Pursuing this metaphor, Wilberforce suggested that this was

the earnest of a joyful rising, which will not be disappointed....
By the power of habit which God has been graciously pleased
to bestow upon us, our work will every day become easier, if
we accustom ourselves to cast our care on him, and labour in
a persuasion of his cooperation.... The eastern nations had
their talismans, which were to advertise them of every danger,
and guard them from every mischief. Be the love of Christ our
talisman.

On January 14, 1786, John Newton received a letter from the poet William Cowper. Newton had been a friend of Cowper's for many years – they had collaborated on a collection of verse entitled *Olney Hymns* – and Newton had been keeping Cowper apprised of Wilberforce's spiritual progress. Cowper wrote, "We were greatly pleased with your account of Mr. W. May your new disciple's conduct ever do honor to his principles and to the instructions of the Spiritual counsellor whom he hath chosen."

Another author whose writings were particularly important to Wilberforce throughout the period of his Great Change was Blaise Pascal. Wilberforce's diary entries reveal that he read Pascal's *Pensées* (or *Thoughts on Religion*) for hours at a time. This work meant so much to him that when agriculturist and travel writer Arthur Young wrote to him many years later, asking for spiritual counsel, Wilberforce wrote, "I think I have recommended to you Pascal's *Thoughts on Religion*. It is a collection of fragments, but they are the fragments of a master like the study of Michaelangelo. I know no book whatever which appears to me to contain such deep views of Christianity." Wilberforce had come to share Pascal's contention that "wisdom ... is nothing if not of God." He wrote, the "basis of all intellectual and moral improvement [is] the Christian religion."

Newton continued to mark his protégé's progress. He wrote to Cowper at Easter: "I judge he is now decidedly on the right track.... I hope the Lord will make him a blessing both as a Christian and a statesman. How seldom do these characters coincide!! But they are not incompatible." To Wilberforce he later wrote: "I hope that great usefulness to the public, and ... the church of God, will be your present reward."

On Good Friday, April 14, 1786, Wilberforce received communion for the first time since the beginning of his Great Change. Two days after Easter, he wrote to his sister Sarah from Stock, where he was staying with the Rev. William Unwin.

Unwin possessed a deep faith and keen mind. The philosopher William Paley was among those who voiced respect for his intellectual gifts. The poet William Cowper was Unwin's close friend. Indeed, it was to Unwin that so many of Cowper's letters – regarded now as some of the best in English prose – were addressed.*

Such a setting was just what Wilberforce needed. He told Sarah:

> About five o'clock yesterday I put myself into a post-chaise, and in four hours found myself safely lodged with the vicar of Stock. It is more than a month since I slept out of town, and I feel all that Milton attributes to the man who has been
>
> > long in populous cities pent,
> > Where houses thick and sewers annoy the air.
>
> I scarce recollect to have spent so pleasant a day as that which is now nearly over. My heart opens involuntarily to Unwin and his wife; I fancy I have been with them every day since we first became acquainted at Nottingham, and expand to them with all the confidence of a twelve years' intimacy. Can my dear sister wonder that I call on her to participate in the pleasure I am tasting?
>
> I know how you sympathize in the happiness of those you love, and I could not therefore forgive myself if I [did] not invite you to partake of my enjoyment. The day has been delightful. I was out before six, and made the fields my oratory, the sun shining as bright and as warm as at Midsummer. I think my own devotions become more fervent when offered in this way amidst the general chorus, with which all nature seems on such a morning to be swelling the song of praise and thanksgiving.... I have been all day basking in the sun.... My eyes are bad, but I could not resist the impulse I felt to call on you and tell you how happy I have been.

---

*The information about William Unwin comes from Goldwin Smith's book, *Cowper*, (London: 1880).

The distress and penitential sorrow that had marked the outset of Wilberforce's Great Change was now behind him. "By degrees," he told his sons many years later, "the promises and offers of the gospel produced in me something of a settled peace of conscience. I devoted myself for whatever might be the term of my future life, to the service of my God and Saviour, and with many infirmities and deficiencies, through his help, I continue until this day."

⌐

The specific results of Wilberforce's Great Change began with the source to which he now looked for his principles: the Scriptures. He contended that "we should really make this book the criterion of our opinions and actions."

He was only too well aware that in doing this he would be subject "to the charge of excess and singularity." Yet he had considered this well. "Singularity for its own sake I grant is worse than folly," he later wrote, "so thought St. Paul also. But we shall find it next to impossible to face [criticism] when it is our duty to do so, unless we diligently cultivate the habit of judgment and feeling, by which we shall alone be able ... to withstand it when duty requires."

Throughout the remainder of his career in Parliament, particularly during the twenty-year fight to secure the abolition of the slave trade, Wilberforce was constantly vilified and excoriated. No less a person than the naval hero Lord Nelson once declared, "I was bred in the good old school and taught to appreciate the value of our West Indian possessions, and neither in the field nor the senate shall their just rights be infringed, while I have an arm to fight in their defense or a tongue to launch my voice against the damnable doctrine of Wilberforce and his hypocritical allies."

Wilberforce grieved to hear such things, but his resolve was unchanged. Others might feel that his philanthropy, as informed by his Christian faith, was strange or extreme. He would not be deterred by the fear of criticism. During one parliamentary debate he stated memorably: "If to be feelingly alive to the sufferings of my fellow-creatures, and to be warmed with the desire of relieving their distresses, is to be a fanatic, I am one of the most incurable fanatics ever to be permitted at large."

Wilberforce's willingness to be thought singular when duty required was not a holier-than-thou attitude donned for public consumption. Over time, humility became one of the most prominent features of his character. Not long before he died, and long after he had been a co-worker with princes, nobles, and senators of all nations, Wilberforce met a beggar while walking on the Isle of Wight. A friend named Joseph Brown recalled that the beggar approached him using the most flattering language. "Do not say this," Wilberforce said gently, "I am only a poor sinner like yourself."

Brown also experienced an instance of Wilberforce's humility that astonished and embarrassed him. One day in conversation, Wilberforce gave him some advice. Brown expressed his thanks and said how much he should feel indebted if, in conversation or correspondence, Wilberforce would at all times be his counselor and, if necessary, correct him and point out all his faults.

Wilberforce suddenly stopped, for they had been walking together, and replied, "I will – but you must promise me one thing."

"With pleasure," Brown answered, little thinking what it was.

"Well, then," continued Wilberforce, "in all your conversation and correspondence with me, be candid and open, and point out all my faults."

The growth of humility in Wilberforce's character meant that for him politics could never again be an arena where he sought "to tear the enemy to pieces." No longer content with acting "tolerably up to his knowledge and convictions," he wished to be faithful to them whatever cost that might entail. He now sought to regulate his conduct by the golden rule – "to do as I would be done by." He was not always successful – on occasion he even sparred with Pitt and other colleagues – but he kept trying.

In practical terms, Wilberforce's resolve to be bound by the golden rule radically changed his political conduct. His dealings with Charles Fox, whom he had attacked so bitterly in 1784, improved so markedly that by 1788 they were working together as "friends of abolition." Fox said in debate that he had once contemplated introducing a measure to abolish the slave trade – but, he affirmed, "It is better that the cause should be in [Wilberforce's] hands than in mine; from him I honestly believe that it will come with more weight, more authority, and more probability of success."

Wilberforce's understanding of calling had also been decisively altered. In general terms, he now rejected the Eusebian temptation and "thought it a great pity that officers in the army and navy should upon becoming religious quit that line of life ... and enter into the Church." He said it was "quite contrary to St. Paul's injunctions who commanded Christians to glorify God in the stations in which they were placed by providence."

To his friend Christopher Wyvill, with whom he had so often worked to promote parliamentary reform, Wilberforce explained that this general understanding of calling had imbued him with a "higher sense of the duties of my station, and a firmer resolution to discharge them with fidelity and zeal."

He then explained his understanding of his call to service in political life: "Not that I would shut myself up from mankind [or confine] myself in a cloister. My walk, I am sensible, is a public one; my business is in the world; and I must mix in assemblies of men, or quit the post which Providence seems to have assigned me."

Wilberforce's Great Change also manifested itself in a very practical and conscientious way. He took greater care to be present for every debate in the Commons. He agreed to serve on countless committees, always a thankless task. His regularity in the House and service on its committees was all the more unique in an age when the chamber was seldom filled. He was there unless sick or obliged to be more than twenty miles from London.

A story has survived about Wilberforce's faithfulness in attending Parliament. As Thomas Price recalled: "When the House of Commons, some years since, was engaged in an investigation that deeply interested George III, the King inquired, from one who had just left the house. 'Who was under examination?' Being told, the King asked which members were taking notes. It was answered, 'Mr. Wilberforce is very busy taking notes.' His Majesty replied: 'Ah, he is a good man – he is a good man.'"

The influence of Wilberforce's new principles was now rapidly pervading all his conduct. A highly intelligent but idle undergraduate when attending St. John's College, he now felt keenly a sense of wasted time and opportunities. "I deeply lamented my idleness at college. For the next seven or eight years, I deemed it to be my duty to redeem the time and prosecute the studies I ought to have cultivated in my earlier years. I made it my object therefore to improve my faculties and add to my slender stock of knowledge."

Wilberforce now spent the greater part of his parliamentary recesses at the house of one friend or another, "where I could have the command of my time and continue my labours with cheerfulness and comfort."

As soon as Parliament was in recess he commonly settled himself (except for occasional stays at Buxton or Bath when his health required it) in the house of some close friend, such as Thomas Gisborne or Thomas Babington. He breakfasted in his own room, dined with the family, and resumed his studies in the evening, joining the family party when he took a little supper half an hour or an hour before bedtime. Within a few years, Wilberforce "repaired in a great degree [his] want of studious habits while at college, by assiduously pursuing an enlarged course of reading." He lived, he said, "as much as I pleased the life of a student."

This devotion to reading and learning persisted for the rest of Wilberforce's life. The essayist Sir James Stephen (grandfather of the novelist Virginia Woolf) vividly described this side of his character. Wilberforce, Stephen wrote, was "the happy comrade, the docile pupil, and the enthusiastic admirer of the greatest. After having lost the sight of one of his eyes, and while sorely annoyed by the ailments of the other, he ran over with eagerness, and appreciated with curious felicity, a greater body of literature than is usually compassed by those who devote themselves exclusively to letters."

Wilberforce read an astonishing variety of books. He took pains to remain well acquainted with works of classical Greek and Roman literature, particularly Horace, Epictetus, and Virgil. He committed long passages of their works to memory, on one occasion proposing to read "at least a hundred lines of Virgil daily – often more." Moreover, he could read, write, and translate Greek and Latin.

He read Boswell's *Life of Samuel Johnson* often, as well as works by Gibbon, Adam Smith, Francis Bacon, David Hume, William Blackstone, Locke, Machiavelli, Montesquieu, Rousseau, Voltaire, and Sir Walter Scott. He memorized many passages from the writings of Shakespeare and Cowper.

The list of Wilberforce's reading topics is impressive. He read memoirs and biographies, biblical and legal commentaries, treatises on economics, essays, histories, collections of letters, linguistic works, novels, philosophical writings, plays, poetry, works on political theory, works of science and theology, and travel books.

"It was not without a certain unity of design," Sir James Stephen concluded, "that these were all in turn either lightly skimmed, or diligently studied.... He learned from them to understand, and so to benefit, mankind."

According to Stephen, Wilberforce's brilliant fancy broke out into a ceaseless conversation with the great masters at whose feet he sat.

He would controvert, interrogate, or applaud in the form of marginal notes, when he was alone; or, if an auditor was at hand, in spoken comments, at one moment so arch and humorous, at the next so reverent and affectionate, and then so full of solemn meaning, that the austere folio, or the saucy pamphlet, became so many characters in a sort of tragicomedy; in which, however, there was usually a large preponderance of the droll above the serious.

Another friend, who traveled with Wilberforce's family observed:

His mental energy never flagged. We were often amused at the capacities of his pockets, which carried a greater number of books than would seem ... credible; and his local memory was such that, drawing out any author, he seemed instantaneously to light on the passage which he wanted.

In addition to the stores of his pockets, a large green bag full of books filled a corner of his carriage, and when we stopped at our inn in the evening it was his delight to have this bag into the parlour, and to spread part of its stores over the table. He kindled at the very sight of books.

Like Benjamin Franklin, from whom he had received such a cordial greeting in Paris in 1783, Wilberforce also developed the habit of keeping lists of virtues he wished to acquire, a program for practicing them, and rules for the best management of his time. Speaking of his practice, Franklin had wryly commented: "I was surprised to find myself so much fuller of faults than I had imagined; but then I had the satisfaction of seeing them diminish."

Wilberforce would have concurred with the first part of Franklin's statement and said that he hoped for the second. He often fell short of his stated goals, but it also is true that he persisted, and so was able to achieve a measure of discipline missing from his younger years.

Another principle that Wilberforce now held to be of "first-rate importance" was "that of bringing together all men who are like-minded, and who may probably at some time or other combine and concert for the public good." As he later urged his son Samuel, "Never omit any opportunity ... of getting acquainted with any good man or any useful man."

Over time, this principle translated into a unique desire and capacity to work together with philosophical opposites. "Measures, not men," became one of Wilberforce's favorite sayings. From abolition to prison reform, and with men of such divergent political views as Charles Fox and Jeremy Bentham, he worked to achieve shared goals. At the heart of it all was his "constant prayer that God will enable me to serve him more steadily, and my fellow-creatures more [diligently]."

John Newton once observed that the characters of a Christian and a statesman seldom coincide. Early on, this posed a puzzle for many of Wilberforce's friends and political colleagues – they believed that these characters were incompatible.

But Wilberforce's later career would show that these roles are compatible and provide solid instruction on how to bring one's faith to bear on society's pressing needs and issues. It is one of the most significant aspects of his legacy. This integration of faith, reform, and leadership was to transform, in profound ways, the society in which he lived.

CHAPTER 4

THE FIRST GREAT OBJECT

*Wilberforce [is] one of the party called in derision
the Saints ... who under sanctified visors pursue worldly
objects with the ardour and perseverance of saints.*

JOHN QUINCY ADAMS

During the most active and productive era of his life, Wilberforce found himself working in circumstances that would have distracted men of lesser conviction. Britain, along with her continental allies, fought what was essentially a world war against France. It was Wilberforce's finest hour.

While Britain and its leaders focused on the war with France, Wilberforce initiated or led an astonishing array of philanthropic projects, public and private, that fostered the rise of the Anglo-American voluntary society movement. He persevered amidst the press of legislative duties and constituent concerns that were his responsibility as an MP for Yorkshire, Britain's most important and powerful county. Added to all these pressures, he faced the cessation and near-severing of vital friendships, a constant stream of false accusations and vitriol, death threats, a challenge to a duel, and serious illnesses – including one that nearly claimed his life.

That Wilberforce might hold to larger goals during this time and see them through was demonstrative of his singular capacity for perseverance. His conversion to Christianity – his Great Change – had altered his destiny and, as events would prove, the destiny of Britain. Scarcely more than a year after his spiritual transformation he found his life's work. On Sunday, October 28, 1787, on a blank page of his diary he wrote, "God Almighty has placed before me *two great objects*, the suppression of the slave trade and the reformation of manners [that is, morals]." From that time forward, he would pursue these objects with remarkable determination.

The first instance of any desire on Wilberforce's part to relieve the sufferings of slaves occurred in 1780, fully six years before his Great Change. "I had been strongly interested for the West Indian slaves," he recalled. "In a letter asking my friend [James] Gordon, then going to Antigua, to collect information for me, I expressed my determination, or at least my hope, that some time or other I should redress the wrongs of those wretched and degraded beings."

Three years passed, and it appears that the urge to aid the slaves waned in light of more personal goals. Then on November 13, 1783, Wilberforce recorded in his diary that he had a conversation concerning the condition of the Negroes with James Ramsay. This was shortly before Ramsay published the first of his two seminal abolitionist works, *An Essay on the Treatment ... of Slaves in the British Sugar Colonies.* Ramsay's writings were the first to document, based on personal experience, the horrors associated with slavery and the slave trade.

By the spring of 1786, however, Wilberforce had undergone his Great Change, and with it his motivation to abolish slavery returned. Had Wilberforce's life not changed so dramatically, it is unlikely he would have been drawn to the circle of social-minded evangelicals at Barham Court in Teston. Barham Court was the home of Sir Charles and Lady Margaret Middleton. Wilberforce had known the Middletons for many years – they were in-laws to his college friend Gerard Edwards – but he now grew close to them. As it turned out, Ramsay also resided at Barham Court.

Largely as a result of Ramsay's experiences while serving as a physician and rector on the Island of St. Kitts, the Middletons had become deeply concerned about Africa and slaves in the British West Indies. Wilberforce's initial interest in bettering the conditions of slaves in the British West Indies now broadened to include conditions in Africa itself and abuses of the slave trade. At this time Wilberforce was also spending a great deal of time with John Newton. The former slave ship captain would have imparted much information about the evils he had seen first hand.

In the autumn of 1786 Sir Charles, a member of Parliament, was urged by Lady Margaret to bring the subject of the slave trade "before the House, and demand parliamentary inquiry into the nature of a traffic so disgraceful to the British character." Sir Charles replied that the cause would be in bad hands if it were committed to him, as he had only made one speech in the House, but he pledged to strenuously support any able member who would undertake it.

When the willingness and fitness of several other members of Parliament was discussed, Wilberforce's name figured most prominently. Known to be one of the closest friends of Prime Minister Pitt, his reputation for eloquence was complemented by a sincere religious faith that was the basis of a growing commitment to philanthropy.

Wilberforce was then at Hull. Lady Margaret prevailed on Sir Charles to write to him and propose that he demand a parliamentary inquiry into the nature of slave trade. They received Wilberforce's reply a few days later. He said he "felt the great importance of the subject," though he "thought himself unequal to the task allotted to him." He stated, however, that he "would not positively decline it;" adding, that on his return to London he would "pay a visit to the family at Teston, and consult with [them]."

Wilberforce took this request seriously. His Great Change had given him a "higher sense of the duties of my station." Now his long interest in conditions among the slaves in the West Indies led him, when he visited the Middletons at Teston, to try to master the subject of the slave trade and to obtain information from every available source.

The small but determined group of abolitionists that had begun to gather at the Middletons' home included a young man named Thomas Clarkson, who in 1785 had written a prize-winning essay at Cambridge condemning the slave trade. Early in 1787 Wilberforce consulted often with Clarkson. Both detested the slave trade, and they now commenced the collaboration to secure its demise for which both their memories are justly celebrated.

In the first months of 1787 Clarkson called at Wilberforce's home, Number 4 Old Palace Yard, every week. They met with other like-minded friends to exchange evidence and information about the slave trade. Wilberforce also vigorously pursued his own research, devoting many additional hours to it.

On March 13, 1787, while at a dinner party at the home of Bennet Langton, Samuel Johnson's great friend, Wilberforce first declared publicly that he was willing to lead the parliamentary effort to end the slave trade. Present on this occasion were several of Johnson's other surviving friends – James Boswell, Sir Joshua Reynolds, William Windham, and Isaac Hawkins Browne. Two of Wilberforce's abolitionist friends were present as well – Sir Charles Middleton and Clarkson.

Indeed, it is to Clarkson that we are indebted for the account of this important event. After dinner, Clarkson recalled, the subject of the slave trade was "purposely introduced." Clarkson was questioned about his knowledge of the trade, and he displayed samples of African cloth. Reynolds, Hawkins Browne, Windham, and Boswell then expressed their decided opposition to the trade.

It was at this point that Langton, the host of the evening, paid Wilberforce a compliment intended to sound out Wilberforce's willingness to lead an effort to end the trade. It was deftly done and provided a catalyst for Wilberforce – who responded that he was willing, if no one better could be found – and after he had more time to learn about the abuses associated with the trade.

Hawkins Browne and Windham then expressed their willingness to support Wilberforce if he took up the task.

Two months later Wilberforce received another, more significant admonition to take the lead in ending the slave trade. On May 12 Wilberforce was at Holwood, Pitt's estate. Pitt's other guest was his cousin, William Grenville. The three friends – one prime minister, another a future prime minister, and the last, Wilberforce, seeking his own great parliamentary cause – walked the sloping hills of the estate. Their talk ranged over various political subjects, but then it turned to the slave trade. Wilberforce recalled:

> I had [by this time] acquired ... much information ... I began to talk the matter over with Pitt and Grenville. Pitt recommended me to undertake its conduct, as a subject suited to my character and talents. At length, I well remember, after a conversation in the open air at the root of an old [oak] tree at Holwood just above the steep descent into the vale of Keston, I resolved to give notice on a fit occasion in the House of Commons of my intention to bring the subject forward.

But when might the fit occasion arise? The final catalyst for Wilberforce came when he met with John Newton on Sunday, October 28. The two friends talked for a long time. Wilberforce now saw his path clearly. After Newton left, he took up his quill pen, and wrote in his diary: "God has set before me two great objects, the suppression of the slave trade and the reformation of manners."

It was a great event in history, this meeting of unlikely friends. Newton was so many things Wilberforce was not. For many years he had led a rough, degenerate, and tempestuous life. He had known times of great destitution and want. He did not possess riches, nor could he ever hope to move in the social circles that Wilberforce did.

Once Wilberforce had looked upon Newton as a father figure. Yet they had been painfully parted, and neither thought he would

The "Wilberforce Oak," the tree under which Wilberforce and Pitt discussed Wilberforce's taking up the fight to end the British slave trade

ever see the other again. In time Wilberforce ceased to care if he ever did.

Nearly fifteen years passed before they were to meet again in December 1785. And it had been Wilberforce who sought Newton out – this man with whom he had so little in common, but who had so much that Wilberforce sensed he needed to hear. Then Newton's counsel had helped him to see he needed to stay in politics. Now, two years later, it was Newton – the former slave ship captain – a man guilty of crimes against humanity – who proved instrumental in setting Wilberforce on the path of service to humanity.

Wilberforce now moved with deliberate speed. Using his influence, he wrote to friends in government and secured permission for Clarkson to examine custom house files and other records pertaining to the slave trade. Wilberforce then met frequently with Clarkson, receiving "detailed accounts of his progress in collecting evidence."

Soon after Christmas 1787 Wilberforce gave notice in the Commons of his intention early in the next session to move for the abolition of the slave trade. In later life he recalled what must have then been immensely gratifying: upon hearing of Wilberforce's notice, his one-time opponent Charles Fox said that "he had himself seriously entertained the idea of bringing the subject before Parliament; but he was pleased to add, that it having got into so much better hands he should not interfere."

Granville Sharp, the elder statesman of the abolitionist cause who served as the chairman of the London Committee for the Abolition of the Slave Trade, sounded a note in unison with Fox. "Mr. W.," Sharp wrote, "is to introduce the business in the House. The respectability of his position as member for the largest county, the great influence of his personal connections, added to an amiable and unblemished character, secure every advantage to the cause."

Wilberforce had originally intended to introduce his motion early in February 1788, but this intention was thwarted when he became seriously ill on February 19 with what appears to have been ulcerative colitis – an excruciatingly painful, stress-induced condition of the digestive tract. He consulted the eminent Scottish physician James Pitcairne. Isaac Milner (whose wide scientific knowledge encompassed medicine) left Cambridge to lend his aid and be by Wilberforce's side.

By March 8 Wilberforce's health was steadily declining. Greatly alarmed, his friends Lord Muncaster and Matthew Montagu called in the celebrated Dr. Richard Warren (George III's physician at the time of his first madness). Warren stated that Wilberforce, "that little fellow with the calico guts, cannot possibly survive a twelve-month." Further discussion of his case with other doctors yielded a more grievous verdict: he "had not stamina to last a fortnight."

Believing he was going to die, Wilberforce summoned the prime minister. He described his meeting with Pitt in a private letter to his friend Christopher Wyvill:

> As to the Slave question, I do not like to touch on it, it is so big a one it frightens me in my present weak state. Suffice it to say ... matters are in a very good train.... Pitt, with a warmth of principle and friendship that have made me love him better than I ever did before, has taken on himself the management of the business, and promises to do all for me if I desire it, that, if I were a [healthy] man, it would be proper for me to do myself.

Pitt acted at once. With the help of Wilberforce's friend Beilby Porteus, the bishop of London, he supervised the Privy Council inquiries into the slave trade that were now in progress. As the session of Parliament advanced, supporters of abolition throughout the country sent one hundred petitions to the House of Commons.

Meanwhile, the London Committee for the Abolition of the Slave Trade had declared that if Wilberforce were unable to resume his post, they would leave to him the selection of his replacement. On April 11 they wrote to him for his directions. Their letter reached him in Bath when he was so weak that he could not read any business letters.

Wilberforce's family and friends now wrote in his name to Pitt and committed the cause into his hands. The letter was written by Wilberforce's mother, his cousin Mary Bird, and Isaac Hawkins Browne – who had been present at Bennet Langton's dinner when Wilberforce first said he would be willing to lead an effort to end the slave trade. Browne had said then he would support

Wilberforce. He had kept his word, and he now performed what he thought was one last act of friendship.

After receiving this letter, Pitt again immediately acted. On April 22 Granville Sharp reported to the London Committee for the Abolition of the Slave Trade that he had been sent for by the prime minister, and he officially informed them of the pledge Pitt had given to Wilberforce.

On May 9 Pitt moved a resolution binding the House to investigate the slave trade early in the following session. In a short speech, he studiously avoided stating his own opinions on the trade. He asserted that a full discussion of the abolition question would serve no useful purpose, as the matter must be considered deliberately and in detail. This, he maintained, could not be done until the inquiry instituted by His Majesty's ministers had been concluded.

Pitt referred to Wilberforce's illness and expressed his hope that his friend would be able to "resume his charge" and introduce the abolition question in the next session. He told his colleagues that in no one else's hands could "any measure of humanity and national interest" be better placed. He concluded by promising to undertake this task himself if Wilberforce had not then recovered.

In reply, Charles Fox stated that he had "unaffectedly rejoiced" when he heard that Wilberforce had resolved to take up the abolition question. He did so "knowing that gentleman's purity of principles and sincere love for the rights of humanity." In contrast to Pitt's official caution, Fox also said, "I have no scruple to declare, at the onset, that my opinion of this momentous business is that the Slave Trade ought not to be regulated but destroyed." Edmund Burke also spoke. Like Fox, he had once thought of taking up the question of the slave trade. He now committed himself to its abolition.

The rest of the debate was remarkable only for the silence of the West Indian party, members of Parliament whose wealth was derived from the slave trade. As this initial challenge came forth they had apparently decided to reserve their defense. Not one West Indian member of Parliament voted against Pitt's resolution. It was summarily carried.

The quiescence of the West Indian party was one major reason for the relative ease with which Pitt's measure passed. They seemed to have been caught off guard by the ardor of Pitt, Fox, and Burke. They may have failed to fully appreciate the nature of the threat that such formidable opposition posed. Then too, they may have chosen to keep their powder dry until a motion that more directly threatened the slave trade had been introduced.

Though the general question of abolition had been temporarily shelved, the parliamentary session would not conclude without a victory in which Wilberforce could rejoice. Sir William Dolben, the member of Parliament for Oxford University, had gone aboard a slave ship that was lying in the Thames. He had been so horrified that he gave notice forthwith of a bill for limiting the number of slaves that a ship should be allowed to carry in proportion to its tonnage.

The bill was read a first time on May 26, and in the debate the supporters of the slave trade tipped their hand. Lord Penrhyn "flatly denied the cruelty and unhealthiness alleged." When questioned by counsel, however, some Liverpool merchants admitted that "the average death rate on the Middle Passage (the most horrific stage of the slaves' transport from Africa) was at least 5 or 10 percent according to its length." They also confirmed that "in one case no less than a third of the slaves had died." This evidence made a deep impression on the House.

The supporters of the slave trade declared that they would accept no regulations. To regulate the trade, they said, would ruin it because "every Negro lost to a British ship by regulation would be a Negro won by a French ship."

Pitt had heard enough. At the start of the debate he had asked the House "to judge the particular regulations proposed in the bill on their own merits, and not to go back on its previous decision to reserve the broader discussion on the fate of the trade as a whole until the next session." But now he "was provoked into taking the wider ground." Pitt said in the closing speech of the debate:

> I have no hesitation to declare that, if the Trade cannot be carried on in a manner different to that stated by the honourable members opposite me, I will retract what I said on a former day against going into the general question [of abolishing it], and, waiving every other discussion than what has this day taken place, I will give my vote for the utter abolition of a trade which is shocking to humanity, is abominable to be carried on by any country, and reflects the greatest dishonour on the British senate and the British nation. The Trade, as the petitioners propose to carry it on, without any regulation, is contrary to every humane, to every Christian principle, to every sentiment that ought to inspire the breast of man.

Pitt's declaration silenced the token opposition. In a thinly attended House, Dolben's bill to limit the number of transported slaves passed by a vote of 56 to 5.

Still, Dolben's bill faced a stiff challenge in the House of Lords. Lord Chancellor Thurlow was indifferent to the fact that Pitt had given the bill such wholehearted support in the House of Commons as almost to make it his own measure. Thurlow derided what he called a "five days' fit of philanthropy," and predicted that on hearing of the debate going on in the British legislature, the slaves would revolt, and that slave-trading merchants would be ruined financially.

The Duke of Richmond and Lords Carlisle, Stanhope, Hopetown, and Townshend supported Dolben's bill. The rest sided with Thurlow. The supporters of the slave trade continued to raise alarmist fears. The Duke of Chandos stated he had just received a letter from Jamaica revealing that the passage of Dolben's bill might lead to an uprising in the West Indies and a massacre of white colonists.

Then came predictable tactics warning that any change in the institution of slavery would wreck the national economy and the British way of life. Lord Rodney warned of losing commerce to the French. He argued that regulating the slave trade might weaken Britain's hold on the West Indies. He also said he "had never heard of a slave being cruelly treated in all the time he had been in the West Indies, and expressed his wish that English laborers might be but half as happy."

It looked as though Dolben's bill was going to be defeated. Pitt, however, hearing how things were going, stated that if it were defeated, he "would not remain in the same cabinet" with its opponents. He then employed all the personal influence he had at his command. Dolben's bill passed, 14 votes to 12. It received the royal assent on July 11, 1788.

⌒

Wilberforce watched and rejoiced from a distance. Beyond all expectation, the first regulation of the slave trade had passed, and he was regaining his health. This was attributed in great measure to the use of opium, a common remedy, which Dr. Pitcairne had prescribed as a last resort. Opium was not a cure for the digestive problems from which Wilberforce suffered, but it did mitigate the symptoms enough for him to recover.

Starting in March 1788, Wilberforce appears to have experienced a dark night of the soul as he wrestled with the initial side effects of taking opium. These may have included hallucinations, for in one prayer he cried out: "Corrupt imaginations are perpetually rising in my mind and innumerable fears close me in on every side."

He also had to cope with the lingering effects of the overwork and stress that had caused his colitis. In a small red leather notebook, he compiled a series of entries that charted his difficulties.

He often copied prayers from the Book of Common Prayer, literary quotations, and other sources, and he composed several informal prayers himself. In one of his own prayers, he prayed:

> Lord, that knowest that no strength, wisdom or contrivance of human power can signify, or relieve me. It is in thy power alone to deliver me. I fly to thee for succour and support, O Lord let it come speedily; give me full proof of thy Almighty power; I am in great troubles, unsurmountable by me; but to thee slight and inconsiderable; look upon me O Lord with compassion and mercy, and restore me to rest, quietness, and comfort, in the world, or in another by removing me hence into a state of peace and happiness. Amen.

Another entry suggested he was dreading the coming fight for the abolition of the slave trade: "Almighty God, under all my weakness and uncertain prospects give me grace to trust firmly in thee, that I may not sink under my sorrows nor be disquieted with the fears of those evils which cannot without thy permission fall upon me."

Gradually, these fears and symptoms began to subside, as reflected in the last pages of Wilberforce's notebook. "O Lord our God," runs one prayer, "thou hast said unto us I will never leave you, nor forsake you ... thou hast supported my spirit in the days of trouble, and has given me many intervals of refreshment, renewing thy loving kindness day by day...." Other entries are petitions "for grace to do his duty, freedom from worldly motives, from desire for applause and from the temptation to depend on human aid alone." One biographer suggests that Wilberforce's "spirit and mind had suffered worse than the body; it had been partly a nervous breakdown."

By the spring of 1789 Wilberforce, now fully recovered, was able to resume leadership of the abolition fight in Parliament. On May 12 he gave an impassioned speech lasting three hours, in which he called for the abolition of slave trade. He remembered:

I opened the question to the House, and the line of argument which I pursued was this: I explained the nature of the traffic for slaves on the African coast – the flagrant evils, the wars, the cruelties, the barbarisms which it engendered – the obstacles which it opposed to the progress of civilisation – and also strongly dwelt on the horrors of the Middle Passage. Finally, I insisted on the impolicy of the trade, since by improving the condition and treatment of the slave population in our islands their numbers might be kept up by natural means.

This summary, helpful as it is, does not convey the eloquence and power with which Wilberforce spoke. After he had come to understand the atrocities of the Middle Passage, for example, he told his colleagues, "I confess to you ... so enormous, so dreadful, so irremediable did its wickedness appear, that my own mind was completely made up for the abolition. A trade founded in iniquity, and carried on as this was, must be abolished, let the policy be what it might – let the consequences be what they would, I from this time determined that I would never rest till I had [secured] its abolition."

Wilberforce was arguing for a sea change in British policy. He had now come to believe that the abolition of the slave trade was "a matter wherein all personal, much more all ministerial, attachments must be as dust in the balance." He drove this point home near the end of his speech in words that can still stir the soul, even when read on the printed page.

> Policy, however ... is not my principle, and I am not ashamed to say it. There is a principle above every thing that is political.... When I reflect on the command which says, "Thou shalt do no murder," believing the authority to be divine, how can I dare to set up any reasonings of my own against it?
>
> And ... when we think of eternity, and of the future consequences of all human conduct, what is there in this life that should make any man contradict the dictates of his conscience, the principles of justice, the laws of religion, and of God....

The nature and all the circumstances of this trade are now laid open to us; we can no longer plead ignorance – we cannot evade it – it is now an object placed before us – we cannot pass it; we may spurn it, we may kick it out of the way, but we cannot turn aside so as to avoid seeing it.... It is brought now so directly before our eyes, that this House must decide, and must justify to all the world, and to their own consciences, the rectitude of the grounds and principles of their decision.

Wilberforce's speech had a powerful impact on the House. Burke stated that the speech "equalled anything he had heard in modern times, and was not, perhaps, to be surpassed in the remains of Grecian eloquence." Pitt knew too the heights of oratory to which Wilberforce could ascend: "Of all the men I knew," he said, "Wilberforce has the greatest natural eloquence."

Despite Wilberforce's speech and the support of Pitt, Burke, Fox, and many great men in Parliament, the House of Commons dissolved itself into a committee to hear further evidence for and against the slave trade. On June 23 the Commons voted to hear more evidence in the next parliamentary session.

⌣

By early 1790 Wilberforce had convinced Parliament to appoint a select committee to continue to hear evidence for and against the slave trade. His chief partner in this investigation was William Smith, the grandfather of Florence Nightingale. In June a general parliamentary election was held, and Wilberforce was reelected member of Parliament for Yorkshire.

Finally, on April 18, 1791, debate on the bill for abolition of the slave trade commenced. It was an event not only anticipated by the politicians who would be taking part but also by abolitionists such as the Quaker William Allen, who arrived early that morning to get a seat in the Stranger's Gallery.

At about five o'clock in the afternoon Prime Minister Pitt and Wilberforce arrived. Shortly after the House resolved itself into a committee of the whole House, Allen recalled, "Wilberforce rose, and in an able speech, which continued for nearly four hours, opened the hidden things of darkness in an admirable manner, exposing the horrid traffic in its native deformity."

When Wilberforce began to speak, Allen noticed that Colonel Banastre Tarleton, a British hero of the American Revolutionary War and implacable opponent of abolition, took up a sheet of paper and a pen – a common tactic used in Parliament to distract and dishearten speakers. Yet Wilberforce had an equally formidable supporter in Pitt, who took out a pen and paper to keep Wilberforce's spirits up. Wilberforce "seemed firm as a rock, and [was] not to be baffled by Tarleton and his company."

Wilberforce had need of such support, for Tarleton was a formidable opponent. He had, in fact, once boasted of killing more men than anyone living and was the basis for the obsessively violent officer depicted in the film *The Patriot*. Tarleton's taking up paper and pen during Wilberforce's speech was intended to distract and dishearten, but it was also intended to send a message: "You don't want to cross swords with me." Pitt's response told Wilberforce that he could count on Pitt – no matter what Tarleton did or might do. It also sent Tarleton a message: "If you cross swords with Wilberforce, you also cross swords with me."

Wilberforce sat on the Treasury Bench, next to the prime minister, who "gave Wilberforce every little assistance in his power with his papers." At one point Allen observed that "when Wilberforce had drawn a strong inference or conclusion … Pitt held up his hands in admiration."

Repeatedly during Wilberforce's speech the cry of "hear him! hear him!" reverberated throughout the house. Allen noted that although Wilberforce "was [feeling] but poorly the day before, yet he exerted his voice in an astonishing manner, speaking with great emphasis all the time, and shining brighter and brighter, after he had been speaking an hour, than at the first, and his voice, so far from failing him, seemed to strengthen as he went on." Wilberforce concluded with moving for leave to bring in a bill for the abolition of the slave trade.

Wilberforce's valiant effort was all for naught. Two days later a vote was taken on the proposed bill: 88 for, 163 against. Wilberforce and his colleagues sought to regroup for a renewal of the fight, which commenced the following year.

Almost one year later, April 2, 1792, Wilberforce again moved for the slave trade's abolition. During the House of Commons debate, he pleaded for the slaves, saying: "Africa! Africa! your sufferings have been the theme that has arrested and engages my heart – your sufferings no tongue can express; no language impart."

Pitt also made a brilliant speech. Wilberforce described it, just afterwards, in a letter to his friend William Hey: "My motion for immediate Abolition was ... supported strenuously ... by Pitt with more energy and ability than were almost ever exerted in the House of Commons.... Fox and [Charles] Grey ... agreed ... in thinking Pitt's speech one of the most extraordinary displays of eloquence they had ever heard. For the last twenty minutes he really seemed to be inspired."

Pitt was concluding his speech as the first rays of sunlight shone through the windows of the House of Commons. Moved by the sight, he cited Virgil in making a stirring appeal to his colleagues to bring a sunrise of happiness to Africa.

Henry Dundas, however, the powerful and influential politician who was then home secretary, rose and proposed that the slave trade be abolished gradually, not immediately. It stole the momentum created by Pitt's eloquence. Many members who were wavering seized upon a solution they thought wisdom itself. After protracted debate, the House of Commons agreed with Dundas and voted to gradually abolish the trade by January 1, 1796.

It was not what Wilberforce had hoped for, and he grew despondent thinking that if the trade were to be abolished gradually, it might never be abolished at all. Upon further reflection, however, he concluded that an important victory had been gained.

It had been the first time Parliament had ever voted for a bill to abolish the slave trade.

At this time he also received encouragement from William Cowper, who had earlier written to John Newton saying he hoped Wilberforce would benefit from Newton's guidance. Indeed Wilberforce had, and Cowper now praised his tireless abolitionist labors.

> *Thy country, Wilberforce, with just disdain,*
> *Hears thee by cruel men and impious call'd*
> *Fanatick, for thy zeal to loose th' enthrall'd*
> *From exile, publick sale, and slavry's chain.*
> *Friend of the poor, the wrong'd, the fetter gall'd,*
> *Fear not lest labour such as thine be vain.*
> *Thou hast achiev'd a part; hast gained the ear*
> *Of Britain's senate to thy glorious cause;*
> *Hope smiles, joy springs, and tho' cold caution pause*
> *And weave delay, the better hour is near*
> *That shall remunerate thy toils severe*
> *By peace for Afric, fenced with British laws.*
> *Enjoy what thou hast won, esteem and love*
> *From all the just on earth, and all the Blest above!*

Not everyone, however, was so complimentary. James Boswell, who had once supported Wilberforce at Bennet Langton's home, had now turned his coat and become a supporter of the slave trade. He penned his own derisive tribute:

> *Go W———with narrow skull,*
> *Go home and preach away at Hull.*
> *No longer in the Senate cackle*
> *In strains that suit the tabernacle;*
> *I hate your little whittling sneer,*
> *Your pert and self-sufficient leer.*
> *Mischief to trade sits on your lip.*
> *Insects will gnaw the noblest ship.*
> *Go, W———, begone, for shame,*
> *Thou dwarf with big resounding name.*

Meanwhile, events on the European continent had worsened. In February 1793 France declared war on Great Britain. As if the outbreak of war were not bad enough, on February 26, 1793, the House of Commons refused to confirm the 1792 vote for gradual abolition. In April 1793 Wilberforce was confronted by rumors that he was abandoning the abolition struggle.

Nothing could have been further from his mind. "In the case of every question of political expediency," he wrote to Dr. James Currie,

> there appears to me room for the consideration of times and seasons – at one period under one set of circumstances it may be proper to push, at another and in other circumstances to withhold our efforts. But in the present instance where the actual commission of guilt is in question, a man who fears God is not at liberty. To you I will say a strong thing which the motive I have just suggested will both explain and justify. If I thought the immediate Abolition of the Slave Trade would cause an insurrection in our [West Indian] islands, I should not for an instant remit my most strenuous endeavours. Be persuaded then, I shall never … sacrifice [this cause] to motives of political convenience or personal feeling.

Wilberforce's resolve notwithstanding, he was soon to receive distressing news. In the summer of 1794, Thomas Clarkson, suffering from ruined health and financial distress, retired from the abolitionist cause. He would not rejoin the fight for twelve years.

⌣

Toward the end of 1794 Wilberforce had also begun to wrestle with another issue that caused him great pain and nearly severed his fifteen-year friendship with Pitt. After much soul-searching Wilberforce resolved to introduce a motion calling for a negotiated peace after nearly two years of war against the French.

Wilberforce offered his motion in December 1794, but for some time he had been wrestling with doubts about the war. "I own my political horizon is much clouded," he had written on November 3 of the same year. "I begin to think we can look for no good from the prosecution of the war."

Wilberforce believed that "at all times, war ought to be deprecated as the greatest of human evils," but he was not a pacifist. In December 1792, on the eve of France's declaration of war against Britain, he had stated, "If we should find ourselves compelled by the obligations of solemn treaties to engage in war, as men of conscience and integrity we must submit to the necessity." He also believed that Scripture allowed for defensive wars. Which is why, in response to a letter he received from Thomas Clarkson in 1820 asking him to support a pacifist society, he replied that he could not because he was not "a condemner of war universally."

Throughout the late autumn and early winter of 1794, Wilberforce sought advice from his friends, seeking to "[make] up my mind cautiously and maturely, and therefore slowly, as to the best conduct … in the present critical emergency." He wrote to several of his oldest friends, including Henry Bankes, whose judgment and independence he highly valued.

Wilberforce told Bankes he was troubled that Pitt's ideas remained so warlike. He acknowledged the strength of the argument that "any peace we could make with a French republic would be insecure, and require an immense peace establishment," but saw "no grounds to hope for a better issue." On the whole, he told Bankes he felt "it might be our best plan to declare our willingness to make peace on equitable terms."

Wilberforce came to the crux of the matter: "I would gladly get an end put to this war without Pitt's being turned out of office, which will hardly be possible I fear if it continue much longer." On private grounds, this weighed on him greatly, but he felt other considerations were far more important. "I am quite sick … of such a scene of havoc and misery," he told Bankes, "and unless I am quite clear I shall not dare vote for [the war's] continuance."

Wilberforce was now under great strain and often unable to sleep. It was not only his friendship with Pitt that was at risk. He feared for his friendship with Pitt's brother-in-law Edward Eliot. Many years before Eliot had, like Wilberforce, embraced evangelical Christianity. Except for his cousin Henry Thornton, there was no one else with whom Wilberforce "was so much in the habit of consulting."

Knowing that he might run the risk of severing this friendship as well, he wrote to Eliot:

> I am sure your affectionate heart will not a little hurt, to hear that I fear I must differ from Pitt on the important point of continuing the war.... Praying to be enabled to decide aright.... I am more and more convinced that we ought to make a general peace, if practicable, on equitable terms.... I need hardly say that the prospect of a public difference with Pitt is extremely painful to me, and though I trust this friendship for me sunk too deep in his heart to be soon worn out, I confess it hangs me like a weight I cannot remove.... My spirits are hardly equal to the encounter. However, I hope it will please God to enable me to act the part of an honest man in this trying occasion.... You and I, my dear friend, have formed, I hope, a connection which will last for *ever*.

On December 29, 1794, Wilberforce met with a group of five friends at his home, Number 4 Old Palace Yard, which stood directly across the street from where the Commons met in St. Stephen's Chapel. All agreed that Wilberforce should propose an amendment to the House of Commons' Address to the King on the conduct of the war. His friend and fellow MP for Yorkshire, Henry Duncombe, would second his motion.

Beyond this, however, Wilberforce's remaining four friends were divided. Bankes and Thornton would vote in favor of his amendment. Lord Muncaster and Matthew Montagu were grieved by the thought of voting against Pitt. As he had for so many nights, Wilberforce slept badly.

The following evening Wilberforce moved his amendment in a speech that greatly affected his colleagues. Shocked, Secretary of War William Windham angrily replied to it. Conversely, Pitt's great political opponent Charles Fox was pleased, thinking he might soon expect Wilberforce to join him and the political opposition. Pitt masked his conflicting emotions, as he was so often able to do, and gave a long speech that struck a moderate tone. Wilberforce's amendment was decisively rejected by a majority of 173.

Pitt's speech that night may have been moderate, but he was greatly hurt and could not sleep himself. Wilberforce's first open opposition was one of only two events in Pitt's public life to have this effect. The other was the mutiny of the British fleet stationed at the Nore in 1797, when the threat of a French invasion was most imminent.

Wilberforce was equally grieved by the ongoing prospect of opposing Pitt. Politics rushed into his mind when he awakened in the night, and prevented his going to sleep again. "No one," he later wrote, "who has not seen a good deal of public life, and felt how difficult and painful it is to differ widely from those with whom you wish to agree, can judge at what an expense of feeling such duties are performed."

Wilberforce's colleagues could not fathom his action. Pitt viewed it as a desertion and betrayal. Fox, equally mistaken, paid Wilberforce a cordial visit, saying, "You will soon see that you must join us altogether." One of Pitt's younger protégés, George Canning, showed the most insight. Based upon Wilberforce's speech and a private conversation afterward, Canning believed that Wilberforce's motion had been an act of conscience. Having made an attempt at peace, Wilberforce and his friends would again support the war.

Canning was right. On January 2 Wilberforce offered an amendment supporting the supply of due resources to carry on the war vigorously if it must continue. This greatly offended the partisans of Pitt's administration, who now thought Wilberforce a hypocrite. Three days later Wilberforce defended the suspension of the Habeas Corpus Act, seeing "no reason to believe that government had abused the power committed to them." This step equally irritated Fox and the Whigs, who thought they had gained a convert to their cause.

Wilberforce's biographer sons rightly concluded that "the politician who truly thinks for himself and takes his own stand, must be assailed with unwelcome judgments on every side."

Wilberforce paid a high price for following his conscience. The Duke of Portland, who was now the Home Secretary, described Wilberforce's defense of Habeas Corpus as "a pretended recantation" and "a ruse which cannot be mistaken." He considered Wilberforce and Henry Bankes "pretended friends." George III had said to Portland: "I always told Mr. Pitt they were hypocrites and not to be trusted." The king's opinion of Wilberforce would later change.

On January 26, 1795, Wilberforce supported Charles Grey's motion for peace with France. (He was the second Earl Grey, for whom the famous tea is named.) Wilberforce, however, offered an amendment to Grey's motion: "That the existence of any particular form of government in France, ought not to preclude such a peace between the two countries, as ... should be otherwise consistent with the safety, honour, and interests of Great Britain."

Following this, Wilberforce suffered an additional humiliation. "When I first went to the levee after moving my Amendment," he wrote, "the King cut me." George III showed his great displeasure by walking right past Wilberforce to the next man in the greeting line without so much as a word or glance.

Still, it was the estrangement with Pitt that hurt most. It ultimately proved to be of short duration, but the pain was no less real. On February 12 he penned a brief diary entry that said much.

There was, he wrote, "a party of *the old firm*" at the home of the Speaker of the House of Commons – "I [was] not there."

As it turned out, Edward Eliot was the catalyst for Wilberforce and Pitt's reconciliation. The affection each felt for Eliot was great. And apart from his deep regard for them both, Eliot's faith furnished him with an additional motive.

Eliot, an able politician whom Pitt later wished to succeed Sir John Shore as governor-General of India, had married Pitt's much-loved sister Harriot. Following her tragic death in September 1786, a few days after she had given birth to a daughter, Wilberforce had done all that he could to comfort Eliot. Not long afterward, Eliot embraced Christianity. "I was little better than an infidel," Eliot wrote, "but it pleased God to draw me by [my bereavement] to a better mind." Eliot died just eleven years later.

"Perhaps no one but myself knew [Eliot] thoroughly," Wilberforce wrote after receiving the news. "Neither in point of understanding, nor of religious and moral character, did he [receive his just recognition]. I can truly say, that I scarcely know any one whose loss I have so much cause to regret. "

Writing to Hannah More, Wilberforce stated: "I feel Eliot's loss deeply.... We were engaged in a multitude of pursuits together, and *he was a bond of connection, which was sure never to fail, between me and Pitt*; because a bond not of political, nor merely of a personal quality, but formed by a consciousness of common sentiments, interests, and feelings."

⌒

Neither Pitt nor Wilberforce could lightly disregard Eliot's efforts to bring them together. Following a dinner on March 21, 1795, Wilberforce met Pitt for the first time since their estrangement. On April 15 Wilberforce called on Pitt for the first time since the beginning of the parliamentary session. Ten days later Wilberforce called on Eliot at Battersea Rise "knowing Pitt was there, and that Eliot knew I knew it, and thinking therefore it would seem unkind not to do it." Initially both Pitt and Wilberforce were "meaning to be kind to each other [and] a little embarrassed," but they were soon walking together and talking openly, as of old.

Pitt had gradually come to understand the reasons why Wilberforce had made his conscientious motion for peace. By May 2 Wilberforce wrote, "All Pitt's supporters believe him disposed to make peace."

Wilberforce was deeply gratified, but his joy was short lived when he discovered that some now believed there had been "a complete understanding" between him and Pitt all the while and that "his opposition was only a pretext."

On May 13 the Duchess of Gordon told Wilberforce that while the Duke of Leeds, the Duke of Bedford, and Lord Thurlow dined with her a few days before, Thurlow said "he would bet, or did bet five guineas that Pitt and I should vote together on my motion ... for peace. This shows he thinks there is a secret understanding between Pitt and me all this time."

Thurlow was mistaken, but it is easy to see why a cynical, calculating politician like him might have thought as he did. The bond between Wilberforce and Pitt was unique and strong, and in time would endure many differences of opinion. Thurlow was therefore baffled when Wilberforce soon felt compelled to oppose Pitt's wishes on another subject: raising the income of the Prince of Wales above all former precedent. On May 14 Wilberforce opposed this grant in a speech, but his opposition produced no unkind feelings.

Two days before the debate on increasing the prince's income, Wilberforce had been invited by Eliot to dine with him at Battersea Rise. Pitt and another old friend, Dudley Ryder, were there as well. Wilberforce called and stayed for two hours, walking, laughing, and reading verses of poetry with his friends, as he had done so often before.

On May 20, as Wilberforce was preparing to introduce another motion for peace with France, he had written: "I had shown my

The library at Battersea Rise, where Wilberforce and his Clapham circle colleagues held so many of what he called their "cabinet councils"

motion to Pitt on Saturday – he [is] very kind now and good-natured." The next day Wilberforce "called at Pitt's to settle with him when [the debate on my motion] should come on."

Wilberforce's motion, a general overture for peace, was rejected. But within six months, he had the satisfaction of hearing from Pitt that he too was convinced of the necessity of peace.

Wilberforce believed Pitt did not arrive at this conclusion sooner largely because of the influence of Henry Dundas, now secretary of state for war. Dundas, Wilberforce thought, had done all he could to foster a thirst for colonial conquest in Pitt. The hope of capturing St. Domingo held out the prospect of gaining a West Indian island whose commerce with France exceeded Britain's whole West Indian trade. Wilberforce contended that Pitt was resolved on continuing the war until he could "make peace on terms which should afford indemnity for the past, and [financial] security for the future."

Wilberforce now devoted a considerable amount of time in the late summer and autumn of 1795 to visits with his Yorkshire constituents, many of whom had been offended by his opposition to Pitt on the question of war. Beginning on August 4, he journeyed throughout much of the county.

Some constituents were "violently incensed by my political conduct." One refused to come down to see him. Still, Wilberforce possessed formidable powers of persuasion and diplomacy. One incident illustrates just how persuasive he could be. Few subjects are as fraught with the danger of sharp disagreement as religion, but Wilberforce once discussed a controversial religious issue with one who did not wish to agree with him: the Poet Laureate Robert Southey.

Southey met Wilberforce for the first time in 1817. He told Wilberforce's sons that they and a group of friends began to discuss the question of Catholic emancipation; "Your father and Sir Thomas Acland taking the one side [in favor of it], and I the other." Southey asserted:

> No person can be more disinclined to disputation than myself ... but if my temper had been likely to hurry me into any unbecoming warmth, your father's manner would effectually have repressed it. His views, when I thought him most mistaken, were so benign ... and [he] argued with such manly yet such earnest sincerity, that if it had been possible to have persuaded me out of an opinion so deeply and firmly rooted, he would have done it. Our discussion, for so it may be called, was protracted till two in the morning.

This conversation was the more remarkable given Wilberforce's admission in early life that his temper was naturally irritable, and when one recalls his bitter, caustic attacks on Fox in 1784.

Few could resist Wilberforce's powers of conversation, wrote his sons. Full of the mirth of childhood, it abounded in stories, reflections, and the allusions of a thoughtful mind. It was continually marked by "humour of the most sparkling quality" – flashes of wit "played lightly over all he touched upon." His fervent imagination was chastened by "the self-restraint of a conscience that could not now bear the offense of giving pain to any." These were gifts he now carefully and conscientiously employed.

Visiting the cities of York, Leeds, Halifax, and Huddersfield, Wilberforce received a cordial welcome from many, and won over others whom political differences had estranged. He returned home to Number 4 Old Palace Yard on October 24, 1795. A letter from Pitt awaited him.

> It would be a great satisfaction to me if you could come so as to allow time for our having some quiet conversation before we meet in the House.... I think our talking over the present state of things may do a great deal of good, and I am sure at all events it can do no harm.... I cannot help thinking that ... shortly ... our opinions [as to the question of peace] cannot materially differ. I need not say how much personal comfort it will give me if my expectation in this respect is realized.

It was immensely gratifying for Wilberforce to learn of Pitt's desire for peace. Many of Pitt's other friends now recognized the principle from which Wilberforce's conduct had arisen. Lord Camden (son of the former Lord chancellor with whom Wilberforce had grown close in the 1780s) wrote:

> We might [have] differ[ed] at the commencement of the last session as to the line which you then thought it right to pursue. I am candid enough to own that I can conceive it not as inconsistent as I then thought it; and that with the explanation your subsequent conduct has given I perfectly understand it. Pitt appears to me to have been more able than ever since the meeting of Parliament, and I have little doubt of his making a peace, and of the country supporting him in it.

The autumn of 1795 marked the beginning of one of the darkest periods of the revolutionary war with France. The French were victorious everywhere. Some Britons, as well as the French, called for the overthrow of the British government – a source of great anxiety. Parliament met on October 29, and Pitt avowed his desire for peace. In this debate Wilberforce declared that all difference between himself and Pitt had ended.

Meanwhile, instances of civil discontent were drawing to a head. The king was violently mobbed on his way to open Parliament. Tumultuous meetings were held in London, and many inflammatory publications were being distributed. On November 18 Wilberforce expressed great concern about the publication of prints depicting the guillotining of the king and others.

As with many subsequent revolutions, cries abounded for the abolition of private property, particularly those lands owned by the rich. There were many levelers in Britain who sought to tear down the existing government and redistribute wealth. Anger against the aristocracy ran particularly high.

In this crisis Wilberforce reluctantly judged it right to arm the executive government with extraordinary powers. On November 10 Pitt proposed legislative measures preventing seditious assemblies, and Wilberforce supported them. His speech, however, which was highly commended, expressly called for maintaining unimpaired the full right of individuals to petition the government concerning any grievances. He wanted to ensure that the voice of the people could be heard in the legislature. "I do not willingly support these Bills," he said, "but I look on them as a temporary sacrifice, by which the blessings of liberty may be transmitted to our children unimpaired."

These bills were fiercely attacked by Fox and other members of the political opposition. Many modern historians have also criticized Wilberforce for supporting what they consider harshly oppressive measures; but in the face of what he considered the real and growing threat posed by revolutionary France and those who would import revolution into Britain, he felt he had no choice. His actions in this regard must be weighed in this context.

Wilberforce worked to structure these bills so that they were no more repressive than necessary. On November 11 he "went to

Pitt's to look over the Sedition Bill [and] altered it much for the better." The next day he again defended these measures, stating that they did, in truth, "raise new bastions to defend the bulwarks of British liberty." In doing so he felt compelled to oppose his friend and colleague Henry Duncombe.

It seemed that at every turn, Wilberforce, in acting according to the dictates of his conscience, had painful differences of opinion with friends.

For Wilberforce, Pitt, and many others, it was a harrowing time. During a meeting at Pitt's about the Sedition Bill on November 16, Pitt stated, "My head would be off in six months were I to resign." "I see that he expects a civil broil," Wilberforce wrote. "Never was [there] a time when [we are] so loudly called on to prepare for the worst."

"Poor Pitt!" he wrote on November 22. "I too am much an object of popular odium. [A] riot is expected from the Westminster meeting.... The printers are all angry at the Sedition Bills.... I greatly fear some civil war or embroilment and with my weak health and bodily infirmities my heart shrinks from its difficulties and dangers."

⌒

Wilberforce's apprehension was heightened by the fact that this latest turn of events was only one of many real and potential threats of physical harm he had endured in recent years. In a diary entry written earlier in 1795, he referred to death threats he had received from supporters of the slave trade: "God protected me from Norris, Kimber, and innumerable other dangers. He is still able to protect me, and will, if it be for my good."

Captain Robert Norris and Captain John Kimber were slave traders whose credibility Wilberforce had destroyed during parliamentary examinations of the slave trade some years before. In 1790 Norris had grown so threatening that Wilberforce feared murder.

Kimber was no less threatening. In April 1792 Wilberforce had charged him with great cruelty in his conduct of the slave trade. Kimber was later capitally indicted for the murder of a slave girl. He was found not guilty, and Wilberforce attributed this to "the shameful remissness of the Crown lawyers, and the indecent behaviour of a high personage, who from the bench identified himself with the prisoner's cause."

Discharged from prison, Kimber sought out Wilberforce, demanding "a public apology, £5,000 [over $1.3 million in today's currency] ... and such a place under government as would make me comfortable." Wilberforce sought Pitt's advice and penned a brief refusal. Kimber decided to resort to violence. He began lying in wait for Wilberforce and continued to do so for the next two years. The intercession of Lord Sheffield eventually terminated this threat, but not before Wilberforce's friend Lord Rokeby had felt it necessary to travel with him for some time as an armed bodyguard.

Then too, in the summer of 1792, just months before the outbreak of war with France, Wilberforce was challenged to a duel by a slave-trading captain named Rolleston. Wilberforce was no coward – the moral courage and determination he demonstrated throughout the fight to abolish the slave trade show he was not – but he was opposed to dueling on Christian grounds. He refused Rolleston's challenge, deeming that a "proper and easy explanation of my determination and views in respect to dueling, might be in all respects [an] eligible [response]." The affair was carried no further.

Wilberforce believed that dueling "is a deliberate preference of the favour of man, before the favour and approbation of God, *in articulo mortis* [at the point of death]." Moreover, dueling was "an instance, wherein our own life, and that of a fellow creature are at stake, and wherein we run the risk of rushing into the presence of our Maker in the very act of offending him."

Wilberforce also felt the practice of dueling mainly rested on "excessive over-valuation of character, which teaches, that worldly credit is to be preserved at any rate, and disgrace at any rate to be avoided." He insisted: "dueling ... has often been shown to be criminal on various principles ... particularly when it has been considered as an indication of malice and revenge."

⁓

Wilberforce's strength of character and determination of purpose belied his appearance. "He seemed the frailest and feeblest of mortals," one friend observed, and so he was in terms of his recurring bouts of sickness and his small stature. But within his spare frame was the stoutest of hearts. He dreaded the scorn he knew his support of the Treason and Sedition bills would bring upon him – but he still gave these measures his full support.

The contest over the Treason and Sedition bills now spread from the Commons to the country at large. Many political observers were concerned because the sentiments of Yorkshire, Wilberforce's constituency, were thought to be hostile to these measures. On November 19, 1795, Wilberforce's friend William Burgh wrote to inform him that "the Bills are obnoxious in this part of the world to an extreme degree."

Wilberforce greatly desired an opportunity to address an open meeting of the freeholders of Yorkshire, but the high sheriff refused to convene one. "The assembling of so large and unwieldy a body," he replied, "would only tend to raise riot and discontent." This decision was quoted triumphantly in the House of Commons as "a strong argument against the Bills." Wilberforce lamented the high sheriff's conduct because it had, in his view, "prevented a full, fair, and free discussion of the subject."

Upon the high sheriff's refusal to convene a meeting, those opposed to the Treason and Sedition bills in Yorkshire had privately resolved to attempt one. To secure the kind of attendance they desired, they waited four days. On Friday, November 27, they issued circulars, requesting "the freeholders to assemble at the Castle

Yard of York, if the sheriff will permit it to be used; and if not; at the guild-hall, upon the Tuesday following."

By this maneuver, those opposed to the Treason and Sedition bills believed they could secure only the presence of their partisans. No newspaper was then published in York on Friday; therefore the announcement would only reach those persons in the county whom they wished to summon.

In London, all that was passing was unknown. At twelve o'clock on Saturday afternoon, November 28, Wilberforce received "a note from Sir William Milner, saying that the York meeting was to be held upon Tuesday next." Wilberforce's suspicions were also aroused by a friend who had written to say, "something extraordinary is certainly designed in Yorkshire." Wilberforce still did not know enough, however, to indicate that his presence would be necessary, until he was in his carriage on his way to church on Sunday morning.

Just as he got into his carriage, an express letter arrived from his friends William Hey and William Cookson, informing him of all that had been done and urging him at all costs to be present at the meeting. He immediately notified Edward Eliot and went to visit him. "He and I, on consideration," Wilberforce wrote, "determined that it would be right for me to go [as] the country's peace might be much benefited by it."

Wilberforce sent his carriage back to be fitted for the journey and then called on Pitt, who was "much disquieted." Wilberforce's servant brought word that his carriage would not be ready when he required it. "Mine is ready," Pitt said, "set off in that." Another guest, upon hearing this, said, "If they find out whose carriage you have got, you will run the risk of being murdered." This fear was not groundless. Some among Wilberforce's Yorkshire supporters had written to him saying that "if he ventured down it would be at the hazard of his life."

By half past two Wilberforce was off in Pitt's carriage and traveled to Alconbury Hill. After a few hours of rest, he was off again early on Monday morning. While on the road Wilberforce busied himself in preparations for the meeting.

Pitt had supplied Wilberforce with samples of the writings by which the public mind was thought to have been poisoned. His mission was deemed so important that the prime minister sent an express after him with further materials. Wilberforce's secretary recalled: "Almost the whole of Monday was spent in dictating; and, between his own manuscripts and the pamphlets which had followed him, we were almost up to the knees in papers."

On Monday, November 30, Wilberforce had sent an express letter to his friend William Hey. "I have made a forced march ... and am going forward.... I am deeply impressed with a sense of the necessity of bold and decided conduct.... *Pray that I may be supported.*" Wilberforce also asked that any friends who were staying away from York be urged to join him there.

Meanwhile the supporters of the government had roused the West Riding section of Yorkshire. The whole county seemed to be pouring into York. One eyewitness recalled: "It was an alarming moment when these immense numbers began to pour in, while as yet we knew not what part they would take. " By Monday evening, however, the supporters of Pitt's government began to feel their strength.

Still, at this point, they lacked an acknowledged leader. The opposition had had time to develop their plans and concentrate their efforts under appointed leaders. The supporters of the government had come together so suddenly that they were not nearly as well organized.

At that critical moment Wilberforce's carriage turned the corner. His approach was not generally known. When he arrived among the thousands gathered outside the guildhall, the street resounded with shouts and hats filled the air. Wilberforce later wrote, "What a row did I make when I turned this corner in 1795, it seemed as if the whole place must [have] come down together."

Alighting from his carriage, Wilberforce pushed through the crowd to address them. He vainly attempted to prevail on Christopher Wyvill – once a close friend, but now a leader of the opposition – to adjourn to the Castle Yard. Wilberforce said he hoped to meet "[them] that day face to face, and convince them of the groundlessness of their prejudices, if they were not prepared to shut up all the avenues to the understanding and all the passages to the heart."

Wyvill and the opposition refused. Wilberforce, his supporters, and many who were undecided or opposed then proceeded without Wyvill and his group to the Castle Yard, where Wilberforce gave a decisive speech.

The crowd that heard Wilberforce's speech was considerable. He convinced many of them to support Pitt and the government. Wyvill and his group were outclassed, and the opposition fell apart.

"It rejoiced my heart to see you at York," a friend wrote later, "and much more to hear you. Your appearance … was wonderfully beneficial to the cause, the country, and yourself. Many who, to my personal knowledge, came decidedly hostile to the Bills, were induced, on hearing your speech, to sign the addresses and petition. You have gained over almost every man in the five great commercial towns of the West Riding."

On Thursday, December 3, Wilberforce received a letter from F. W. Cookson, an influential merchant from Leeds. "Your York expedition … confirmed the staunch, fixed the neutral, and deterred the speculative.... The bells were ringing till midnight on Tuesday.... Twenty King's men to one Jacobin was the cry, and *the glorious first of December* to be an era."

Wilberforce's success was complete. Risking physical harm, he followed his conscience against what at the moment seemed to be his personal interest. When he left London he did not know which way popular sentiment ran. His friends had warned him to expect opposition and that he risked losing the next general election.

Beyond all expectation, he returned to London more popular than ever and safe from all possibility of political rivalry.

A constituent wrote long after, "I never saw you but once. That day you won my heart, and every honest heart in the county.... I never felt the power of eloquence until that day.... The contrast of your address, and the mellow tone of your voice ... with the bellowing, screaming attempts at speaking in some others, was most wonderful. You breathed energy and vigour into the desponding souls of timid loyalists, and sent us home with joy and delight."

On December 7, Wilberforce sent word of his success to Pitt by express letter. The following morning, he set off for London. By Friday, December 9, he got to the House with the petitions from the Yorkshire meeting. He told his tale with effect and was received with great gratitude.

Wilberforce assured the House that the north approved of the Treason and Sedition bills. Every day confirmed his statements in the unanimous petitions that followed him from Yorkshire. Pitt deeply felt the importance of his effort. In time, other counties followed Yorkshire's lead, "proving the justice," Wilberforce remembered, "of what Fox often said, 'Yorkshire and Middlesex between them make all England.'"

⌣

Wilberforce now sought to use this success to bolster his efforts to end the slave trade. Whereas he had been previously charged with being an irresponsible radical whose abolitionism could undermine the British economy and perhaps the nation, no one could now question his support of the established political order.

His old friend William Burgh wrote, "Your giving notice at this time that you intend to bring the Slave Trade again before the House ... will ... snatch [the question] from that odious connexion in which those who contend for the Trade have endeavoured to place it before the public eye."

Burgh's reference to an odious connection concerned recent events in the West Indies. The French government, finding it impossible to defeat Britain's navy, incited the entire black population of the French West Indian islands to foment rebellion in the English West Indian colonies. Uprisings took place in Grenada, Dominica, and St. Vincent's. Anti-abolitionists alleged that such occurrences were indicative of the true intentions of Wilberforce and his friends – that violence and the abolitionist cause were directly related – that abolitionists were revolutionaries at heart.

Notwithstanding these charges, the violence that erupted in the British West Indies was indeed fearful, prompting some friends of abolition to suggest that any motion to abolish the slave trade be set aside and taken up again at a more opportune time.

Wilberforce disagreed. On December 15, 1795, he gave notice that early in the next parliamentary session he would propose his motion. "Now is the very time to show our true principles," he asserted, "by stopping a practice which violates all the real rights of human nature."

⌒

The year 1796 would prove to be the one in which Wilberforce came closest to securing abolition prior to 1807. The failure of his motion at this time was the most devastating defeat of the entire twenty-year fight to abolish the slave trade.

The initial signs were promising. On January 6, Wilberforce went to town to attend a royal levee. Unlike the levee he attended in 1795, he received a far more positive reception from George III. Very likely the King had heard of Wilberforce's great success in defending the Treason and Sedition bills, for he spoke with Wilberforce cordially. They chatted about a new book written by Wilberforce's friend Thomas Gisborne – *The Principles of Moral Philosophy* – a literary reply to philosopher William Paley's *Moral and Political Philosophy*. Then Wilberforce set off for Pitt's, where he likewise received a warm welcome.

Parliament met on February 2, 1796. On February 18, Wilberforce introduced his motion for a bill to abolish the slave trade. The time stipulated for the bill to take effect was March 1, 1797. Roused by an unusually animated debate, Wilberforce judged he had spoken "warmly and well."

Robert Banks Jenkinson (the future prime minister and second Earl Liverpool), professed to join in Wilberforce's condemnation of the slave trade. Yet he made a speech that contributed to the opposite result. "I anxiously wish that the question were postponed at least till the return of peace," he said in his closing remarks.

Wilberforce rose to reply: "There is something not a little provoking in the dry calm way in which gentlemen are apt to speak of the sufferings of others. The question suspended! Is the desolation of wretched Africa suspended? Are all the complicated miseries of this atrocious trade – is the work of death suspended? No, sir, I will not delay this motion, and I call upon the House not to insult the forbearance of Heaven by delaying this tardy act of justice."

In response to the charge that the slaves were well fed, Wilberforce cried: "What! are these the only claims of a rational being? Are the feelings of the heart nothing? . . . So far from thanking the honourable gentleman for the feeding, clothing and lodging of which he boasts, I protest against the way in which he has mentioned them as degrading men to the level of the brutes, and insulting all the higher qualities of our common nature."

When Banastre Tarleton (as formidable a Wilberforce foe as ever) made a motion for an adjournment, it was voted down by a majority of 26. Wilberforce felt "surprise and joy in carrying my question."

Wilberforce now worked on the language of his abolition bill and consulted often with Pitt at 10 Downing Street for that purpose. On Monday, February 22, Wilberforce crossed the street from his home at Number 4 Old Palace Yard to oversee the bill's further legislative progress. Finding the House in a good state, he brought in his bill without opposition and returned home.

Wilberforce did not continue unopposed for long. March 3 had been fixed for the second reading of his bill. After a morning spent consulting about it at Pitt's, he was dining in Palace Yard with a party of friends from the Commons. Early in the evening a supporter of the slave trade moved the second reading of his bill, hoping by this maneuver to prevent its further progress. Wilberforce defeated this attempt, hurrying from dinner over to the House and speaking until his supporters could arrive. The second reading of his bill was carried 63 to 31.

On March 7, 1796, the bill was placed in committee. Wilberforce then got the bill through committee by a majority of 76 to 31.

At its third reading, however, his hopes were disappointed. A terse diary entry described his devastating defeat. "I dined before [going to the] House," he wrote on March 15. "My Slave Bill was thrown out by 74 to 70.... Ten or twelve of those who had supported me [were] absent in the country, or [away] on pleasure. Enough [were] at the Opera to have carried it. [I am] very much vexed and incensed at our opponents."

Wilberforce was crushed, and it was probably the carelessness of his absent supporters that hurt most. His opponents, never ones to miss an opportunity, had given free opera tickets to some whom they knew would support his abolition bill. A writer for the *True Briton* wrote on March 16, "A new comic opera was brought forward last night, under the name of *I Dui Gobi* [*The Two Hunchbacks*], the music of which was composed by Portugallo.... There was a large and splendid audience."

Wilberforce's grief over this narrow loss now gave way to serious physical illness. The strain of all that had transpired since December 1794 had taken its toll. He came down with a severe fever followed by excruciating intestinal troubles. On April 12 he wrote that he had "never suffered so much." By May 6 he was still feeling so poorly that he feared a relapse of his earlier illness.

Wilberforce's friend and spiritual mentor Isaac Milner (with his wide knowledge of medicine) hurried to treat him. Slowly Wilberforce recovered, considering Milner's treatment instrumental: "He was the means, if not of saving my life, at least of sparing me a long and dangerous fit of sickness."

Describing this period, one biographer has rightly observed, "It says much for Wilberforce's courage that throughout this illness he kept working as best he could." Indeed it does.

On March 5 Wilberforce somehow found the strength to form and implement a scheme for relieving the poverty and distress of emigrant clergy who had fled the terrors of the French revolution – and the guillotine. Unable to sleep at night, he used even these sleepless hours to reflect and draw up his plan. During daylight hours he interviewed the Bishop of St. Pol de Leon and several others. He went with his cousin Henry Thornton to visit Lady Buckinghamshire and other guests in an effort to solicit the aid of prominent persons.

As if this weren't enough, in May Wilberforce faced the taxing demands of a general election. He had to secure his own seat, but he also actively campaigned for two of Pitt's supporters. One of them, Wilberforce's cousin Samuel Thornton, won reelection with difficulty. The other, Walter Spencer Stanhope, lost.

Wilberforce now attended to his own election. He canvassed hard for a fortnight, feeling "much fatigued." He managed on June 1 to secure a few days' rest in the home of his friend Ralph Creyke, who had kindly pressed him to come. He felt "excessively comfortable from [the] calm after [a] fortnight's turbulence and bustle," and was grateful for the "peace and rationality" of Creyke's home.

The election at York Castle followed on June 7. Wilberforce spoke for about twenty minutes, was reelected and chaired through the streets. He described the scene: "[The] people whilst half down Coney Street tore off the ribbons from my chair, and almost threw me down – [I got] safely out." A dinner at the York Tavern followed, with sixty-five or seventy of his supporters. He returned home about seven and prayed. "[I was] much affected, and shed many tears."

On April 17, 1796, Wilberforce had written in his diary that he had been gravely ill "for ten days and have had my head a good deal weakened." What is most significant about this diary entry, however, is its last sentence: "I have lately felt and now feel a sort of terror on reentering the world."

The years of constant struggle, the strains on long-standing friendships, the continuing threats of personal violence, and the weight of oft-disappointed hopes concerning abolition had taken their toll.

Gravely ill, exhausted, and emotionally spent, Wilberforce suffered what appears to have been a second nervous breakdown. Any thought of reentering the political fray, which had dealt him so many setbacks and blows, filled him with anxiety.

As a twenty-five-year-old, Wilberforce had brimmed with self-confidence. No cloud of political or personal discord darkened his horizon. He championed no unpopular causes and enjoyed wide political support. But after his Great Change in 1786, he had chosen a road less traveled. It had proven a difficult road.

On July 21, 1796, he wrote a letter to John Newton that expressed his willingness to consider retirement from public life. Newton's reply demonstrates why so many valued his pastoral counsel. Urging his friend to stay the course, Newton once again proved pivotal in keeping Wilberforce in political life. If he had concurred with Wilberforce's inclination to retire, Wilberforce very likely would have. Newton wrote:

> If, after taking the proper steps to secure your continuance in Parliament, you had been excluded, it would not have greatly grieved you. You would have … considered it as a providential intimation that the Lord had no farther occasion for you there. And in this view, I think you would have received your [dismissal] with thankfulness.
>
> But I hope it is a token for good that He has not yet dismissed you. Some of [God's] people may be emphatically said not to live to themselves. May it not be said of you? …

You meet with many things which weary and disgust you ... but then they are inseparably connected with your path of duty; and though you cannot do all the good you wish for, some good is done....

It costs you something ... and exposes you to many impertinences from which you would gladly be exempted; but if, upon the whole, you are thereby instrumental in promoting the cause of God and the public good, you will have no reason [for] regret....

Nor is it possible at present to calculate all the advantages that may result from your having a seat in the House at such a time as this. The example, and even the presence of a consistent character, may have a powerful, though unobserved, effect upon others. You are not only a representative for Yorkshire, you have the far greater honour of being a representative for the Lord, in a place where many know Him not, and an opportunity of showing them what are the genuine fruits of that religion which you are known to profess.

Though you have not, as yet, fully succeeded in your persevering endeavours to abolish the slave trade, the business is still in [process]; and since you took it in hand, the condition of the slaves in our islands, has undoubtedly been already [improved].... These instances, to which others ... might ... be added, are proofs that you have not laboured in vain.

It is true that you live in the midst of difficulties and snares, and you need a double guard of watchfulness and prayer. But since you know both your need of help, and where to look for it, I may say to you as Darius to Daniel. "Thy God whom thou servest continually is able to preserve and deliver you."

Daniel, likewise, was a public man, and in critical circumstances; but he trusted in the Lord; was faithful in his department, and therefore though he had enemies, they could not prevail against him.

Indeed the great point for our comfort in life is to have a well-grounded persuasion that we are where, all things considered, we ought to be. Then it is no great matter whether we are in public or in private life, in a city or a village, in a palace or a cottage. The promise, "My grace is sufficient for thee," is necessary to support us in the smoothest scenes, and is equally able to support us in the most difficult.

Happy the man who has a deep impression of our Lord's words, "Without Me you can do nothing" – who feels with the Apostle ... likewise a heartfelt dependence upon the Saviour, through whom we can both do and bear all things that are [part of] the post allotted us.

He is always near. He knows our wants, our dangers, our feelings, and our fears. By looking to him we are enlightened and made strong out of weakness. With his wisdom for our guide, his power for our protection, his fullness for our supply, and proposing his glory as our chief end, and placing our happiness in his favour, in communion with him, and communications from Him, we shall be able to "withstand in the evil day, and having done all to stand."

... May the Lord bless you my dear Sir. May he be your sun and shield, and fill you with all joy and peace in believing.

Such an appeal could not fail to strike a chord in Wilberforce's heart. Newton wisely reminded him that he had already accomplished a great deal – something often lost on those who strive for great things – only to find that their progress is incremental at best.

Newton's citation of the biblical story of Daniel was also a masterstroke. Like him, Wilberforce knew the loneliness of being a trailblazer. There were few members of Parliament publicly known to be evangelicals. It would have been a source of great comfort to recall a scriptural precedent of someone serving long, faithfully, and well under trying circumstances. Wilberforce had not been imprisoned in a lions' den, but he had faced the threat of death several times in recent years. Unlike Daniel, he had not been called to literally serve in exile, but he had been a political pariah for some time when he had opposed Pitt.

Newton also added his voice to that of John Wesley, who wrote just days before his death in 1791 to Wilberforce, commending his abolitionist labors: "Unless God has raised you up for this very thing," Wesley had written, "you will be worn out by the opposition of men and devils; but if God be for you, who can be against you?"

Newton had closed his letter by saying: "Happy the man who has a deep impression of our Lord's words, 'Without Me you can do nothing.'" This might seem a self-serving platitude. But for Wilberforce, who sincerely believed that God had set before him the object of suppressing the slave trade, Newton's last words of advice would have had the strongest appeal and offered the greatest comfort.

From Wilberforce's faith perspective, this served as a reminder that it was his responsibility to be faithful in discharging the call to service in political life. Ultimately, the affairs of nations were in the hands of the "Disposer of all human events," not his or anyone else's. This should not, and did not, breed indifference within Wilberforce; rather, it helped him to understand that there was only so much he or anyone else could really do about so many aspects of service in political life.

Wilberforce resolved to stay the course. If nothing else, Newton's letter served as a reminder that he had many good friends – friends who had been and would be there for him in the years ahead. Since 1792 Wilberforce, his cousin Henry Thornton, Edward Eliot, and several other evangelicals serving in Parliament had been living as neighbors in Clapham, then a pastoral village just outside London.

Eliot, it will be remembered, had been instrumental in healing the breach between Wilberforce and Pitt in 1795. Thornton and Wilberforce's other friends were a daily reminder that he had a circle in whom he could confide, consult, and set aside the cares of political life. All things considered, he was indeed blessed. Years later he would insist that this network of support had been indispensable in enabling him to serve effectively in politics.

Others might dismiss such a seemingly trivial notion, but Wilberforce knew that his friendships were one of the most important parts of his life. Tragically, toward the end of his political career, several of Wilberforce's colleagues in the House of Commons committed suicide. He lamented that they had no group of friends such as he had at Clapham.

By September 7, 1796, Wilberforce was able to place his grievous defeat and the other trials he had endured in perspective. Undertaking a thoughtful review of "the notables in my life," he drew up a list of all the blessings he felt he had experienced during his years in politics. He cited "my being providentially engaged in the slave trade business," and recalled, "how often [have I been] protected from evil and danger!" His illness, though it "might have been fatal, [was] well recovered from." He concluded: "It is Thou, O Lord, that hast given the very small increase there has been, and that must give all if there be more."

Looking to "the state of public affairs" in a letter to his friend Lord Muncaster, Wilberforce conceded that "seldom have they offered a more gloomy spectacle." In words reminiscent of Thomas Jefferson's statement regarding slavery, "I tremble for my country when I reflect that God is just, and that His justice cannot sleep forever," Wilberforce asked Muncaster if he didn't agree that "the slave trade ... when estimated by the Scripture standard ... may well strike terror into the heart of every serious man?" Yet the remainder of Wilberforce's letter clearly indicated that, while he was grieved over the slave trade, he had regained his emotional equilibrium.

⌐

The fight to abolish the slave trade would go on for another eleven years. Every year, from 1797 to 1803, Wilberforce suffered abolition related setbacks. From 1797 to 1799 his annual motion for abolition was defeated. For two years, starting in 1800, his motion was deferred in expectation of a general conference of European powers regarding the continuance of the war against Napoleon's France. No further progress was made in 1802. In 1803 Wilberforce's motion was again postponed because an invasion of French forces was expected.

Other events during this period caused Wilberforce much concern, including one in which he faced accusations that he was fomenting mutiny and sedition.

In May 1797, while the naval mutiny at the Nore had yet to be put down, other discontents broke out amongst the military in the neighborhood of London. It was at this moment, wrote Wilberforce's sons, "it was buzzed about that Mr. Wilberforce had written to the soldiers to express his sympathy and promise to bring their complaints before the House of Commons."

This rumor ran riot. It was so widespread, in fact, that on May 13 Pitt sent for him and William Windham (the secretary of war) did the same. "I have no intention of making any motion on the subject,' Wilberforce stated emphatically. "To do so at this time and in such a manner I should deem little short of positive insanity." Still, it was asserted that a representative from Wilberforce had brought a message to the London barracks, read aloud his letter, and actually shown them his signature.

How this matter was finally laid to rest said much about Wilberforce and the vexing harassments to which he was periodically subjected.

The story is as follows. An Anglican clergyman named Williams had been recommended to Wilberforce as a deserving recipient of his charity. Though Williams had been reduced to dire financial straits through immoral excess and possible mental imbalance, he was now thought penitent. Wilberforce began assisting Williams.

Williams was anything but penitent, however. He was as immoral and apparently unbalanced as he had ever been. During one interview he spat in Wilberforce's face and grew so violent that a Bow Street warrant had to be sworn out against him to prevent him from further acts of violence. Finding him at last irreclaimable, Wilberforce had written to refuse him any further aid.

But Williams was not done. Still filled with spite and resentment, he took Wilberforce's letter down to the London military barracks. There, before the illiterate soldiers, he pretended to read a seditious message from Wilberforce, after which he showed the genuine Wilberforce signature. Several trying days were to unfold – and Wilberforce received not a few anxious letters from Pitt – before the mutinous seeds sown by Williams were thoroughly and finally quashed.

One year later, on May 25, 1798, Wilberforce received another shock. Pitt had fought a duel with a political opponent named George Tierney.

Thankfully, both men survived – indeed, neither was hurt. In Pitt's case (as the newspapers of the day joked) this was understandable, for he was so thin that standing sideways no one, no matter how good a shot, could have hit him. In Tierney's case, his emerging unscathed was rather miraculous, for he was so large a man that Pitt could hardly have failed to hit him.

For Wilberforce it was no laughing matter. He was horrified that a prime minister could have so recklessly put the welfare of Great Britain at risk during a time of war. So great was Wilberforce's aversion to this so-called "system of honour," that he talked seriously of introducing a parliamentary motion to outlaw dueling. This alarmed Pitt, who quickly wrote:

> My dear Wilberforce, I am not the person to argue with you on a subject in which I am a good deal concerned. I hope too that I am incapable of doubting your kindness to me (however mistaken I may think it).... I feel it a real duty to say to you frankly that your motion is one for my removal. If any step on the subject is proposed in parliament and agreed to, I shall feel from that moment that I can be of more use out of office

than in it.... I state to you, as I think I ought, distinctly and explicitly what I feel. I hope I need not repeat what I always feel personally to yourself. Yours ever, William Pitt.

After receiving Pitt's letter, Wilberforce began to doubt the wisdom of persevering in his motion. Following consultation with Pitt as well as his Clapham friends, Charles Grant and Henry Thornton, he resolved to give it up. The next day he wrote:

My dear Pitt ... I have given the most serious and impartial consideration to the question whether to persist in bringing forward my intended motion or to relinquish it. My own opinion as to the propriety of it in itself remains unaltered. But being also convinced that it would be productive on the whole of more practical harm than practical good ... I have resolved to give it up.... I cannot hesitate a moment in sending you word of my determination....

I am sure ... I need not tell you that the idea of my being compelled by duty to do any thing painful or embarrassing to you has hurt me not a little, but I know you too well not to be sure that even you yourself would not wish me to be influenced by this consideration against the dictates of my conscience. I will only hint the pain you have been the occasion of my suffering on [this] subject....

It is my sincere prayer, my dear Pitt, that you may here be the honoured instrument of Providence for your country's good ... much more that you may at length partake of a more solid and durable happiness and honour than this world can bestow. I am and I trust I ever shall be your affectionate and faithful Friend.

Pitt responded:

My dear Wilberforce, I cannot say to you how much I am relieved by your determination which I am sincerely convinced is right on your own principles as much as on those of persons who think differently. Much less can I tell you how sincerely

I feel your cordial friendship and kindness on all occasions as well where we differ as where we agree. Ever affectionately yours, W. Pitt.

Wilberforce knew how to speak truth to kings. He was willing to pay a steep personal and political price to act according to his conscience. At times his call to political life was a very difficult one indeed.

⌒

In 1801 the war with France and bad harvests led to widespread hunger in Britain. Deeply concerned, Wilberforce demonstrated his extraordinary personal generosity by giving away £3,000 more than he earned (nearly $800,000 today) to help meet the needs of those who were suffering.

The British government faced an additional crisis when, on March 15, 1801, Pitt resigned as prime minister over the question of Catholic Emancipation. Less than sixty years before, Bonnie Prince Charlie, the Catholic pretender to the English throne, had led the Jacobite Rebellion in an attempt to regain the throne. The Protestant King George III was vehemently opposed to any measure that might, in his eyes, give too much political power to Catholics. The Catholics had threatened the monarchy before; they might do so again.

Another of Wilberforce's friends, Henry Addington, succeeded Pitt. The commencement of Addington's administration seemed to signal that a peace with France might be achievable and that this might bode well for the abolition of the slave trade.

On January 2, 1802, Wilberforce learned that a general agreement on abolition might be achieved. Addington was now engaged in peace treaty negotiations with France. In a remarkable demonstration of selflessness, Wilberforce offered the leadership of the abolition cause to Addington.

It is not ... without emotion that I relinquish the idea of being myself the active and chief agent in terminating the greatest of all human evils. ... I hope I can truly assure you also, that it helps to reconcile me to *my* loss on this occasion, that it would be *your* gain. ... I should look on with joy, if the Disposer of all human events, who had already rendered you the instrument of good to mankind in the termination of one of the most bloody wars that has raged in modern times, should further honour you, by making you His agent in dispensing to the world this greatest and most extended of all earthly benefits.

This act was one of the finest in the long abolition struggle. Wilberforce had invested fifteen years of his life in this fight, but he was willing to relinquish his leadership to serve a greater good. Its nobility is not diminished in the least by the fact that Addington, though touched by Wilberforce's offer, declined it, stating that the conclusion of a peace with France should be the only issue on the negotiating table. Sadly, the peace that Addington negotiated with France was short-lived, lasting only about a year. On May 16, 1803, the war with France began again.

On May 7, 1804, the British government again underwent a change of leadership when Addington resigned, and Pitt became prime minister for a second time. Later that year Wilberforce, supported by Pitt and Fox (still a leader of the political opposition), carried an abolition motion by a substantial majority. Though this motion didn't ultimately carry the day and secure the end of the slave trade, it now seemed apparent that abolition would take place within a few years. Popular support for abolition had been steadily growing, in great part due to the sustained campaign to convince the public of the slave trade's immorality. Many in Parliament felt the shift in momentum, or were themselves convinced, and began to support Wilberforce. Overjoyed by this prospect, Newton wrote his friend:

Though I can scarcely see the paper before me I must attempt to express my thankfulness to the Lord, and to offer my congratulations to you for the success which he has so far been pleased to give to your unwearied endeavours for the abolition of the slave trade.... I have considered [it] a millstone, sufficient of itself ... to sink such an enlightened and highly favour'd nation as ours to the bottom of the sea.... Whether I, who am within two months of entering my eightieth year, shall live to see the accomplishment of that work, is only known to Him in whose hands are all our times and ways, but the hopeful prospect of its accomplishment will, I trust, give me daily satisfaction so long as my declining faculties are preserved.

Wilberforce was incredibly busy, but his affection for Newton, who had so often helped him to stay the course, was such that he immediately wrote back:

I steal one moment from business and bustle to thank you most cordially for your kind congratulations.... O my dear sir, it is refreshing to me to turn away my eye from the vanities with which it is surrounded, and to fix it on you, who appear in some sort to be already enlightened with the beams of that blessed day which is beginning to rise on you, as you approach the very boundaries of this world's horizon. May you soon enjoy its meridian lustre. Pray for us, my dear sir, that we also may be enabled to hold on our way, and at last to join with you in the shout of victory.... I shall ever reckon it the greatest of all my temporal favours that I have been providentially led to take the conduct of this business.

⌒

During the next two years, however, Wilberforce faced two of the most difficult crises that took place in his political career. In 1805 Henry Dundas, now Lord Melville and First Lord of the Admiralty, was charged with permitting the embezzlement of funds by a subordinate. Pitt stood by Lord Melville, saying he had not pocketed public money, although he had acted like a fool.

Pitt's kinsman Lord Rosebery described what happened in the subsequent debate over Melville's impeachment:

> The speech of Wilberforce was ... eagerly looked for; he was one of Pitt's dearest friends, but one also whom, in a matter of public morals, friendship could not sway.
>
> As he rose, Pitt bent forward and fixed an eagle glance of inquiry upon him. Wilberforce felt all that mute appeal implied, but did not waver. He declared that he must vote for [impeachment]. Not in his slave trade triumph did he hold a prouder position.

"It is we who are now truly on our trial before the moral sense of England," Wilberforce said, "and, if we shrink from it, deeply shall we hereafter repent our conduct." Wilberforce's speech was decisive and was said to have swayed forty votes. An even division followed, and the Speaker of the House of Commons gave a casting vote against Melville. Pitt sat in his place and wept.

The impeachment of Lord Melville followed, yet Wilberforce stayed his hand. He told his colleagues that the sentence of the law should be sufficient and asked not to be included in its execution. "Is it to be expected of me," he asked, "that I am to stifle the natural feelings of the heart, and not even to shed a tear over the very sentence I am pronouncing? ... Christianity ... requires us indeed to do justice but to love mercy. I learn not in her school to triumph even over a conquered enemy ... must I join the triumph over a fallen friend?"

Wilberforce was deeply grieved – remembering the days twenty years before when he, Pitt, and Dundas had been together so often at Wimbledon – but he felt bound to do his duty. As he wrote two years later: "The author of all moral obligation has enjoined us to renounce certain actions, without an inquiry as to reasons or consequences."

Lord Melville resigned in disgrace. To all appearances, Britain had lost the services of the one man who was deemed indispensable to the British war effort against Napoleon. In the words of one biographer, "Wilberforce's speech may have altered the destiny of Britain."

Melville's successor was none other than Sir Charles Middleton, who had first solicited Wilberforce's leadership for an effort to end the slave trade in 1786. Middleton, a devout Christian, had served a long and distinguished career in His Majesty's Navy.

In the view of many military historians, it was Middleton's leadership and grasp of strategy that laid the foundation for Admiral Horatio Nelson's celebrated victory at Trafalgar. Britain's supremacy at sea would never again be challenged by Napoleon; and France's defeat at Trafalgar set the stage for Napoleon's complete defeat at Waterloo.

Despite Wilberforce's relief that Middleton had assumed Melville's duties, a grievous loss was soon to follow. Pitt, whose health had been steadily declining, died early in 1806 due to complications resulting from a severe case of gout. He was forty-seven.

Wilberforce was heartbroken when he heard the news – all the more because he had not been able, as Lord Rosebery said, "to renew the sacred conservation" – to have one last talk with Pitt about his faith. During Pitt's funeral procession Wilberforce, at the family's request, carried a banner as he walked behind the coffin. In tribute to Pitt and his political achievements, Wilberforce later wrote a brief memoir.

After Pitt's death, Lord Grenville became prime minister. It was he who, along with Wilberforce and Pitt, had sat under the oak tree on Pitt's estate when Wilberforce agreed to take up the abolition of the slave trade in 1787. An ardent supporter of abolition, Grenville began at once to try to secure passage of Wilberforce's oft-defeated motion to abolish the slave trade.

It is one of the great ironies of the British abolition story that Grenville was now such a pivotal figure in the struggle to end the slave trade. Most would have assumed that the end of the slave trade would have taken place under Pitt's administration. For so many years he had been zealous for abolition, and for so many years he had been one of Britain's most powerful prime ministers. In contrast, Grenville's administration barely survived for a year.

Moreover, Wilberforce had not always liked Grenville. They had known one another since their youth, and in better times Wilberforce once told Rufus King – the American minister to Great Britain – that Grenville "had seedlings in his character ... as the acorn contains the Oak." By the early years of the abolition struggle, however, Wilberforce had considered him "a shabby man – bent upon amassing money."

It was strange indeed that Grenville was now the man indispensable to the cause of abolition. Wilberforce himself observed, "How wonderful are the ways of God, and how are we taught to trust not in man but in Him! Though [close to] Pitt for all my life since earliest manhood, and he [was] most warm for Abolition ... yet now my whole human dependence [for the success of my bill] is placed on Fox, to whom through [my political] life [I have been] opposed, and on Grenville, to whom [I was] always rather hostile till of late years." In the 1790s Pitt himself had spoken of Wilberforce's dislike of Grenville: "You don't like Grenville, and Grenville knows that you don't."

It was a further irony, but an altogether fitting one, that Charles Fox was also now so necessary in aiding Wilberforce. Fox, whom Wilberforce had so violently attacked in 1784, also came into office as part of Grenville's administration. Wilberforce and Fox now consulted with one another about matters of legislative strategy, and Fox secured a promise from the Prince of Wales that he would not adversely stir up the opposition of the royal family to abolition.

It was yet another fruit of Wilberforce's Great Change that it was now possible to have such a close working relationship with

Fox and Grenville, men with whom he previously had decided personal and political differences.

The abolition cause was further aided by a brilliant legislative strategy – suggested by Wilberforce's brother-in-law James Stephen – that successfully outflanked the parliamentary opponents of abolition. Wilberforce, again demonstrating one of his greatest assets as a leader, deferred to Stephen's plan. Prime Minister Grenville also agreed and, in a speech given in the early stages of the abolition bill's debate, offered an eloquent tribute to Wilberforce:

> I cannot conceive any consciousness more truly gratifying than must be enjoyed by [my honourable friend] on finding a measure to which he had devoted his life, carried into effect – a measure so truly benevolent, so admirably conducive to the virtuous prosperity of his country and the welfare of mankind – a measure which will diffuse happiness among millions now in existence, and for which his memory will be blessed by millions yet unborn.

The night of February 23, 1807, was unforgettable. As Wilberforce's motion was being debated, excitement began to grow throughout the House of Commons. Most of the speeches supported abolition; as soon as one member had finished speaking, several others would jump to their feet wishing to add their voice to those who had gone before.

The evening reached its climax when the solicitor-general, Sir Samuel Romilly, came to the closing remarks of his deeply moving speech. He contrasted Napoleon and Wilberforce, painting a picture of the reception each would receive as they returned home after the day's labors. Napoleon would arrive in pomp and power, a man who knew the height of earthly ambition, yet as one tormented by bloodshed and the oppressions of war. Wilberforce would come home to "the bosom of his happy and delighted family," able to lie down in peace because he had "preserved so many millions of his fellow creatures."

The House of Commons rose nearly to a man, turned to Wilberforce, and began to cheer. The chamber was swept again and again with sustained applause.

Wilberforce sat with his head bowed and wept.

Thereupon the Commons voted to abolish the slave trade by an overwhelming majority, 283 to 16. This fight, led so nobly, had taken twenty years.

It was, as Sir Hugh Thomas wrote, "one of the most remarkable examples of the triumph of an individual statesman on a major philanthropic issue, and at the same time one more reminder that individuals can make history."

On December 21, 1807 – within a few months of the abolition of the slave trade – John Newton, who had wondered if he would live to see such a day, died. The man who perhaps more than any other had been responsible for helping Wilberforce to stay the course had shared in the joy of final victory.

The distinguished historian G. M. Trevelyan has eloquently summarized the magnitude of Wilberforce's achievement:

Thus was Wilberforce rewarded for his complete honesty of purpose. He had never shrunk from the pursuit of his great humanitarian object even when after the French Revolution it had become for a while extremely unpopular in the world of politics and fashion; he had always been ready to work with persons of any party, class or religion who would support the cause.

He was an enthusiast who was always wise. He was an agitator who always retained his powerful gift of social charm.... He could not have done what he did if he had desired [high political] office. With his talents and position he would probably have been Pitt's successor as Prime Minister if he had preferred party to mankind. His sacrifice of one kind of fame and power gave him another and a nobler title to remembrance.

CHAPTER 5

THE SECOND GREAT OBJECT

... bind the task assign'd thee to thine heart.
WILLIAM COWPER

By ending the slave trade, Britain had become a more enlightened and civilized nation, an example to other nations of the power of principled politics. Many wondered how Britain's opinion could be so totally changed within one generation. A major reason why a legislated end to the slave trade was possible was the flowering of Wilberforce's second great object: the reformation of manners.

The goal of the reformation of manners was to turn the tide of immorality in Britain. The profligacy and moral decay that marked the Regency era (when Wilberforce first entered public life) gave way to the moral integrity and concern for others that was a hallmark of the Victorian era (which began in 1837, just a few years after his death). Wilberforce and his fellow reformers were salt and light in their generation, setting on foot an incredible array of charitable initiatives. Their collective legacy turned around a society and a culture.

When Wilberforce commenced his political career in 1780, Britain was in the early stages of its industrial revolution. In that year industrialist and inventor Richard Arkwright built his first cotton mill. A process of urbanization followed as many laborers suffered the loss of their agricultural jobs and journeyed to cities in search of employment. Increasingly, men and women found work in factories.

In 1750 London was the only city with a population of more than fifty thousand. By 1801 eight cities had surpassed this number – in 1851 twenty-nine had done so. Many who worked in the factories, women and children included, lived in squalid and impoverished conditions. Cheap gin purchased relief from these hardships, and this became a plague, alongside poverty and the difficulties of factory life.

Alongside industrialization, clerical apathy afflicted many quarters of the Church of England, marked by nominal belief in the Christian creeds and widespread corruption. Wilberforce's sons wrote that "the deadly leaven" of latitudinarian views had spread to an alarming extent. Many clergymen did not hold orthodox views, and few were honest enough to resign their church positions.

Foreign missions had diminished, while in Britain itself, "a vast population was springing up around our manufactories, but there was no thought of providing for them church accommodation."

Many clergy were either greatly neglecting or not ministering at all to the needs of their congregations as they were absent from their churches. "Non-residence without cause ... was spreading through the church," the Wilberforces stated, "and all the cords of moral obligation were relaxed as the spirit of religion slumbered." Morally, many took their lead from the Church of England – and its morality was sorely lacking.

Joseph Milner, the vicar of Hull whom Wilberforce so admired, had described the state of things starkly in 1789: "It is an affecting consideration to reflect what a number of clergymen there are whose lives demonstrate them to be wholly devoid of any religious sensibility whatever, with whom 'to pray and sermonize' is the same thing as to till the ground or to navigate the seas, a mere secular trade, and unconnected with any concern for their own salvation or that of the flocks committed to their charge."*

---

*See *Works of the late Joseph Milner*, ed. I. Milner (1810), viii, 279.

The experience of Wilberforce's fellow reformer Hannah More, who commenced her educational reforms in the late 1780s, demonstrates just how apathetic and immoral some clergymen serving in the Church of England had become. In the town of Axbridge she discovered to her dismay that a preacher named Gould was "drunk about six times a week, has kept a mistress in his House, and very frequently is prevented from preaching by two black eyes got by fighting."

The lower class languished in moral apathy, and the middle class – of which Wilberforce was a member – was no better. Wilberforce remembered the days of his youth as a time when adultery and dueling were common. Prior to his Great Change, he himself drank hard and gambled often, though not as often or as disastrously as the aristocratic Charles Fox who, along with his brothers, lost the fantastic sum of £140,000 at the gambling tables (a sum in the tens of millions today).

Some of Wilberforce's colleagues in Parliament sold their votes to finance lavish lifestyles. They frequented luxurious clubs, played at cards, or gambled as they pleased. The spirit of the age was characterized as one of moral expediency, which it was "so much the fashion of our days to make the standard and test of morals." In his novel *Roderick Random*, Tobias Smollett put it more tersely and vividly. "London is the devil's drawing-room." The England of *The Pilgrim's Progress* had become the England of *The Rake's Progress*.

Wilberforce's interest in moral reform appears to have arisen in the mid-1780s. As early as 1785 he had been disturbed by signs of cultural malaise. It was then that he wrote to his friend Lord Muncaster: "It is not the confusion of parties, and their quarrelling and battling in the House of Commons which makes me despair of the republic ... but it is the universal corruption and profligacy of the times, which taking its rise amongst the rich and luxurious – has now extended its baneful influence and spread its destructive poison through the whole body of the people."

Hannah More (1745–1833), the celebrated poet, playwright, and reformer whose schools were financed by Wilberforce. Thousands of children were educated as a result.

Wilberforce's moral awakening was fueled by his knowledge of friends whose lives had been shattered by immoral conduct and the consequences that flowed from it. Fox was one example. Unlike many of his day, Wilberforce was not indifferent to scenes that others found easy or convenient to ignore.

By 1787 Wilberforce had begun his work for moral and cultural renewal. His Great Change had convinced him of his own need for transformation. He became equally burdened for his fellow citizens.

His first thought was to focus on the proclamations issued when a new monarch assumed the throne. A new sovereign always issued a proclamation "for the encouragement of Piety and Virtue; and for the Preventing of Vice, Profaneness and Immorality." This was often a mere formality, but Wilberforce discovered that the proclamation issued by William and Mary in 1692 had been much more effective than any issued since.

The reason, Wilberforce learned, was that in the 1690s local "Societies for the Reformation of Manners" and "Religious Societies" were formed about the time that William and Mary's proclamation was issued. Societies for the Reformation of Manners were formed in greater London to assist magistrates in the detection of crime and the enforcement of criminal laws. Other religious societies arose in towns and villages throughout the nation. Groups of young men gathered to consider the implications of Scripture for their lives. This attention to Scripture, and increased religious devotion, was in fact a religious revival. All of these factors worked in concert.

In 1697 the Reverend Josiah Woodward traced the history of these reform movements in his book *An Account of the Rise and Progress of the Religious Societies in the City of London [and] Endeavours for Reformation of Manners*. He wrote, "The Societies for Reformation bent their utmost Endeavours from the first to suppress publick Vice ... [Secondly] the Religious Societies endeavour'd chiefly to promote Religion in their own Breasts."

Wilberforce embraced this dual emphasis – to eliminate public corruption and promote religion in the hearts of the people – and sought to revive it. His reading of Woodward's book prompted him to form a similar association – a new Society for the Reformation of Manners.

On June 12, 1787, Wilberforce wrote to his friend William Hey, an eminent surgeon in Leeds, "I am conscious that ours is an infinitely inferior aim, yet surely it is of the utmost consequence, and worthy of the labours of a whole life."

At this early juncture, Wilberforce was downplaying his expectations. He hoped for great things, but he thought he would do well to begin modestly. He began by trying to enlist the aid and support of those among his numerous friends who were also determined to resist the growing lack of morality and integrity.

Wilberforce spoke of his concerns about regulating external conduct and changing the hearts of his fellow citizens. "In our free state," he asserted, "it is peculiarly needful to obtain these ends by the agency of some voluntary association; for thus only can those moral principles be guarded, which of old were under the immediate protection of the government."

Voluntary societies were his chosen vehicle because he thought that the good obtainable through political means had its limitations. He believed that laws could not counteract the nature of things, or, more simply, that one could not legislate morality. His own moral transformation had not taken place because Parliament had passed a law.

This issue was one of basic freedom. As he phrased it: "Compulsion and Christianity! Why, the very terms are at variance with each other – the ideas are incompatible. In the language of Inspiration itself, Christianity has been called 'the law of liberty.' Her service in the excellent formularies of our Church has been truly denominated 'perfect freedom'; and they, let me add, will most advance her cause who contend for it in her own spirit and character."

Bearing in mind what he perceived to be the necessity of free and voluntary initiatives, Wilberforce conceived a plan to promote moral reformation that to modern ears seems impossible: he would endeavor to make goodness fashionable among the leadership class.

He shared his plan with his friend Beilby Porteus, the Bishop of London. The first step was to persuade George III to reissue the "Proclamation for the Encouragement of Piety and Virtue," which had marked his rise to the throne in 1760.

Porteus described his consultation with Wilberforce: "The design appeared to me to be ... of the greatest importance and necessity, but I foresaw great difficulties in the execution of it unless conducted with great judgment and discretion, especially in the first outset." And so Porteus advised Wilberforce to begin cautiously and privately, mentioning his plan in confidence to leading figures in church and state, particularly the Archbishop of Canterbury, Prime Minister Pitt, and later others among the nobility, clergy, and gentry.

It was a sound strategy, though not one without risk. It was possible that Pitt would be unwilling to back Wilberforce on such a potentially divisive issue. If Wilberforce had not secured Pitt's approval initially, his plan might have come to nothing. By the same token, if the Archbishop of Canterbury had been lukewarm, the plan could also have been stillborn. He needed the endorsement and commitment of both leaders. This was particularly the case because Wilberforce hoped to be able to set two good moral examples before the people of Britain: a government committed to justice and a church committed to faithfulness and first principles.

After Wilberforce secured Pitt's approval and that of the Archbishop of Canterbury, the Archbishop then spoke with Queen Charlotte, the wife of George III. This step succeeded admirably, and on May 29, 1787, Wilberforce was able to report to William Hey:

> I trust in a very few days you will hear of a Proclamation being issued for the discouragement of vice, of letters being written by the secretaries of state to the lords-lieutenant, expressing his Majesty's pleasure, that they recommend it to the justices throughout their several counties to be active in the execution of the laws against immoralities, and of a society's being formed in London for the purpose of carrying into effect his Majesty's good and gracious intentions.
>
> I have been some time at work ... and the persons with whom I have [coordinated] my measures, are so trusty, temperate, and unobnoxious, that I think I am not indulging a vain expectation in persuading myself that something considerable may be done.

It would give you no little pleasure, could you hear how warmly the Archbishop of Canterbury expresses himself.... [T]he interest he takes in the good work does him great credit, and he assures me that [the King], to whom he has opened the subject in form, and suggested the measures above mentioned, is deeply impressed.

On June 1, 1787, George III published his "Proclamation for the Encouragement of Piety and Virtue." Few who read this document knew that Wilberforce had been the prime mover behind it. He was only twenty-seven and had "no rank or political office. But he was determined to change the moral climate of his age [and] thus reduce serious crime. His motives were humane, not repressive."

"Men of authority and influence," Wilberforce was to write later, "may promote the cause of good morals. Let them in their several stations encourage virtue and [discourage] vice.... Let them favour and take part in any plans which may be formed for the advancement of morality. Above all things, let them endeavour to instruct and improve the rising generation."

Once the Society for the Reformation of Manners had grown sufficiently, Wilberforce published a list of its members and an account of how it had been formed. Persons from every walk of life – representatives from both houses of Parliament, city merchants, tradesmen, and aldermen – had all lent their support. The Duke of Montagu accepted the office of president. The Archbishop of Canterbury put the power of his name behind the society, and the rest of the bishops followed his example.

Wilberforce next sent out circulars that described how local reformation societies might be formed throughout the country. He urged his correspondents to do as he had done – draw together like-minded associates to further the work of reform.

The parent Society for the Reformation of Manners was soon in active operation. For many years, the Duke of Montagu opened his house for its reception and presided over its meetings. At these gatherings legislative strategies were discussed, as were ideas for voluntary organizations – everything from schools to lending libraries and soup kitchens – that could better the lives of Britons. The society obtained many valuable acts of Parliament and was also a center from which scores of other useful plans proceeded.

The voluntary societies that sprang up from 1780 to 1830 numbered in the hundreds. There were groups dedicated to publishing and distributing Bibles, educating the blind, promoting animal welfare, treating ailing seamen, sponsoring vaccination efforts, and easing the plight of the poor and those in debtors' prison.

Believing charity for the poor should not be confined to home, Wilberforce was also a vice president of the Friends of Foreigners in Distress, a group whose distinguished members included a Wilberforce friend who was not British: John Quincy Adams, the sixth president of the United States. During his time as America's ambassador to Britain, Adams said that he greatly respected Wilberforce and was grateful for opportunities "of consulting with him … upon subjects so interesting to humanity as those upon which [his] exertions have been so long and so earnestly employed."

Occasionally endorsements from society's upper echelon were marked by a certain degree of irony. King George IV, a man known for his many mistresses, was induced to become a patron of the London Female Penitentiary. While not always supplied by persons who were paragons of virtue, these endorsements nonetheless had the effect of greatly diminishing potential opposition to the various reforms advocated by Wilberforce and his fellow reformers.

Wilberforce was not an elitist, but in the highly aristocratic society of his day, he recognized that one of the most effective ways to promote moral renewal was to pursue it in this way. Indeed, this strategy was so successful that it greatly reinforced the philanthropic tradition of noblesse oblige in Britain during his lifetime.

Such reform initiatives might have found a measure of general acceptance, but several among Wilberforce's contemporaries criticized him in varying degrees. Sydney Smith, the celebrated wit and essayist, satirized the Society for the Suppression of Vice (which Wilberforce helped establish) as "the Society for the Suppression of Vice among those with less than £500 a year." Wilberforce's goals may have been laudable, Smith said, but in pursuing endorsements from the leadership class, he believed Wilberforce had left himself open to the criticism that he did not care about vice among middle- and upper-class Britons.

This, however, was not the case. Wilberforce's bestselling book, *A Practical View of Christianity*, set out a vision of the "good society" written specifically for "the Higher and Middle classes." He sought to promote moral reformation among all classes of British society but sought to work with the leadership class to secure as broad a base of support as possible.

It is worth noting too that Smith did not dislike Wilberforce – quite the contrary. Though at times critical of Wilberforce and his reformer colleagues, Smith would later write to Lady Holland: "Little Wilberforce is here, and we are great friends. He looks like a little spirit running about without a body, or in a kind of undress with only half a body."

Not all of Wilberforce's critics were so friendly. The satirist William Hazlitt was particularly harsh. In his *Spirit of the Age*, a collection of contemporary biographies, he pilloried Wilberforce, saying,

> Mr. Wilberforce's humanity will go to all lengths that it can with safety and discretion; but it is not to be supposed that it should lose him his seat for Yorkshire, the smile of [His] Majesty, or the countenance of the loyal and pious. He is anxious to do all the good he can without hurting himself or his fair fame ... [He] is, [I] think, as fine a specimen of moral equivocation as can well be conceived.... He carefully chooses his

ground to fight the battles of ... religion and humanity; and as such it is always safe and advantageous to himself.

Hazlitt criticized Wilberforce from a distance. Unlike Smith, he never met or personally corresponded with Wilberforce. He was something of a bomb thrower, criticizing prominent men of many political persuasions, including Jeremy Bentham, Samuel Taylor Coleridge, Sir Walter Scott, Lord Eldon, and others.

Hazlitt considered Wilberforce a man whose name was "a sort of bye-word for affectation, cant, hollow professions ... fickleness, and effeminate imbecility." His faith was "a mixture of fashion and fanaticism." His patriotism was servile.

Wilberforce's leadership of the fight to end the slave trade was not beyond the range of Hazlitt's acid pen. When much of the English-speaking world knew that Wilberforce had persevered despite chronic illness, vitriol, and threats to his life, Hazlitt insisted Wilberforce had taken on the fight to gain political popularity. Once "the gloss of novelty was gone from it," he became "half inclined to surrender it into Mr. Pitt's dilatory hands." Hazlitt surely knew, for it was a matter of parliamentary record, that Wilberforce had for a brief time surrendered leadership of the cause to Pitt because he had very nearly died.

Just before Hazlitt's *Spirit of the Age* was published in 1825, Wilberforce was castigated in verse by Lord Byron in his epic poem *Don Juan*. Within this work, which traced the travels of an unprincipled young man throughout Europe, Byron interspersed digressions on subjects of all kinds. In three places, he spoke of Wilberforce.

Byron's satire is most pointed in the last of his references. Describing Wilberforce as having nearly miraculous powers with which to change the world, Byron uses Wilberforce's true moral authority as a foil with which to skewer those he most wishes to criticize, specifically King George IV. In the first line of this passage, Byron perpetrates a tasteless pun:

O Wilberforce, thou man of black renown,
Whose merit none enough can sing or say,
Thou hast struck one immense Colossus down,
Thou moral Washington of Africa!
But there's another little thing I own,
Which you should perpetrate some summer's day,
And set the other half of earth to rights;
You have freed the blacks – now pray shut up the whites....
Shut up – no, not the King, but the Pavilion,
Or else 'twill cost us another million.
Shut up the world at large, let Bedlam out;
And you will be perhaps surprised to find
All things pursue exactly the same route,
As now with those of [so-called] sound mind.

It is not completely clear why Byron so often set up Wilberforce as a straw man. The most likely possibility is that Byron resented Wilberforce as a hypocrite and a personification of the established order. After his marriage in 1816 to Anne Isabella Milbanke (a woman sympathetic to evangelicals), Byron left England and never returned. He was deeply embittered, and he rejected the moral constraints of conventional society.

What is clear is that Byron was often bitterly sarcastic at Wilberforce's expense. The most glaring instance of this is a remnant of Byron's table talk, which has been preserved. It was of a piece with things that had been said about Wilberforce ever since he had taken up the cause of abolition. As one of Byron's friends, John Galt, recalled:

[Byron] delighted in mystifications, especially when he thought any one could be taken in. Accordingly, in one of his playful fits, he told me very gravely that his mother had been a pupil of Miss Hannah More's, but left her [school].

"Why," said I.

"Because it was reported that Hannah had a child by Wilberforce."

Another story about Wilberforce was one of Byron's favorites, and it was Wilberforce's reputation for saintliness that gave the story its point. It seems that one night the playwright Richard Sheridan was incredibly drunk and found lying in a gutter. When asked by the constable what his name was, Sheridan – a great wit – gathered himself and said in thickly slurred speech, "*Wilberfoss!*"

One could be forgiven for thinking that on the basis of this story, Sheridan heartily disliked Wilberforce, but he didn't. In fact it was Sheridan who so gallantly expressed regret at the thought of Wilberforce retiring altogether from political life in 1812. Wilberforce remembered:

> On my way to the House of Commons one day – soon after my having exchanged my seat for Yorkshire for the borough of Bramber – I met Sheridan. After we had exchanged salutations [he said], "Do you know that I was near to writing to you some little time ago?"
>
> On my asking the occasion of his intended letter [he said], "Why, I read in the newspaper your farewell *Address to the Freeholders of Yorkshire*, and though you and I have not much agreed in our votes in the House of Commons, yet I thought the independent part you acted would render your retirement from parliament a public loss. I was about therefore to write to you, to enforce on you the propriety of reconsidering your determination … when I was informed that you were to come into parliament for Bramber."

Wilberforce was grateful for Sheridan's kindness, and when it came to Byron, Wilberforce took time to read his poems. This showed a charitable side of his character that his critics have often overlooked. Throughout his long career in Parliament, Wilberforce could feel warmth and affection for any person who supported abolition. Richard Sheridan, Henry Brougham, and Jeremy Bentham were all humanitarians and men of genius, but many evangelicals of Wilberforce's day would have considered them respectively as a drunken playwright, an unprincipled Scottish adventurer, and an atheist. One biographer has concluded, "But after their services to abolition Wilberforce could regard them all with … affection. He was probably the only man in England who read [about] Lord Byron in the hopes of finding 'good feeling.'"

Wilberforce's neighbor Lady Raffles recalled that during a visit to his home, Highwood Hill, in 1828, she had read passages to him from Thomas Moore's *Life of Lord Byron*. That evening Wilberforce paced up and down the room as she read. "What struck me particularly," she remembered, "was his anxiety to find out any thing in Lord Byron's favour. 'There now,' he would stop and exclaim, 'surely there is good feeling there!'"

There was, wrote Wilberforce's sons, a desire in their father "of finding some favourable points in every character." The importance of this trait cannot be overstated. The first impulse of many would-be reformers is to focus on points of disagreement. Wilberforce strove to find common ground and build consensus whenever he could. He did not always succeed, but his willingness to try made him many friends when others would only have made enemies.

This side of Wilberforce's character was not a natural inclination. He always admitted that he struggled with his temper, and the invective he used in his early political career shows he knew how to devastate an opponent with criticism. After his Great Change, he increasingly refused to take the easy way out and give in to the win-at-all-costs path. Acting upon the golden rule, he dedicated himself to the more difficult task of cultivating a charitable demeanor.

⌣

Perhaps the best example of Wilberforce's commitment to this task lay in his dealings with William Cobbett, a gifted writer committed to political radicalism and economic theories. To Cobbett, Wilberforce was the ideal symbol of the established order, and he attacked Wilberforce on numerous occasions – for supporting the peace administration of Prime Minister Henry Addington, for his desire to abolish bear baiting, for advocating smallpox inocula- tion, and for his campaign to encourage the growth of potatoes.

When Habeas Corpus was suspended in Britain in 1817, Cob- bett fled to America, fearing arrest because of his subversive writings. To his fellow political agitator Henry "Orator" Hunt, he wrote, "Think of it. A hundred brace of woodcocks a day. Think of that! No Alien Acts here. No long-sworded and whiskered cap- tains. No Judges escorted from town to town and sitting under a guard of dragoons.... No Cannings, Liverpools, Castlereaghs, Eldons, Ellenboroughs, or Sidmouths.... No Wilberforces. Think of *that!* No Wilberforces!"

Characteristically, Wilberforce found a way to be charitable to Cobbett, or at least to think charitably of him. Writing to his friend William Jay, he said: "I have not seen 'Cobbett' for some time. My chief reason for ever taking his [*Political Register*] was, that I could not otherwise see it; and I thought it right to know what were the lessons of a very able and influential political teacher on the pass- ing events of the day."

On another occasion Wilberforce waxed philosophical about Cobbett's hatred of him: "Cobbett has publish[ed] a very clever letter to me, full, as you may suppose, of falsehood and mischief. Well! remember good old [Martin] Luther, in worse times, when assailed by enemies who could burn as well as write."

Later biographers have noted the injustice of Cobbett's feelings and writings about Wilberforce. The Oxford scholar Sir Reginald Coupland observed:

> Quick haters like Cobbett hated Wilberforce; Hazlitt drew a rancorous portrait of him in *The Spirit of the Age....* [But they] ignore the liberal side of Wilberforce's politics – his ap- peals for the public relief of poverty and for state employment, his demands for popular education, his persistent attacks on

the [injustices] of the Penal Code ... his denunciations of the Transportation system and the condition of English prisons, his support of factory legislation on behalf of the children, his pleas for the wretched ... chimney sweeps.

Wilberforce cared for the working classes as deeply as Cobbett or Hazlitt – though they refused to believe him or acknowledge his compassion for the poor and many initiatives on their behalf. More tellingly, Wilberforce did far more than either Cobbett or Hazlitt to actually relieve the burdens of the poor and improve their lives. Cobbett and Hazlitt wielded their pens far more effectively than they set on foot schemes that achieved true and lasting reforms.

Contrary to what Cobbett and Hazlitt wrote, Wilberforce was not averse to working with political radicals. He always sought to be a bridge builder and would work with anyone in pursuit of common philanthropic goals. His relations with Jeremy Bentham and Charles Fox (men with whom he had little in common philosophically or politically) attest this.

Critics like Cobbett let personal animosity preclude any acknowledgment that good had been done by Wilberforce's efforts to promote a reformation of manners. What is worse, by constantly attacking Wilberforce, Cobbett destroyed any opportunities to aid him in helping the working classes.

Cobbett's most damning charge against Wilberforce came in 1823, four years after Cobbett's return to Britain. In this year Wilberforce published his last major abolitionist work, *An Appeal ... in Behalf of the Negro Slaves.* Cobbett attacked Wilberforce in an open letter that began, "Wilberforce, I have you before me in a canting pamphlet." In racist language, he wildly accused Wilberforce of being "totally ignorant of the subject on which you are writing," and railed against him saying: "You seem to have a great affection for the fat and lazy and laughing and singing and dancing negroes." Cobbett concluded his diatribe with one of the greatest political lies of the era: "Never have you done one single act in favour of the labourers of this country."

When it came to helping the poor, Cobbett talked a good game. But in criticizing an opponent, his care for the poor, to say nothing of slaves, took a backseat to his desire to discredit those he considered enemies.

And yet it was Wilberforce, as biographer John Pollock has written, who was "the man identified, more than any other public figure ... as the friend of the poor." Indeed, in 1796, Jeremy Bentham, whose worldview differed so widely from Wilberforce's, had dedicated an early draft of his *Essay on the Poor Laws* to him – a mark of the nearly universal recognition Wilberforce enjoyed as a friend of the poor.

"Strengthening the hands of the poor" was central to Wilberforce's life.

His sons Robert and Samuel report that their father's annual philanthropic contributions were given to nearly every charitable institution in London and Yorkshire. He also supported a number of individuals, often anonymously. Many of them, his sons assert, "afterwards acquired independence and wealth [and] were indebted to his support for carrying them through their early struggles."

Many young men of promise preparing to take Holy Orders also received financial support from Wilberforce. Students preparing for other careers received his patronage as well, and he gave moral power to the work of reforming manners through his determination to designate a set amount of his annual income for charitable giving. In order to make this amount as high as possible, Wilberforce exercised "self-denial in small things."

The young Wilberforce had dipped into his purse freely, hosting lavish parties and gambling. Though always social and amiable, he now hosted dinner parties that were much more modest. The table he set was relatively simple in nature. When visiting Wilberforce, one guest remarked that one went for the sparkling conversation, not for the items on the menu.

Though Wilberforce was often in demand as a dinner guest himself, he attended parties less than he had before. Parties before had been a way for him to advance himself socially; they were now opportunities to deepen friendships. In an intensely class-conscious age, Wilberforce forsook the amenities of traveling in his own comfortable and expensive carriage. Instead, he began to travel by coach, the equivalent today of taking a taxi instead of a limousine. Before his marriage in 1797, he was able to give at least one-fourth of his annual income to charitable organizations. Using an incomplete record for one of the years between 1785 and 1797, his sons report that £2,000 – well over half a million dollars now – was set aside by their father yearly for charitable purposes.

Wilberforce was also devoted to charitable works among his family. To one relative, he wrote:

> Never distress yourself my dear Mary ... on the ground of my being put to expense on account of yourself.... You give what is more valuable than money – time, thought, serious, active, persevering attention.... It has pleased God of his good providence to bless me with affluence, and to give me the power, and I hope the heart, to assist those who are less gifted with the good things of this life.... I am willing to take charge of Charles' education for two or three years.

Like John Thornton before him, Wilberforce often gave sums to active clergymen to distribute among needy parishioners. He also visited prisons in London and relieved the financial distress of people imprisoned for debt. Sometimes his family would accompany him to the prisons. In 1818 his wife, Barbara, and some other friends went with him to witness the work of prison reformer Elizabeth Fry among female prisoners at Newgate. Thereafter he became an ardent supporter of her work.

On one occasion Wilberforce's philanthropy resulted in a victory at sea. A friend told him of an officer who was under a heavy burden of debt and asked him to intercede on the young man's behalf. He told Wilberforce that at times officers' pockets were not very deep and that his own were not very full. "Leave that to me," Wilberforce replied. The officer's debt was paid, he was outfitted, and Wilberforce used his influence to obtain a command for him.

Some time later this officer engaged an enemy ship, captured it, and was given a promotion. When he returned home, he called on Wilberforce in the uniform of a newly promoted post captain to thank him.

Nor was this the only instance of Wilberforce's philanthropy extending to those who followed the sea.

In the wake of the Napoleonic Wars, Wilberforce worked with his Clapham colleague Zachary Macaulay to establish the charity that was the forerunner of the London School of Hygiene and Tropical Medicine. This initiative began in 1818, when Wilberforce and Macaulay launched an appeal for "relief of distressed seamen." Three years later, in 1821, the committee Wilberforce and Macaulay had formed became the Seamen's Hospital Society (SHS). Wilberforce's influence with high-ranking government officials was instrumental in obtaining a hospital ship, the *Grampus*, on loan from the British Admiralty. Ten years later, the *Grampus* was replaced by a larger ship, the *Dreadnought*. This name was the name adopted for subsequent hospital ships and finally for the Society's onshore hospital buildings at Greenwich, established in 1870.

In the year 2000 Wilberforce's philanthropic legacy touched that of two modern philanthropists; for in that year the Bill and Melinda Gates Foundation awarded the London School of Hygiene and Tropical Medicine $40 million for a major program of work on malaria. This led to the creation of the school's Centre on Globalization, Environmental Change and Health.*

---

*The information about Wilberforce and the history of the London School of Hygiene & Tropical Medicine comes from Lise Wilkinson and Anne Hardy, *Prevention and Cure. The London School of Hygiene and Tropical Medicine. A 20th Century Quest for Global Public Health*. 2001. Kegan Paul, London.

⌣

Wilberforce also remained dedicated throughout his political career to education for the poor. He took particular interest and pleasure in educational programs for indigent or friendless boys who were the sons of dead or destitute clergymen or military officers. One young man he assisted, Gordon Smith, became an army doctor. Wilberforce also founded schools and institutions for the education of the deaf and blind.

"Assistance to young men of promise had always been with him a favourite charity," wrote Wilberforce's sons,

> but ... he gave more than merely money – he made his house the home of one or two youths, the expense of whose education he defrayed; all their holidays were spent with him; and hours of his own time were profusely given to training and furnishing their minds. Nor were the poor forgotten – they were invited to join in his family worship on the Sunday evening, and sought out often in their cottages for instruction and [financial relief].

Wilberforce took a lively interest in the Elland Society, donating £100 per year to it – well over $26,000 today – with the proviso that "my name must not be mentioned." This society, run by his friend William Hey, was devoted to identifying poor but promising students and educating them, or as Wilberforce phrased it: "catching the colts roaming wild on Halifax Moor, and cutting their manes and tails, and sending them to college."

In addition to this, Wilberforce often welcomed these young men to his home to arrange for their employment. He took pains to personally place young men under tutors until they were ready for college. It was one of his consistent interests to see young men educated and placed in clerical positions. Once these men had embarked on their ministries, he would at times sort out the occasional difficulties that might arise between a young minister and his superior. And while he also believed that funds spent training clergymen born in humble circumstances would help to spread the gospel – he also felt it would aid the poor because in his mind "such men will always be advocates for them."

Wilberforce's sons maintained that no one recognized promise, though marked by rough edges, more readily than their father. "We have different forms assigned to us in the school of life," he once said, "different gifts imparted. All is not attractive that is good. Iron is useful, though it does not sparkle like the diamond. Gold has not the fragrance of a flower. So different persons have various modes of excellence, and we must have an eye to all."

Wilberforce's personal and public endeavors were beginning to bear fruit. Though his personal charities were often anonymous and behind the scenes, he was gaining a widespread reputation for compassion. Increasingly people would seek him out should they find themselves, a family member, or a friend in distress. Those seeking reforms in other areas of Britain's national life sought out Wilberforce as well. Much work remained to be done to make British society more humane, but substantial progress arose from his growing stature as a philanthropist.

These early successes encouraged Wilberforce and his colleagues to attempt to export the work of moral reform. One example is the founding of the British and Foreign Bible Society in 1804, in which Wilberforce had been instrumental.

Because his own life had been transformed through the reading of the Scriptures, he believed that the distribution of them could impart similar blessings of the Judeo-Christian heritage throughout the world. This belief spread, and consequently the American Bible Society owed its formation in 1816 to the example set by the British and Foreign Bible Society.

In its early years the president of the ABS was Wilberforce's old friend and correspondent John Jay, one of America's most important founding fathers and the author of some of the *Federalist Papers*.

The two men appear to have met for the first time in the spring or early summer of 1794, when Jay held jointly the posts of chief justice of the Supreme Court and American ambassador to Great Britain. Their correspondence commenced about six months later, after Jay received copies of a report from Wilberforce on the colony of freed slaves in Sierra Leone. From this time forward until October 25, 1810, they engaged in a friendly, lengthy, and significant correspondence. Jay also possessed a deeply held Anglican faith, giving him and Wilberforce ample ground for agreement on many issues.

Jay admired Wilberforce. In May 1822, in an address to the American Bible Society, he praised Wilberforce's leadership of the struggle to end the British slave trade: "Considerations of a higher class ... finally prevailed, and the parliament abolished that detestable trade. Well-merited honor was thereby reflected on that Legislature; and particularly on that excellent and celebrated member of it, whose pious zeal and unwearied perseverance were greatly and conspicuously instrumental to [its] removal."

Wilberforce's support of Christian missions was linked to his commitment to make the Scriptures available throughout the world. Beginning in 1793 he led another arduous but ultimately successful twenty-year effort to convince the British government to allow the introduction of Christian missions into India. He was no cultural imperialist, but his Christian faith had prompted him to commence the work of abolition and various humane projects. Christianity, he believed, had done so much to humanize and better the lives of his fellow Britons, he wished the same for the people of India.

Wilberforce had been deeply concerned for them ever since he had learned of the horrible human rights abuses associated with some pagan religious practices. He decried the practice of suttee, whereby Indian widows were "compelled or seduced into consenting to be burnt alive on the death of their husbands," or the "great annual festival ... at the temple of juggernaut [during which] gigantic idols [are] placed on a stupendous car sixty feet in height, and drawn along by six cables, preceded by elephants ... when a wretched victim offer[s] himself [as] a voluntary sacrifice, and throw[s] himself on the road before the tower, the multitude leaving a space clear for his passage, he [is] crushed to death by the wheels."

⌐

The process of moral reform was uneven at times. There were great victories but also great disappointments. For years Wilberforce supported Jeremy Bentham's panopticon prison reform plan. At his own expense Bentham built a model prison, designed and constructed to provide a more humane environment. When the government refused to pay Bentham for this work, Wilberforce came to his aid. Only after many years was Bentham finally reimbursed, but the plan itself never caught on.

A ledger listing Wilberforce's personal charities has survived from the year 1798, revealing that he was sometimes frustrated by his own generosity. He reluctantly lent one man £100, realizing the man was living beyond his means. Wilberforce expressed doubt that the man's promises to pay off his debts would lead to him cutting expenses. Another man had either taken or borrowed £63 he could never repay. Wilberforce had grave misgivings about helping, writing:

I do it only because it would be ruin to him to withhold it. I doubt if even under these circumstances [my decision is] quite right. I have solemnly assured him it should be the last time of my assisting him and have given him parting advice. He has treated me ill ... applying only £21 of the last £70 I gave him to this purpose. As I have told him plainly, I fear he cannot be saved from ruin. I have had much anxiety and vexation from him.... My only comfort is that I treat him like a Christian, he [treats] me as a man of the world. He dislikes me and feels no gratitude to me, I know, for what I have done.

Such treatment could easily sour a charitably minded person. Wilberforce was bothered at times by ingratitude, but he considered it a sacred duty to conform to the golden rule. God had given him ample resources, and it was his belief that he was to give and leave the results with God.

Some results of his efforts were disappointing and at times frustrating, but far more of them yielded good fruit. In November 1821 Wilberforce penned a revealing summary of the successes that had transpired during the previous thirty-four years. "It pleased God to diffuse a spirit," he wrote,

> which began to display its love of God and love of man by the formation of societies of a religious and moral nature, which have already contributed in no small degree to bless almost all nations.... The blessings of religious light and of moral improvement [have resulted in] the growing attention to the education of our people, with societies and institutions for relieving every species of suffering which vice and misery can ever produce among the human race.

The Cambridge historian F. K. Brown described Britain during the fifty-year period preceding the start of the Victorian era as "the Age of Wilberforce." During this time, Brown wrote, and under the leadership of Wilberforce, there was probably no benevolent project that was not brought to his attention, and

> probably not a week of his life passed without appeals for help from private persons he had never heard of. His name was on the contribution lists of some seventy evangelical societies, his private charities were constant, and there were not many biographies of evangelical clergymen of the day who needed help that do not mention gifts from him. How much he gave beyond this to build churches and help such projects as Hannah More's schools will probably never be known.

Wilberforce's epitaph in Westminster Abbey, composed by a young Thomas Babington Macaulay, speaks of "the abiding eloquence of a Christian life." This speaks to the profound ways Wilberforce was able to touch the hearts and minds of his contemporaries. At times he did so individually, as with Czar Alexander of Russia (who admired his abolitionist labors) or the young men of humble means whose education he supervised late in his life. On other occasions, his moral example had an impact on groups of people, as through the writing of his widely read book *A Practical View of Christianity*.

Ultimately, in concert with fellow reformers, Wilberforce achieved remarkable success in making goodness fashionable. And yet he was profoundly aware that true lasting reform took place in the hearts and minds of individuals, one person at a time. Each of these persons then became an agent of change and renewal in his or her own right. Wherever they found themselves within society – rich, poor, or middle class – and with whatever gifts or talents they had been given, they could unite their energies with those of their fellow citizens and follow through on their duty to work toward making the good society. Wilberforce described this process eloquently in *A Practical View*:

> If any country were indeed filled with men, each … diligently discharging the duties of his own station without breaking in upon the rights of others, but on the contrary endeavoring, so far as he might be able, to forward their views and promote their happiness, all would be active and harmonious in the goodly frame of human society. There would be no jarrings, no discord. The whole machine of civil life would work without obstruction or disorder, and the course of its movements would be like the harmony of the heavenly spheres.

Four central ideals are set forth in this passage: stewardship, respect for the rights of others (a key concept for a pluralistic society), forwarding the views of others, and the promotion of the happiness of others. And it should be remembered that these ideals were not utopian flights of fancy; they produced tangible results and ultimately the rich legacy of moral renewal and philanthropy associated with Wilberforce's name. Each of these four ideals is a foundation pillar of his political thought.

Stewardship, as defined by Wilberforce, meant that each person was endowed by the Almighty with "means and occasions ... of improving ourselves, or of promoting the happiness of others." To whom much was given, he also believed, much was required. "When summoned to give an account of our stewardship," he wrote, "we shall be called upon to answer for the use we have made ... of the means of relieving the wants and necessities of our fellow-creatures." It was, then, a sacred duty to use the gift of life well.

For Wilberforce, respect for the rights of others meant the application of the golden rule to every area of life. It was the basis for every human rights and philanthropic issue with which he was involved in public life. "Let every one," he wrote, "regulate his conduct ... by the golden rule of doing to others as in similar circumstances we would have them do to us; and the path of duty will be clear before him, and I will add, the decision of [a] legislature would scarcely any longer be doubtful."

The golden rule also was directly linked to the third of Wilberforce's ideals: forwarding the views of others. In his abolitionist writings, he stated directly that it was the golden rule that informed his opposition to the slave trade.

> As to the arguments in favour of the slave trade, deduced from the Holy Scriptures, [I am] not much disposed to enter into a discussion of them, because [I] can scarcely believe they are urged seriously.... He who can justify the slave trade from the practice of Joseph, might justify concubinage and capricious divorces from that of the patriarchs. With regard to the passages referred to in the New Testament, our blessed Saviour's grand practical rule, of doing to others as we would have them do to us, as it is the shortest, so it is perhaps the best refutation of all such laborious sophistry.

Of the four Wilberforcian ideals, the promotion of the happiness of others is in some respects the most striking. It neatly turns Jefferson's ideal of "the pursuit of happiness" on its head. Wilberforce believed that when individual citizens promote the happiness of others they are most truly promoting or pursuing their own. Every individual becomes a powerful agent of social change in this sense, and the power for positive social change is multiplied to the extent that more people pursue or, more properly, promote the happiness of others. This fourth ideal is an affirmation of our common humanity and of the ties that bind us together as fellow citizens.

Wilberforce did not reject the individual pursuit of happiness in the Jeffersonian sense. He readily acknowledged the importance of improving ourselves, which is a pursuit of one's own happiness. But he also felt that when it comes to promoting a good society, there should be more to achieving true happiness than the Jeffersonian model affords. In doing so, Wilberforce made an original, uniquely Judeo-Christian and sadly overlooked contribution to Anglo-American political thought.

"Why do we make laws to punish men?" Wilberforce wrote. "It is their interest to be upright and virtuous without these laws: but there is a present impulse continually breaking in upon their better judgment; an impulse contrary to their permanent and known interest, which it is not even in the power of all our laws sufficiently to refrain." He also asserted: "The maladies of a state, however they may break out in political effects, will generally be found to arise from moral causes. It is only therefore by carefully studying those causes, that we can hope to detect the true nature of the diseases which afflict the political body, and consequently how best to produce a cure."

Wilberforce believed that the long-term cultivation of character, apart from political considerations, produced long-lasting benefits to society. He supported the view that politics should be rooted in the moral consensus of cultures. Politics should not, he believed, shape the culture – the culture should shape politics.

Wilberforce was also able to serve effectively in a political climate deeply skeptical about and often hostile to the evangelical Christianity that he espoused. As the apostle Paul had done in Athens, Wilberforce invoked the literature and philosophy of the times to make points without imagining a large sympathetic majority standing behind him. This served to generate recognition and support for the vital role he believed religion and morality could play in society.

"The legislators of antiquity," he wrote, "[made it] ... their deepest study, and primary aim, to preserve from deterioration the public morals." To support this contention he would often cite political theorists like Cicero, Locke, Machiavelli, and Montesquieu.

The latter two philosophers were very important to Wilberforce, and he invoked their authority:

> It is a truth attested by the history of all ages and countries, and established on the authority of all the ablest writers, both ancient and modern [among them] Machiavelli and Montesquieu ... that the religion and morality of a country, especially of every free community, are inseparably connected with its preservation and welfare; that their flourishing or declining state is the sure indication of its tending to prosperity or decay. It has even been expressly laid down, that a people grossly corrupt are incapable of liberty.

One need not be particularly religious to value the role of religion in society, Wilberforce believed. Machiavelli, he said,

> was not considered either as a religious or moral authority, but ... was eminently distinguished for political knowledge and sagacity. [He] stated, that "the rulers of all states, whether kingdoms or commonwealths, should take care that religion should be honoured, and all its ceremonies preserved inviolate,

for there was not a more certain symptom of the destruction of states, than a contempt for religion and morals."

Wilberforce's life and work was also a testament to the idea that promoting moral renewal takes time. One need only consider how long the Victorian era endured – from 1837 until 1901. Because Wilberforce and his contemporaries labored long and built a solid foundation for moral renewal, the societal benefits continued for many years after their deaths.

Wilberforce's life, as John Pollock has written, "gives us an example of how to create the momentum that leads to positive change.... It is a matter of history that for two generations at least after Wilberforce, the British character was molded by attitudes that were essentially his. Under his leadership, a Christian social conscience attacked prevalent social ills while at the same time seeking to better the lives of those affected by them."

The reformation of manners, the second of Wilberforce's two great objects, is not as well remembered as the first, the abolition of the slave trade. But the latter would have been impossible without the former.

It was not mere happenstance that the two objects were combined in Wilberforce's celebrated diary entry. The linkage was deliberate and Wilberforce believed the abolition of the slave trade could not have taken place without a concurrent moral reformation to strengthen the consensus that the British slave trade was a tragic national sin. He realized that "attempts at political reform, without changing the hearts and minds of people at the same time, were futile."

CHAPTER 6

THE WASHINGTON OF HUMANITY

That good and great man, William Wilberforce.
THOMAS BABINGTON MACAULAY

In March 1818 the Italian statesman Count Pecchio was visiting Britain. He was in London on the day Parliament opened its new legislative session. During the day's proceedings, he witnessed Wilberforce's entrance into the House of Commons. He never forgot the scene. "When Mr. Wilberforce passes through the crowd," he wrote, "every one contemplates this little old man, worn with age, and his head sunk upon his shoulders, as a sacred relic; as the Washington of humanity."

What was it about Wilberforce that moved everyone in the room to contemplate his arrival? Why would someone like Count Pecchio take note of this?

The answer lies in a unique fact: from the abolition of the slave trade in 1807 until his death, Wilberforce was accorded a measure of personal and moral influence without precedent in British political life. Sir Winston Churchill once said that Wilberforce, in the early years of his political life, was "the keeper of Pitt's conscience." After 1807 Wilberforce had in many ways become the nation's conscience.

His contemporaries knew that the struggle against the slave trade had required great fortitude and perseverance. Many also understood that Wilberforce's faith had imbued him with a willingness to stay the course in the face of great physical debility, vitriol, and threats against his life. His service to something larger than self, amidst all of these circumstances, was the reason why he came to be venerated as "a sacred relic."

This is not to say that there were not other highly regarded men in the British government during Wilberforce's lifetime. Pitt and the Duke of Wellington also commanded great and abiding respect. But Wilberforce operated on a different kind of scale. His interest was England, but also Europe as a whole and Britain's colonies. He wasn't focused on winning military battles (as with Wellington's victories) or solving a budget problem (such as Pitt's great retrenchment of Britain's finances after the disastrous war with America), important as those things undoubtedly were. He was interested in solving a humanitarian issue – one that affected millions around the globe.

This unique influence made what happened after the abolition of the slave trade all the more remarkable. For within weeks of this great victory, Wilberforce's seat in Parliament was seriously threatened.

It all began when the short-lived ministry headed by Lord Grenville, which had been so instrumental in helping the abolitionists achieve victory, came to an end in late March 1807. It had lasted a little more than a year, having been formed after the death of Pitt in January 1806. The new ministry was headed by Spencer Perceval (an evangelical like Wilberforce) and had a large electoral majority. But despite these promising signs, Wilberforce was deeply chagrined to receive a letter from Perceval shortly thereafter announcing a parliamentary dissolution. He was now forced to contend with the rigors of a general election.

Wilberforce's place in the legislature as MP for Yorkshire was a highly coveted one. In 1784 he had displaced the favored candidate of the landed aristocrats who had formerly controlled Yorkshire's parliamentary representation. While Pitt lived, Wilberforce received his ardent and powerful support. Now that Pitt had died and the Grenville ministry had proved to be of such short duration, the wealthy aristocrats, who had in a very real sense been biding their time, believed Wilberforce might be vulnerable.

This was especially so because the strength of the newly formed Perceval administration was relatively untested. The landed aristocratic interests in Yorkshire had exercised great control and influence for many years prior to Wilberforce's upset victory twenty-three years before. True enough, Wilberforce had represented the county with distinction, but from their perspective his seat was really theirs. It was only a question of time and the right circumstances until it would be theirs again.

Wilberforce learned that he would have two rivals in the upcoming Yorkshire election: Henry Lascelles and Lord Milton. Lascelles' family was extremely wealthy, and he had formerly been an MP for the county of Yorkshire. His father, Lord Harewood (a West Indian slave plantation owner) was ready, Wilberforce noted, "to spend in [the contest] his whole Barbadoes [sic] property."

Lord Milton had even deeper pockets. The heir of the second Earl Fitzwilliam, Milton had access to the virtually inexhaustible wealth of his family. Wilberforce's middle-class, mercantile fortune was substantial, but it paled in comparison to those of his opponents.

Many of Wilberforce's friends were so demoralized by this that they urged him to forgo the idea of seeking reelection altogether. As Wilberforce's sons wrote, however, "the moral importance which he attached to it determined him to venture the attempt." It was true that he had secured the abolition of the slave trade, and many public and private philanthropic projects close to his heart were underway. But he firmly believed there was more for him to do.

He very nearly lost his chance. A cryptic entry in his diary states that he left London for the campaign trail on April 28 "after a narrow escape from breaking my leg when just setting out." The diary says no more about the nature of the accident, but it would have certainly ended his hopes of reelection, as a candidate was expected to travel widely and conduct a vigorous campaign. His diary entry concluded with "*Deo gratias* – how are we always in His hands!"

Wilberforce arrived in Yorkshire on April 29. He began his tour in the West Riding section of the county, where he believed he could count on strong support. His campaign swing there was rapid and successful.

In years past, the society-loving Wilberforce "did not dislike such scenes" and took pleasure in speaking many times to large crowds each day. Now, the prospect of being away from his home and family, and conducting a lengthy, taxing campaign, had lost much of its former appeal. Still, though he wished to be home, it must have cheered his spirits when he learned that Prime Minister Perceval was campaigning earnestly for him.

Nomination day was May 13, and when Wilberforce's name was called "nearly every hand was held up in his favour." This was promising, but securing funds to cover the expenses of the approaching elections weighed heavily on him. After the nomination Wilberforce's friends held a meeting during which this subject was raised. As the *Annual Register* reported, Wilberforce declared a firm resolve not to let his seat go to the highest bidder. He said he was willing to risk much of his personal fortune to serve the larger end of securing reelection. He then thanked his friends for the generous promises of support that had already been made, and called upon the county "to assert its independence" in the face of the moneyed interests.

Wilberforce, the veteran legislator, was essentially running as a political outsider – an interesting turn of events to say the least. His was the wealth and social standing of a merchant family, that is to say, new wealth. The landed aristocratic interests opposing him were old money, part of the established order in the minds of the people. In running as an outsider, Wilberforce had dusted off a page from the playbook of his highly successful 1784 campaign.

One man present that day long remembered the effect produced by Wilberforce's appeal. Another gentleman rose as soon as Wilberforce sat down and said: "It is impossible that we can desert Mr. Wilberforce ... put down my name for £500." About £18,000 ($4.7 million in today's currency) was immediately pledged. It was also resolved that securing Wilberforce's reelection was in the best interests of the county and that Wilberforce should not be permitted to spend one pound of his own fortune in the campaign. They would do all that was needed to secure his reelection.

The next day, May 14, Wilberforce set off to spend the few days before the election in a campaign tour of the East Riding section of Yorkshire. Reaching his home city of Hull, he was met by a great crowd of his constituents. An eyewitness recalled the scene.

> When standing up to address them it seemed as if he was struck by the scene before him – the fields and gardens where he had played as a boy now converted into wharves or occupied by buildings.... [He poured] forth the thoughts with which the change impressed him – the gradual alteration of external objects and the still greater alteration which had taken place in themselves – he addressed the people with the most thrilling effect.

Wilberforce himself was deeply moved. "Every object," he said, "and many of the faces I behold around me, are such as were familiar to me in my earliest years.... I am reminded of many friends and connexions, some of them near and dear to me, who are now no more.... Feelings of gratitude and attachment ... at this moment powerfully affect my heart."

He then reminisced about "the period when I first became the object of your public notice.... It was your kindness, gentlemen, which first called me into public life, and ... placed me in the honourable situation of your representative.... I [have] endeavoured to discharge its duties with industry and fidelity."

Wilberforce spoke of the principles he strove to follow in his parliamentary career. "My conduct has been open to you all," he stated, "and I have the satisfaction of knowing that in general it has been honoured with your approbation. I was no party man – *measures, not men*, were the object of my concern." He then paid tribute to the memory of Pitt, who had been very popular in Yorkshire. He spoke of their early, enduring friendship, expressing gratitude that he was generally able to approve Pitt's measures and know "the satisfaction of finding the dictates of public duty coincide with the impulse of private friendship."

Grateful as he was for this, Wilberforce alluded to the times when he and the prime minister had differed. "I never addicted myself to him so closely as not to consider every question and every measure with impartiality and freedom," he asserted, "and I supported or opposed him as my judgment and conscience prescribed.... Great however as was [my] respect and attachment I ... sometimes opposed his measures, at no small cost of private feeling." Wilberforce then stressed that Pitt, for "his part, was liberal enough to give me credit for my motives, and to continue to receive me with unabated confidence and regard."

Wilberforce spoke next of his recent visit to the West Riding section of Yorkshire County. He marveled at "the effects of manufacturing industry [and] those of commercial enterprise [in the] very fields in which I so often walked and played." He then sounded a recurring theme of his political life, one of his most valued ideals of political service, commending his constituents upon finding that they were "not so absorbed in the pursuit of ... particular schemes, or the promotion of ... personal interests, as not to be attentive also to the public welfare."

Wilberforce concluded his speech by reflecting on "the happy effect of our free constitution." Under the blessing of Providence, he maintained, it had been "the instrument of dispensing greater civil happiness for a longer period, and to a greater body of men, than any system of political government in any other age or quarter of the world." He finished with a call for responsible citizenship that is evergreen.

"Gentlemen, so long as you thus understand the constitution under which you live, and know its nature ... you will be safe and happy ... notwithstanding the varieties of political opinion which will ever exist in a free country.... While this spirit of patriotism and its effects continue to flourish, you may with the favour of Providence, bid defiance to the power of the greatest of our adversaries."

Wilberforce returned to York on the day of election, Wednesday, May 20. Following a show of hands, he was shocked to learn that he was second, the next lowest, on the poll. Things looked so bad that when his friends met at dinner after the poll, a barrister who had come from London to advise him remarked: "I can see clearly enough how this will turn out. Mr. Wilberforce has obviously no chance ... the sooner he resigns the better."

Yet neither Wilberforce's advisors, nor his opponents, had reckoned on the strength of popular support in his favor. His supporters had a kind of undaunted respect for him and would let no obstacle stand in the way of their casting votes for his reelection.

Wilberforce had need of determined support. Lascelles and Lord Milton were playing political hardball and had hired virtually all the carriages in the county, leaving Wilberforce's supporters without transportation. Necessity being the mother of invention, his supporters seized on other means to come and cast their votes. As one observer wrote, "Boats are proceeding up the river heavily laden with voters: farmers lend their waggons; even donkeys have the honour of carrying voters.... No money can convey all the voters; but if their feelings are roused [Wilberforce's] election is secure."

A vast number of freeholders from the North Riding of Yorkshire, headed by Sir Robert Hildyard, entered York determined to vote for Wilberforce. A member of Wilberforce's election committee met another large body, chiefly middle-class voters from

Wensley Dale. "For what parties, gentlemen, do you come?" they were asked. "Wilberforce, to a man!" they replied.

Such parties continued to arrive at York at every given hour, day and night, by land and by water. Drained as he was by the rigors of this contest, Wilberforce wrote to his beloved wife, Barbara, then at home in Clapham.

> My having been left behind on the poll seemed to rouse the zeal of my friends (I should rather say of my fervent adherents); they exerted themselves, and have mended my condition.... Affection ... is borne me by many to whom I am scarcely or not at all known. Even those who do not vote for me seem to give me their esteem. I am thankful for the weather [the preceding days had been rainy and boisterous] and indeed I am thankful for a quiet mind which is placed above the storm.

The tally for the poll had now shifted.

Date of Polling	Wilberforce	Lascelles	Milton
Friday, May 22	2847	2698	3032
Saturday, May 23	4260	3894	4158

Now at the head of the poll, Wilberforce wrote again to Barbara on Sunday night, May 24. The comfort he had from the change of his standing in the election poll was tempered by his longing for his wife and children.

> I am robbed of the time I meant to spend in writing to you ... but you will be glad to hear that I have spent on the whole a very pleasant Sunday, though this evening is of necessity passed in my committee room.
>
> I have been twice at the [York] Minster, where the sublimity of the whole scene once nearly overcame me. [The cathedral] is the largest and finest Gothic building probably in the world. The city is full of freeholders, who came in such numbers as to cover the whole area of the place (a very large one) where the service is performed and every seat and pew were filled. I was exactly reminded of the great Jewish Passover in

the Temple in the reign of Josiah.... I am now writing in a front room, and I sat in one for two hours last night, and there was not the smallest noise or disturbance....

[Referring to his home, Wilberforce continued:] How beautiful Broomfield must be at this moment! Even here the lilacs and hawthorn are in bloom in warm situations. I imagine myself roaming ... with you and the little ones.... indeed I have joined you in spirit several times today.... Surely the universal kindness which I experience is to be regarded as a singular instance of the goodness of the Almighty. Indeed no one has so much cause to adopt the declaration that goodness and mercy have followed me all my days. I bless God my mind is calm and serene and I can leave the event [of my reelection] to Him without anxiety desiring that in whatever state I may be placed I may adorn the doctrine of God my Saviour and do honour to my Christian profession.... I must say Good night. May God bless you. Kiss the babes.

Looking back on this stormy election many years later, Wilberforce recalled: "All possible tricks were played to deprive me of votes." The most damaging of these was the charge that Wilberforce and Lascelles had formed a secret coalition. It was patently false, since anyone who consulted the official campaign paperwork could easily ascertain that Wilberforce was not in any way connected with Lascelles.

Not wishing to rely on this alone, Wilberforce strove to actively refute the charge. His opponents, anticipating this and knowing of Wilberforce's formidable oratorical skills, had hired a "rent-a-mob" to keep him from being heard.

It was only Wilberforce's great skill in managing unruly audiences that allowed him to get his message out. While attempting to explain a point on which he had been misrepresented, he was repeatedly shouted down by a mob hired by Lord Milton. Again and again he tried to be heard, to no avail. "Print, print," cried one of

Wilberforce's friends from the crowd, "print what you have to say in a handbill and let them read it since they will not hear you."

"They read indeed," cried Wilberforce. "What, do you suppose that men who make such a noise as those fellows can read? No men that make such noises as those can read I'll promise you. They must hear me now or they'll know nothing about the matter." Wilberforce's sons reported: "Immediately there was a fine Yorkshire grin over some thousand friendly faces."

One of Wilberforce's election agents, a man named Russel, marveled at Wilberforce's composure during these trying days. "It was necessary," Russel recalled, "that I should have some private communication with him every day.... When he came in from the hustings to dress for dinner ... each day ... I perceived that he was repeating to himself what seemed the same words.... At length I was able to catch them and they proved to be that stanza [from] Cowper's [*Olney Hymns*]:

> *The calm retreat, the silent shade,*
> *With prayer and praise agree,*
> *And seem by Thy sweet bounty made*
> *For those that follow Thee.*

By the twelfth day of the poll, Wilberforce's reelection was certain. He experienced a severe gastric attack, however, which confined him to his room for the remaining four days of the poll. Lord Milton's supporters now resorted to a desperate tactic and circulated a rumor that he was dead. The rumor of his demise was, to say the least, greatly exaggerated, and it did not affect his election.

The entire country had followed this hotly contested election. "Nothing since the days of the [glorious] revolution [of 1688]," a reporter for the *York Herald* stated,

has ever presented to the world such a scene as this great county for fifteen days and nights. Repose or rest have been unknown in it, except it was seen in a messenger asleep upon his post-horse, or in his carriage. Every day the roads in every direction to and from every remote corner of the county have been covered with vehicles loaded with voters; and barouches, curricles, gigs, flying waggons, and military cars with eight horses crowded sometimes with forty voters have been scouring the country leaving not the slightest chance for the quiet traveller to urge his humble journey or find a chair at an inn to sit down upon.

Wilberforce's cousin Henry Thornton described the Yorkshire election in terms that would have gratified Wilberforce's feelings more than the article in the *York Herald*, affirming the power of his political independence and integrity.

It was a great victory and strikingly refutes the favourite argument of those who maintain stoutly the necessity of party connexion for political efficiency. "No man," they allege, "in this country ever obtained any great personal power and influence in society, merely by originating in Parliament measures of internal regulation, or conducting with judgment and success, improvements however extensive, that do not affect the interests of one or other of the two great parties in the state."
… Wilberforce may perhaps be mentioned as an exception – and certainly the greatness, the long endurance and the difficulty of the struggle which he at last conducted to so glorious a termination have given him a fame and popularity which may be compared in some respects with that of a [great] party leader.

The personal wealth spent by Wilberforce's political opponents dwarfed the money raised by voluntary donations in his support. Lascelles and Lord Milton each spent £100,000 ($26 million), Wilberforce £28,600 ($7.5 million). Wilberforce's contributors, many of whom gave though unasked, sent funds from all over England and from as far away as Edinburgh, Scotland. Because a total of £64,455 (just under $17 million] was raised, the overage was returned. Though outspent by a margin of over three to one, Wilberforce had triumphed. It was a tribute to the moral authority and influence that he commanded that he could fend off such a powerful and well-moneyed political challenge.

⌒

A little more than a year later, on November 19, 1808, Wilberforce took possession of a new house at Kensington Gore – a site now occupied by the Royal Albert Hall and not far from the lovely and extensive grounds of Hyde Park. He had purchased a twenty-five-year lease on the property the preceding spring.

Wilberforce gave up Broomfield with great regret. It was a home endeared to him by many happy moments and great natural beauty. Much of his regret stemmed from leaving a home so close to his Clapham friends. There was John Venn, the rector of Holy Trinity Church, Clapham, whose rich pastoral ministry drew standing-room only crowds. Others to whom Wilberforce was particularly close included his cousin and fellow MP Henry Thornton; Lord Teignmouth and Charles Grant (with their distinguished careers in India); the brilliant lawyer James Stephen; Zachary Macaulay (possessed of wide learning and great administrative gifts); and Hannah More – "the Bishop in petticoats" – who though she didn't reside at Clapham worked closely with Wilberforce and the others to implement educational reforms.

Wilberforce had lived in Clapham since 1792, when he and Thornton had resolved to start "a chummery" there as bachelors. Sixteen years of deep friendship and philanthropic collaboration had followed. He would miss it all greatly. "I give up ... living near my friends in this circle," Wilberforce wrote, "yet I trust my connexion with them is so firm that the removal will not weaken it."

A London house was essential to Wilberforce's parliamentary attendance, but his strong desire to be with his family more often was the most important factor in his decision to reside at Kensington Gore. There, within a mile of Hyde Park Corner, he was

within walking distance of home, which afforded health benefits and much pleasure, because he could enjoy the gardens for
which Hyde Park was famous. "During the long days at the close
of spring," Wilberforce's friend John Harford recalled,

> [he] sometimes went into the garden at a late hour to listen to
> the nightingales which then abounded at Kensington. None
> but a few select friends who liked to spend their time as he
> did were invited to his house on Sundays. In the evenings he
> sometimes read aloud fine passages from his favourite poet,
> Cowper, imparting to them the fullest effect by the tones of
> his musical voice, and he was always ready for conversation at
> once elevating and instructive.

Wilberforce also exchanged his house across the street from
the Commons, Number 4 Old Palace Yard, for more modest lodgings, which he described as "a nest close to the House of Commons." He planned to use the money saved by this step to support
his ample charities.

Wilberforce's change of residence proved wise. He was with
his family more often, and the size of his new house enabled him
to exercise with greater comfort the hospitality in which he delighted. Kensington Gore was seldom free of guests when he was
in it. It was said that a cheerful and enlightened atmosphere per-
vaded the house and grounds.

The first hours in the morning were the only ones that Wilberforce could strictly call his own. He spent these in devotional
exercises. "I always find that I have most time for business and it
is best done, when I have most properly observed my private devotions," he observed. "In the calmness of the morning, before the
mind is heated and wearied by the turmoil of the day you have a
season of unusual importance for communing with God and with
yourself."

After his devotions, Wilberforce joined his assembled household for morning prayer. He conducted this service himself. A late

breakfast followed, during which he would receive his first set of visitors. The anteroom in this new residence was no different than the anteroom at Number 4 Old Palace Yard, which Hannah More had once described as being "like Noah's ark – full of beasts clean and unclean." To this Wilberforce had replied archly that Parliament was like Noah's ark – "many beasts and a few humans."

Wilberforce's social gifts were put to good use at Kensington Gore, "drawing out and harmonizing all the shades of character and feeling," which were often brought suddenly together there. Once, he sought to relax the stiffness of "a starched little fellow" who was overly class conscious. The Baptist theologian Andrew Fuller was announced – a man of considerable intellect but one "who bore about him very plainly the *vestigia ruris* [the vestiges of the country]."

Before Fuller came in, Wilberforce said to his little friend, "You know Andrew Fuller?"

"No, I never heard his name."

"Oh, then you must know him, he is an extraordinary man whose talents have raised him from a very low situation." This prepared the way for Fuller, a brawny, robust man who walked in looking very much like a blacksmith.

As ever, Wilberforce remained dedicated to his charities, though they sometimes played havoc with his schedule. Once a houseguest forced his way into Kensington Gore but was not any the less welcome for his rudeness. "E. forced his way in to see me," Wilberforce told his diary, "the poor midshipman who about eight months ago wrote to me from Morpeth gaol [about] the suit of a tailor for [a] uniform.... I got [him] released and sent him a few [pounds]. He called to thank me and said he should never forget my kindness – [he was] not ashamed of it and [said he] would subscribe five pounds per annum to [the] Small Debt Society." On another occasion, a man whom Wilberforce helped regain a lucrative estate gratefully sent a turkey that graced the dinner table that evening.

Gore House, sometimes called Kensington Gore, the home where Wilberforce lived from 1808 to 1821

Two months before moving into Kensington Gore, Wilberforce had written to James Monroe, later America's fifth president. On June 7, 1803, Wilberforce wrote what appears to have been his first letter to Monroe, alarmed by rumors that some American states had renewed the slave trade after having "prohibited it for several years." Monroe, serving as one of two American commissioners sent to Britain to negotiate a commercial treaty, wrote a kind, reassuring reply. Wilberforce quickly wrote back and praised the United States, saying, "Without having so much light thrown on the subject [of the slave trade] as has been cast on it here, you have seen enough to induce you to do your utmost to put a stop to this unjust traffic." Shortly thereafter, they met and remained friends.

In 1807, when the British slave trade abolition bill was being debated, Wilberforce received word that the American Congress had also brought in an abolition bill. He wasted no time in writing to Monroe, overjoyed at "the concurrence of our two countries in carrying into execution this great work of Beneficence."

Wilberforce's cousin, fellow abolitionist and member of Parliament, Henry Thornton, captured the significance of this historical moment when he wrote: "I hope and trust that tomorrow will be an era for old England, and the [House of] Lords will do that in England which the descendents of the Puritans in America are now doing in Congress, for me Trade is surely as ignoble and ungentlemanly as it is un-Christian."

This incident, and the enduring friendship that resulted from it, was a vital connection between the British and American abolitionist movements. One biographer has observed that though "Wilberforce never visited the United States … he remains a figure of great importance to American history, since without his twenty-year campaign in Parliament against the British [slave] trade it is doubtful whether the American slave trade would have been simultaneously abolished by Congress in 1807."

The U.S. Constitution, ratified in 1787, stipulated in section 9 of Article I that Congress would not be able to prohibit the importation of slaves before 1808. During January and February 1807, the House of Representatives and the Senate worked to develop mutually acceptable bills. The final vote in the House on March 2 was 63 for, 49 against. President Thomas Jefferson signed the bill into law within a month of the British bill abolishing the slave trade. As of January 1, 1808, the American slave trade would be no more.

The passage of abolition bills by the American and British legislatures, important as they were, did not forestall an unforeseen threat that arose in the summer of 1808. British slave traders had begun to evade capture by disguising themselves as American ships, while American slavers disguised their vessels as British ships. Wilberforce, horrified at the prospect of "a subterfuge by which the whole effect of our [abolition] law may be defeated," resolved to make a direct appeal to the U.S. government.

He wrote to Monroe, saying, "All our hopes of success in our endeavours for the internal benefit of Africa must be grounded on our preventing these infractions of the law." Wilberforce also enclosed another letter to President Thomas Jefferson. And though by this time he was known the world over for having led the fight to abolish the British slave trade, Wilberforce modestly asked Monroe to "make my name known to Mr. Jefferson."

Wilberforce told Jefferson of his fear that a large British contraband slave trade could develop under the protection of the American flag. He pleaded for Jefferson's intervention on behalf of "the unknown multitudes whose fate is involved in the decision you may form on this particular case." Lastly, he suggested an Anglo-American convention to secure the liberation of these human cargoes, regardless of which Navy came to their rescue or the flag that American or British slavers might fly. "I am now writing to Jefferson in America," he wrote, "to obtain some agreement between the two nations for giving effect to Abolition by allowing each country to take the other's slave ships."

Wilberforce set forth a compelling case to Jefferson. He told Jefferson in the conclusion of his letter,

> A compact formed between our two countries for the benevolent purpose of stopping, perhaps, the most destructive scourge that ever afflicted the human race, may lead to similar agreements with other countries, until at length all the civilized nations of the earth shall have come into this *concert of benevolence*. It was by a compact of a similar nature, established between a number of different independent states, that in the darkness and anarchy of the middle ages, the ravages of private war were arrested in a great part of Europe for near three centuries; during which period political order, respect for the laws, together with the equal administration of justice, made a considerable progress. Surely a better precedent cannot be followed. Surely there can never exist an occasion more proper for resorting to such a measure; and may we hope that

the adoption of it would now be followed in Africa by the same happy consequences which it formerly produced in Europe.

Though Jefferson did not act on Wilberforce's suggestion, Wilberforce persisted, next writing to his friend John Jay.

I [do not] see any prospect of preventing this abuse, unless a convention could be made between the two countries, by which the ships of war of each should be authorised, and even encouraged (by the hopes of gaining by the forfeitures) to seize and bring in for adjudication the vessels of the other, when prosecuting this unlawful commerce. I rather believe there is another particular in which it still remains for your country to render its law similar to ours, by subjecting to forfeiture any slave-ship of any country, and under any flag, which is fitted out in and cleared out from an American port. Now, my dear sir, may I hope for your assistance towards the production of the effects I have specified?

Jay's reply to Wilberforce on November 8, 1809, was all Wilberforce could have wished for. Jay began by paying tribute to the abolitionist endeavors of Wilberforce and his colleagues, who were trying to end the slave trade even as the interminable war against Napoleon's France continued.

"The patrons of the Abolition Act," Jay wrote,

and of the African Institution certainly do honour, and will probably do more than ordinary good, to Great Britain, against whom complaints have ascended both from Asia and Africa. It is pleasing to behold a nation assiduously cultivating the arts of peace and humanity in the midst of war.... That your and our governments should co-operate in rendering their respective laws against the slave-trade effectual, is to me very desirable, and I believe that a convention for the purpose would be approved by all who think and feel as you and I do respecting that base and cruel traffic.... They who offer to do what is fit and right to be done, cannot be losers by it. I can do but little – that little shall be done.

Despite Jay's intercession with the American government on Wilberforce's behalf, the American government again did not act on Wilberforce's proposal. It was not until 1824, during the presidency of James Monroe, that the Anglo-American convention Wilberforce had so greatly desired was finally passed.

⌣

Apart from his efforts to secure an Anglo-American anti-slave-trade cooperation agreement and his great victory in securing the abolition of the British slave trade, Wilberforce spent many years during the period from 1807 to 1822 doing all he could to convince other European nations to abolish the slave trade as well. His major effort to secure this goal was in 1814 – before, during, and after the peace negotiations at Amiens – after the first defeat of the French, which sent Napoleon into exile on the Island of Elba.

Upon hearing that Napoleon had accepted the emperor of Russia's offer that he renounce the French throne and retire to Elba, Wilberforce wrote to Hannah More, "So the dynasty of Bonaparte has ceased to reign, as Talleyrand informs us. This God hath done. How can I but wish that my old friend Pitt were still alive to witness this catastrophe of the twenty-five years drama (since 1789)?" Wilberforce confided to his diary: "I am delighted Paris is spared. Oh for the general abolition of the slave trade!"

On April 11, 1814, while his wife and children went out to see the illuminations celebrating Napoleon's defeat, Wilberforce resolved to push as hard as he could for a general abolition of the slave trade. He wrote to the prime minister, Lord Liverpool, expressing his opinion that Britain's ally Emperor Alexander of Russia "was doubtless in full unison with all grand and humane proposals." He told Liverpool frankly that "we should look to government alone for not restoring any slave colony [to France] without [an] abolition condition." He received "a very pleasing answer" from Liverpool, asking that he furnish British foreign secretary Lord Castlereagh with a copy of his 1807 anti-slave-trade manifesto *A Letter to the Freeholders of Yorkshire*.

Writing to his old friend Thomas Gisborne, Wilberforce revealed how deeply his hopes to secure a general abolition of the slave trade ran.

> It would be too shocking to restore to Europe the blessings of peace with professions of our reverence for the principles of justice and humanity, and at the same moment to be creating (for so it would really be doing wherever the slave trade is [now] extinct), this traffic in the persons of our fellow-creatures. We are much occupied with the grand object of prevailing on all the great European powers to agree to a convention for the general Abolition of the Slave Trade. Oh may God turn the hearts of these men!

Wilberforce's hopes were dashed. The new French government refused to voluntarily abolish the slave trade. The French trade continued until 1815, when Napoleon, briefly restored to power, proclaimed a total and immediate abolition of the slave trade to try to curry favor with the British government. After his defeat at Waterloo and the restoration of the Bourbon monarchy by Britain, the victorious powers did not allow King Louis XVIII (a constitutional monarch) to revive the trade.

Still, prior to Napoleon's seizure of power and defeat at Waterloo, Wilberforce experienced one of the great privileges of his life. During the peace negotiations after France's first defeat in 1814, Russia's emperor Alexander proved he was indeed favorable to grand and humane proposals by announcing that he would personally seek a general convention to abolish the slave trade.

In June 1814 Alexander was in Britain. The king of Prussia and many other European statesmen had assembled there after the first capture of Paris to congratulate the prince regent of England

and the British nation upon the termination of war with France. On June 11 John Harford was present at a dinner party at Kensington Gore when a note was delivered to Wilberforce. Wilberforce read it and handed it to Harford, whispering that he should not mention its contents to anyone else.

The note was from one of the officers of state attendant to Alexander, expressing His Imperial Majesty's wish that Wilberforce visit him the next day. Harford handed the note back to Wilberforce, who expressed his hope that he might be able to use this high honor to further the general abolition cause. Wilberforce made no mention of this invitation to his other guests, a measure of forbearance Harford thought "perfectly in unison with [Wilberforce's] simplicity of character."

Early on June 12, a Sunday, Wilberforce appeared at breakfast in his court dress. He told Harford that prior to coming downstairs, he had earnestly been "imploring the blessing of God upon the approaching interview."

Alexander received him kindly and cordially. As Wilberforce entered the room, he knelt and was about to kiss the emperor's hand. Alexander caught Wilberforce by his own hand and shook it in "a most friendly manner." Wilberforce recalled that Alexander "was much interested (in abolition), and very glad to see me." Wilberforce stated that the French would not abolish the slave trade when they had said they would. Alexander replied forcefully: "We must make them." Correcting himself, he then said, "We must keep them to it."

Wilberforce and Alexander's efforts proved ultimately to be a dead letter, but this does not detract from the importance of their meeting. Alexander, as a leader who had led the fight to defeat Napoleon, was one of the grand men of Europe at this time. His standing in the European community rivaled that of the Duke of Wellington. There was no reason for him to have sought out Wilberforce, who held no official government post, other than an honest belief that consulting with him would produce some

good result for the sake of a general abolition agreement. Wellington may have been the era's greatest soldier; Alexander's actions
showed that Wilberforce was the era's greatest humanitarian.

This reputation for social justice and fair dealing moved many
people to seek Wilberforce's counsel and trust in his integrity. The
poet Robert Southey, for many years one of Wilberforce's friends,
judged that while Wilberforce's parliamentary influence was great,
it was exceeded by "the weight with which his opinion came to the
public; [it was] far greater than of any other individual."

～

Another poet whom Wilberforce had known for many years was
William Wordsworth. When Wordsworth's first collection of poetry, the *Lyrical Ballads* (on which he collaborated with Samuel
Coleridge) was published in 1798, he had sent a copy of the book
to Wilberforce, asking him to accept it. He praised Wilberforce's
book, *A Practical View of Christianity*, saying he and Wilberforce
were "labourers in the same vineyard."

Wordsworth was the nephew of William Cookson, one of Wilberforce's tutors at St. John's College. This was but one of many
points of connection between the Wordsworths and Wilberforce.

Just before Christmas in 1789, Wilberforce had been staying
with Cookson and his family at the Forncett Rectory in Norfolk.
Wilberforce had gone there in keeping with his resolution to pursue self-education. Cookson, like Wilberforce's friend Thomas
Gisborne, supervised Wilberforce's studies.

Cookson's niece, Dorothy Wordsworth, was also there. She was
quite taken with him and thought him "one of the best of men."
She must have been noticeably smitten, for her friend Jane Halifax suggested she marry Wilberforce. Dorothy demurely replied:
"Mr. W. would, were he ever to marry, look for a lady possessed
of many more accomplishments than I can boast, and besides he
is as unlikely as any man ever to marry at all as any I know."
Given Dorothy's response, Wilberforce was probably unaware of

her affection for him. Down through the years, however, the ties between him and the Wordsworths endured, largely because of a shared love of the beauty of Britain's Lake District.

In the late summer and early autumn of 1818, Wilberforce was able to keep an old promise he had made to his family to take them to his beloved Lake District, which he had toured so often as a young bachelor. He wrote to William and Dorothy Wordsworth for help in securing lodgings. They located two small homes near their own home at Rydal.

When Wilberforce's large entourage arrived (nineteen people plus their horses), Dorothy Wordsworth went to visit them. Wilberforce and his two youngest sons, Samuel and Henry, had not yet arrived, but the rest of the family had. They walked about the houses and their gardens, enchanted by all they saw. Wilberforce's carriage pulled up a short while later, and everyone dashed out to meet him.

It had been almost twenty-five years since Dorothy had last seen Wilberforce. She was moved when she saw his feeble appearance. She soon learned, however, that while his appearance may have been feeble, he was still able to, and indeed insisted upon, walking great distances during the family's six-week stay. He walked up hills and mountains with his family, even the formidable Skiddaw, though once caught in a rainstorm. His resolve recalled his earlier tour of this region in 1779.

On September 7 Wilberforce and his family boated on Lake Winandermere. They dined in the boat, under the lee of the great island. They arrived home late, after a "delightful evening when they had walked out at night and saw the moon and a flood of light."

When the Wilberforces departed, Dorothy committed her reflections about their visit to paper. She noticed, perhaps wistfully – given her own former attachment to Wilberforce – that Barbara Wilberforce called her husband "Wilby" continually. She concluded: "There never lived on earth, I am sure, a man of sweeter temper than Mr. Wilberforce. He is made up of benevolence and lovingkindness, and though shattered in constitution and feeble in body, he is as lively and animated as in the days of his youth."

Dorothy was right. On September 5 Wilberforce had taken a two-hour walk by Rydal and Grasmere, arriving home "a good deal tired." With great delight, he retraced all the haunts he had so loved in his youth. He pointed out to his children every well-remembered beauty. At the close of one day, he wrote, "It doubles my own enjoyment to see my dear children enjoy these scenes with me."

It was easy to see that Wilberforce was deeply attached to his family. And the nation of Britain was deeply attached to Wilberforce. He had taken a country that had been broken into pieces morally and labored unstintingly to create a moral consensus with regard to abolition. That the British Empire during the Victorian era was more humane than it might have been otherwise was due in no small measure to him.

His is the story of a man illuminated with the convictions of faith who persevered through trial and hardship. His focus, though consistent and plain, wasn't single-minded. He was involved in war efforts, many kinds of legislation, and myriad philanthropies. Still, historically, he is not an enigma.

This point was made powerfully by Benjamin Hughes, a pioneering African-American educator. He delivered an address on Wilberforce's life and character at the request of the people of color in New York City on October 22, 1833, almost three months after Wilberforce's death. "The statues of heroes and princes," Hughes stated, "and the [commendations] of statesmen have proclaimed their worth, as the martial prowess of the one, or the brilliant genius of the other, may have fired the world, or attracted the admiration of men."

Hughes then described the "splendid achievements of Napoleon," achieved amid "the bristling points of countless bayonets" and "deluged fields of blood." It was true enough, Hughes said,

Napoleon was unrivaled in the annals of war. Yet Napoleon was no more; and with him, Hughes continued, "sleep those vast designs, which convulsed the world in bloody contest for empire."

Hughes then made an arresting statement, one that showed how clearly he understood why someone like Wilberforce might not be estimated at his true worth. "There is a charm," Hughes observed, "that attracts the admiration of men to their destroyers; a propensity to applaud those very acts that bring misery on the human race; and on the other hand to pass by unheeded, the placid and even tenor of the real benefactors of their species."

Warming to this thought, Hughes asserted that

> the moral sublimity ... of philanthropy and virtue, have no allurements, and are of no consideration. But there is a spectacle more glorious and venerable than the transient blaze of a meteor; or the triumphant entry of a conqueror. It is the benign manifestation of those nobler feelings of our nature in behalf of the oppressed.... [It] is that species of love to man, [called] philanthropy ... [which is] not circumscribed within the narrow precincts of country, restricted to religion or party; – it is co-extensive with the world. Hence, of all men, it is to the Philanthropist that we are chiefly indebted; it is upon his disinterested deeds that we are to stare; – and his is the memory for which we should cherish the fondest recollections.

Hughes was able to see the things that really matter. Leaders with a great appetite for power do leave their mark, but it is those who do the work of justice who change the flow of humanity. We may be more naturally drawn to Napoleon, but his hands were stained with blood. Wilberforce's hands were unstained and his memory was enshrined in the hearts of Hughes and his fellow African-Americans.

CHAPTER 7

NATURE, MORALS, AND IDEAS

How can we judge fairly of the characters and merits of men,
of the wisdom or folly of actions, unless we have ... an accurate
knowledge of all particulars, so that we may live as it were
in the times, and among the persons, of whom we read,
see with their eyes, and reason and decide on their premises?
WILLIAM WILBERFORCE

Though his body was often weak, Wilberforce's mental energy was nearly inexhaustible. Following his Great Change in 1786, he became a student in earnest, turning nearly every moment to account.

"My business," he wrote some years later, "was to employ as diligently as I could in study as much as possible of my recesses from Parliament.... As I knew I could [study] far less in any house of my own, for many years I quartered myself for nearly all the time Parliament was not sitting with different friends.... [They] suffered me to breakfast in my own room, and live as much as I pleased the life of a student.... Thus I went on until I married in 1797."

As one of two MPs for Yorkshire for most of his political life, Wilberforce represented the most powerful constituency in England. Ambitious and driven by the desire for distinction in his early political life, he had cultivated his natural gift for eloquence. His oratory could sway the counsels of government and often the hearts of those who disagreed with him. Now, convinced of the need to cultivate other gifts and humbled by his waste of time and opportunities during his formal education, he would study with his learned friends. Staying in their homes for a month or two at a stretch, he studied for nine or ten hours a day with William Cookson, Thomas Gisborne, and Thomas Babington (the uncle of historian, poet, and politician Thomas Babington Macaulay).

Instead of dancing the nights away, Wilberforce took better care of himself, exercising by taking long walks alone. He reveled in the beauty of the forests, hills, and fields surrounding the homes of his friends. In these places, his eye would wander

> ... *unsated with delight from shade*
> *To shade, from grove to thicket, from near groups*
> *To yon primaeval woods with darkening sweep*
> *Retiring; and with beauty sees the whole*
> *Kindle, and glow with renovated life!*

There was a profoundly spiritual aspect to Wilberforce's program of self-education. This sounds rather mysterious, but he viewed it in practical terms. "My religion," he wrote, "taught me the duty of devoting all my faculties and powers as a debt of gratitude to my reconciled Father in Christ Jesus, as well as of reasonable service to my Creator, Preserver, and continual Benefactor."

In discharging this grateful service, Wilberforce sought to measure his progress as a Christian through what he called "improvement in love to God and man." Love to man meant that he was to "employ ... his talents for the benefit of his fellow-creatures." Love to God meant that he ought cultivate his talents and realize his potential as an act of devotion.

Seasons of study, rest, and renewal furthered the transformation that had commenced with Wilberforce's Great Change. He had always admired his friend Pitt's scholarly training and intellect, and he moved to cultivate this side of his own character. In study, he found he reconnected with all he truly valued in life. He had discovered God to be his "patron and benefactor and friend, 'who loved us, and gave himself for us.' " The "labours of a whole life," he wrote, are "but an imperfect expression of ... thankfulness."

And so Wilberforce viewed his continuing interaction with great books, persons, and ideas as a blessing – and he reveled in it. He ranged at will over the whole cultural landscape available to him with a zest that rivaled his love of the outdoors.

⌐

One measure of how comprehensive Wilberforce's journeys of the mind were is to consider the major writers of English prose with whose works he was familiar. Covering a literary period ranging roughly from 1550 to 1830, he read authors ranging from reformation theologian Richard Hooker to the essays of Thomas Babington Macaulay.

Moving out beyond literature to other areas of cultural achievement, Wilberforce's familiarity with the world of the visual arts, for example, was impressive. He was a founder of Britain's National Gallery and counted among his friends the American-born artist Benjamin West, president of the Royal Academy from 1792 to 1805 and again from 1806 to 1820.

Wilberforce also knew West's predecessor at the Royal Academy, Sir Joshua Reynolds, and they met on many occasions. It was Reynolds who had been present with several other surviving friends of Samuel Johnson's at the dinner hosted by Bennet Langton in 1787 – when Wilberforce first avowed his willingness to take up the abolition of the slave trade. Thus Reynolds had played a role helping Wilberforce to take up his great cause.

In one of history's fascinating moments, Wilberforce was with Reynolds when news of the mutiny on the *Bounty* first reached England. On March 27, 1790, Wilberforce attended a dinner at the Bishop of Salisbury's. Present on this occasion was Wilberforce's friend Hannah More, the poet and playwright; the noted botanist, explorer and president of the Royal Society, Sir Joseph Banks; Eva Maria, widow of the celebrated Shakespearian actor David Garrick, and Reynolds. "We talked of Captain Bligh's affair," Wilberforce wrote, "and Sir Joshua (like myself) was not surprised at it." The assembled guests then spoke of Otaheite (Tahiti) as a kind of Calypso's island – the place in Homer's Odyssey to which Ulysses had been lured by the nymph Calypso. Under an enchantment, Ulysses had remained there seven years.

Wilberforce was also a close friend of the landscape painter Joseph Farington, who, in addition to being a member of the Royal Academy, was a noted diarist. The two did one another good service as friends. Farington was deeply influenced by his reading of Wilberforce's *Practical View of Christianity*, while some of the best prose portraits of Wilberforce that have come down to us were penned by Farington.

Wilberforce's friendship with Samuel Morse, the brilliant American painter whose achievements in so many fields – including the invention of the telegraph – earned him great fame as "the American da Vinci," resulted in one of the most poignant recollections historians have of Wilberforce's home life. Earlier, Morse had written a letter to his father, Jedidiah (famous as "the father of American geography"), which demonstrated his profound respect for Wilberforce. "Mr. Wilberforce," Morse wrote,

> is an excellent man; his whole soul is bent on doing good to his fellow men. Not a moment of his time is lost. He is always planning some benevolent scheme or other, and not only planning but executing; he is made up altogether of affectionate feeling. What I saw of him in private gave me the most exalted opinion of him as a Christian. Oh, that such men as Mr. Wilberforce were more common in this world. So much human blood would not be shed to gratify the malice and revenge of a few wicked, interested men.

When, on June 18, 1815, news reached Wilberforce of Napoleon's final defeat at Waterloo, ending twenty years of war with France, his reaction was recorded by Morse.

[This] incident ... well illustrates the character of [Mr. Wilberforce]. As I passed through Hyde Park on my way to [his home at] Kensington Gore, I observed that great crowds had gathered, and rumors were rife that the allied armies had entered Paris, that Napoleon was a prisoner, and that the war was virtually at an end; and it was momentarily expected that the park guns would announce the good news to the people. On entering the drawing room at Mr. Wilberforce's I found ... Mr. [Zachary] Macaulay, Mr. [Charles] Grant ... his two sons Robert and Charles, and [the social theorist] Robert Owen of Lanark, in quite excited conversation respecting the rumors that prevailed.

Mr. Wilberforce expatiated largely on the prospects of a universal peace in consequence of the probable overthrow of Napoleon, whom, naturally, he considered the great disturber of the nations. At every period, however, he exclaimed: "It is too good to be true, it cannot be true." He was altogether skeptical in regard to the rumors.

The general subject, however, was the absorbing topic at the dinner table. After dinner the company joined the ladies in the drawing room. I sat near a window which looked out in the direction of the distant park. Presently a flash and distant dull report of a gun attracted my attention, but was unnoticed by the rest of the company. Another flash and report assured me that the park guns were firing, and at once I called Mr. Wilberforce's attention to the fact. Running to the window he threw it up in time to see the next flash and hear the report. Clasping his hands in silence, with the tears rolling down his cheeks, he stood for a few moments perfectly absorbed in thought, and, before uttering a word, embraced his wife and daughters, and shook hands with every one in the room. The scene was not one to be forgotten.

⌣

Three years earlier, on December 30, 1812, Wilberforce had met Robert Owen for the first time. Owen was just one year away from publishing his classic treatise, *A New View of Society*, a work containing ideas some scholars believe anticipated the theories of Karl Marx. On the occasion of their first meeting, Wilberforce and Owen had a breakfast meeting at Wilberforce's London home, Kensington Gore.

Owen stayed for several hours, discussing his ideas about educational reform and of "rendering manufactures and morals compatible." For the then relatively unknown Owen this was a wonderful opportunity to seek support from Wilberforce, who had long been recognized as a champion of educational reform and of better working conditions in factories.

Ten years earlier, in 1802, Wilberforce had helped Sir Robert Peel (father of the prime minister) secure passage of an act designed to limit excessive working hours in factories and improve the conditions of children working in cotton mills. Wilberforce was also a cofounder of the Society for the Relief of the Manufacturing Poor.

Soon after his breakfast visit Owen was a dinner guest at Kensington Gore, along with Wilberforce's Clapham circle colleagues Charles Grant and Henry Thornton and their wives. As Owen began to describe his ideas about educational reform, he hinted that the ladies present should retire from a discussion "which must prove beyond their comprehension." Wilberforce "eagerly dissented from the proposition." The ladies stayed.

It was well that they did, for before long Grant, Thornton, and Wilberforce were "all fast asleep, and the ladies were [Owen's] only real audience." Before the men had dropped off, however, Owen had stated to Wilberforce, "One of my great principles is that persons ought to place themselves in the situation of others, and act as they would wish themselves to be treated."

"Is that quite a new principle, Mr. Owen?" Wilberforce replied archly. "I think I have read something very like it in a book called the New Testament."

Unperturbed, Owen gravely answered, "Very possibly it may be so."

After his Great Change Wilberforce was nearly always able to dissent from the opinions of others with tact and kindness. This trait grew gradually within him; it was not instantaneous, nor did he always act as charitably as he might have wished on some occasions. But he kept trying.

Wilberforce had shown Owen great kindness in granting two interviews and introducing him to Grant and Thornton, two influential and powerful politicians in their own right. Owen mistook this kindness for approval and left Kensington Gore believing Wilberforce was charmed with his theories about reform. Wilberforce was not – writing in his diary about Owen's "strange, fanciful speculations" and his "new view of man." Still, he tried to maintain an open mind, also writing: "I kept [Owen's] paper and ran over it afterwards."

When Owen published his *New View of Society*, his respect for Wilberforce and hopes of obtaining his political patronage remained. Owen dedicated the essay to Wilberforce. Despite the wishful thinking expressed in such statements as "no one ... appears to have more nearly adopted in practice the principles which the Essay develops than yourself," Owen showed that he was well aware of Wilberforce's reputation for fair-mindedness. "In all the most important questions," Owen wrote, "which have come before [Parliament] since you became a legislator, you have not allowed the mistaken considerations of sect or party to influence your decisions; so far as an unbiased judgment can be formed of them, they appear generally to have been dictated by comprehensive views of human nature, and impartiality to your fellow-creatures."

Wilberforce's response to Owen's dedication does not appear to have survived. But some idea of what it might have been can be gauged from an incident that took place five years after the *New View* was published. On June 16, 1818, Wilberforce's friend and fellow abolitionist William Allen (who initially supported some of

Owen's educational reforms) gave him a briefing on Owen's work among the people of New Lanark.

Wilberforce was gratified to hear that good was being done, but wrote in his diary that he believed this was "not owing to [Owen's] lessons." Rather, he thought that the good work being done resulted from the fact that "there are several good people there" – men like Allen whom he greatly respected. Still, as he had written after his first meeting with Owen in 1812, Wilberforce found it "strange that the Quakers, even the sensible Allen" admired the paper Owen had left for him to read over.

Wilberforce may have had serious misgivings about Owen's ideas, but his interest in all things related to aiding the poor continued unabated. After Allen had left him that day in 1818, Wilberforce had his reader read John Davison's *[Considerations] on the Poor Laws* to him "for an hour and a half out of doors." He judged it "very clever," and wrote in his diary that it contained "some masterly passages."

～

Intellectual curiosity remained a constant in Wilberforce's life. Sir James Mackintosh – the historian and philosopher who was one of Wilberforce's most learned political colleagues – was struck by this side of Wilberforce's character. Mackintosh had important friendships with many great men, among them Edmund Burke; but there was something, Mackintosh felt, altogether singular about Wilberforce – a kind of intellectual vitality. In 1830, three years before Wilberforce's death, he wrote:

> If I were called upon to describe Wilberforce in one word, I should say he was the most *amusable* man I ever met with in my life. Instead of having to think what subjects will interest him, it is perfectly impossible to hit on one that does not. *I never saw anyone who touched life at so many points*; and this is the more remarkable in a man who is supposed to live absorbed in the contemplation of a future state. When he was in

the House of Commons, he seemed to have the freshest mind of any man there. There was all the charm of youth about him. And he is quite as remarkable in this bright evening of his days as when I saw him in his glory many years ago.

As Mackintosh and many other friends knew, Wilberforce loved to spend time among the volumes housed in his well-stocked library. For him books and periodicals were treasured companions. As one of his younger friends, John Harford, recalled:

I almost seem, at this moment, to behold him ... passing through the anteroom of his library, when about thus to retire, with a folio under his arm, and stopping me to tell me that his companion was a volume of [Richard] Baxter's *Practical Works*.

Baxter was one of his favourite divines, and he shared this preference with [Samuel] Johnson, who, as Boswell tells us, on being asked what works of Baxter he would most recommend replied, "Sir, all that he has written is good."

Richard Rush, the third son of American founding father Benjamin Rush, was yet another contemporary who was impressed with Wilberforce's intellectual interests and wide knowledge of men and affairs. Appointed Minister to Great Britain on October 31, 1817, Rush was one of the most efficient and well-liked ministers to the Court of St. James. He possessed a deep regard for the British people and for Wilberforce in particular. His book, *Memoranda of a Residence at the Court of London*, reveals that he too had noticed Wilberforce had much in common with Samuel Johnson.

Rush described one visit with Wilberforce as an "evening rich in topicks in which all took part." Wine was poured into everyone's glasses, but the conversation proved so interesting that it sat there, forgotten. The conversation turned to the life and character of Johnson. Rush was "surprised to learn that Mr. Wilberforce knew nothing of Johnson personally," although they were contemporaries. This was the more surprising, Rush continued, for "both [were] social in their habits."

Rush's next observation is as enigmatic as it is brief: "Their political creed was also much the same." Had Rush recorded more, in specific terms, about Wilberforce's political creed and Johnson's, our understanding of Wilberforce's political ideas might have been uniquely enhanced. We are left only with this tantalizing sentence.

Rush's book contains other revealing insights into Wilberforce's thought and opinions. The two first met on April 12, 1818, when Rush dined at Wilberforce's home. A large party was there, including Lord Teignmouth, Lord Rocksavage, Thomas Babington, and several other guests. Many inquiries, Rush reports, were made about the United States: its commerce, revenue, population, literature, and state of religion. "A friendly spirit characterized the inquiries and remarks," Rush wrote. "Mr. Wilberforce's fame as a philanthropist and Christian had been known to me. His parliamentary labours and those of his pen had probably been more diffused over the United States than any other country out of England."

Rush was well acquainted with Wilberforce's "long and zealous exertions ... to put an end to the slave trade." Rush had "expected to find [Wilberforce] grave; [but] on the contrary, he was full of animation. He led, without engrossing the conversation. His manner gave point to all that he said, and in his voice there were peculiarly eloquent intonations."

The party also discussed the "ease with which some persons wrote, and the labor that composition cost others.... 'Burke, Pitt, Windham, and Lord Ellenborough, were all great blotters,' [Wilberforce] said; 'Burke had begun a history of England, but gave it over.... What a mine of reflection it would have contained!'"

One guest mentioned a gentleman who had large possessions in the West Indies, following which Wilberforce made an observation that showed how skilled he was in diplomacy. "There is in

grammar," Wilberforce said, "what they call a *disjunctive conjunction* ... so there is in society; it is thus with that gentleman and
me – he is so great a slave holder ... but we do very well when
we meet; we pass by topics upon which we should not agree, and
exchange the small shot of conversation."

Rush noted that "these things all flowed from [Wilberforce]
very happily.... We were invited and arrived at an early hour;
but it was midnight when we got home, so agreeably had the time
passed. Most of the company were public professors of religion,
always the more attractive, when in alliance, as on this occasion,
with genius and accomplishments."

⌒

Wilberforce was an insightful judge of men, events, and ideas.
His recollections and writings reveal much about what he was like
as a person, his views of morality, and the ideas he championed.
John Harford's book *Recollections of William Wilberforce* affords
another rich store of knowledge. He was for Wilberforce what Boswell was for Samuel Johnson.

The *Recollections* are a painterly evocation of the friend Harford
knew so well. They are based upon correspondence, dictations,
and extensive notes taken during Wilberforce's lifetime. Following
the onset of blindness in 1862, Harford, an artist and biographer
of Michelangelo, used these earlier prose sketches and studies to
craft a memoir rich in Wilberforce's own words. It was a fully
realized portrait. Like Boswell before him, Harford was a gifted
stylist and chronicler. Through him, we see Wilberforce as he was
in life.

In his preface Harford took note of Wilberforce's "eminent talents as an orator and a statesman" – and his "admirable qualities,
both of head and heart." These qualities, Harford said, "procured
for [Mr. Wilberforce] also an influence for good, both in and out
of Parliament, and among men of all parties, scarcely equaled by
any of his contemporaries."

Wilberforce's close friend John Harford, author of Recollections of William Wilberforce, *published in 1864*

Harford observed that some aspects of oratory came naturally to Wilberforce; others he carefully cultivated. From his earliest years, he had a wonderfully expressive voice – so much so that people referred to him as "the nightingale of the House of Commons." Wilberforce was also preeminent as a speaker and debater in an age that had some of history's best: William Pitt, Charles Fox, Edmund Burke, and Richard Sheridan.

Still, it was eloquence that Harford felt was the foundation of Wilberforce's skill as a debater. Another friend, J. B. S. Morritt, agreed, saying that Wilberforce's colleagues were often moved by "passages of ... brilliancy" in his speeches.

When forced to defend his views, Wilberforce also proved himself to be "a complete master of the science of defence." George

Canning, the best orator of the generation that succeeded Wilberforce, concurred. "If there is any one," he said, "who understands thoroughly the tactics of debate, and knows exactly what will carry the House along with him, it certainly is [Wilberforce]."

Edward Everett, who rivaled Daniel Webster as the greatest American orator of the first half of the nineteenth century, furnished a telling description of Wilberforce's oratorical gifts.

Everett, best known today for the eloquent oration he gave prior to Lincoln's *Gettysburg Address*, met Wilberforce in April 1818. He was taken with many aspects of Wilberforce's character, among them his intellectual curiosity. When they first met, they had an animated meeting. Everett described his two-year continental tour and the year and a half he had spent at Gottingen University in Germany. "Wilberforce," he recalled, "asked an infinity of questions about Germany and German theology." He told Everett that nothing was known of German theology in England and exhorted him to write a book on the subject.

When Wilberforce learned of Everett's wide-ranging interest in European culture, he wrote a letter to the Reverend William Bean to gain Everett admission to a noted London museum. He directed Bean to inform him of "any other step I can take [which] would be useful for him." Wilberforce was taken with Everett, whom he described to Bean as "a young man of very superior attainments."

One month later, on May 5, 1818, Everett heard Wilberforce give a speech at a meeting of the Church Missionary Society. Wilberforce, Everett recalled,

> spoke to great effect. His manner, as far as respects movement and gesture are bad – his figure quite diminutive and unprepossessing, and his air much hurt by his extreme nearsightedness. But his fluency – happy use of metaphor – affectionate and cordial manner of allusion to the persons or topicks in question – make him one of the happiest speakers I ever heard: nothing can be imagined more hearty than the welcome given

him: and to one, who has only seen him in private, nothing can be more unexpected than his power as an orator.

In private, he is distracted – flies from topick to topick – seems whirled around in a vortex of affairs: nervous and restless. When he gets up, all this subsides – he rises above himself and his immediate personality, and reminds one of that image in [Oliver] Goldsmith,

> To them his hopes, his fears, his cares were given
> But all his serious tho'ts found rest in heaven.

It is a curious reverse of what happens in most men, who, though they be calm and tranquil in private, are thrown into trepidation whenever they address the publick, or rise to do it. Mr. Wilberforce has the consolation of having done more good than any man living. I bear him this testimony the more readily, because I differ from him myself on most of his religious opinions; and the more pointedly because the miserable infection of party spirit goes so far here that it is getting to be quite fashionable to abuse him in the papers, and ... speak contemptuously of him.

⌒

John Harford was also keenly interested in Wilberforce's understanding of oratory, or, as he described it, "the science of speaking." Wilberforce, Harford wrote, laid great stress upon "the influence which a man of ability and judgment may acquire by cultivating this talent."

Were Wilberforce giving counsel to a young member of Parliament, he said he would "particularly caution him against courting applause ... by ambitiously aiming to make what is called *a fine speech*." There were two reasons for this. First, should the attempt to make a fine speech prove successful, an undue estimate might be formed of the speaker's abilities. This, he held, would render any subsequent and less studied efforts failures. Second, he warned that should a young member consumed by nervousness unfortunately break down – a case by no means uncommon – "vexation and dis-appointment might possibly seal his lips for ever."

In a related vein, Wilberforce had also thought much about "preparation for the style of speaking most adapted to the House." Diligent attendance on committees, he asserted, and "careful at-tention to the details of business and evidence which come before them," was a key to success. In this way, "a great fund of useful practical knowledge on various important topics might thus be ac-quired, which would qualify a man, whenever the reports of such committees became the subject of debate, to supply the House with what it especially valued – accurate and useful information."

Wilberforce believed too that "the discussions carried on in committees frequently resembled in every particular, except … the excitement of a great popular assembly, the debates of the House itself." By frequent participation in committee discussions, he maintained, "a man of any ability for speaking would soon acquire the habit of reasoning and expressing himself correctly and with parliamentary tact." He stated that he had known "many gentlemen who, though labouring at first under much embarrass-ment and difficulty, had thus successfully made their way, and risen at length into consequence and consideration."

Wilberforce also placed a premium on the "logical arrange-ment of ideas" when speaking. The cultivation of "elegant and cor-rect writing," he believed, also was essential to success. In this, he shared common ground with Pitt, with whom he also agreed that young speakers should "commit to memory a few striking thoughts with reference to any debate in which they proposed to take a part, in order to have something ready to retreat upon, in ease of difficulty or nervous embarrassment." Wilberforce found it particularly useful "to engage a friend to read aloud to him suit-able passages out of any distinguished author, and then to repeat them as nearly as possible in the same words." To make this point, he cited William Windham's speeches. These, he knew, had been "prepared with assiduous care, and, though interspersed with anecdotes which seemed spontaneous, to have been written down before delivery."

Another colleague whom Wilberforce admired was Richard Sheridan, whose speeches were so "diligently elaborated, that he had often been known, before the occurrence of a great debate, to shut himself in his room, day after day, where he was heard declaiming for hours together."

⌐

As an accomplished classicist, Wilberforce was steeped in the writings of the great authors of Greek and Roman antiquity. Of all "the rhetorical treatises of the ancients," he said he most preferred "Tully's *De Oratore* – which well deserved to be carefully studied as an admirable epitome of the science of speaking."

Not surprisingly Wilberforce also believed that a good sense of humor was a valuable asset for public speakers. He had a deep appreciation for what he called "the fine edge" of George Canning's humor and, indeed, Canning was in his judgment the most talented all-around orator he ever heard. "You see the joke sparkling in [Canning's] eye before he gives it utterance," Wilberforce said. "It appear[s] to me to furnish a sort of intellectual parallel to the natural fact that light travels quicker than sound – you behold the flash before you hear the report."

There were moments, Wilberforce said, "when Pitt and Fox carried their listeners along with them with a power that appeared at the time almost irresistible," but, he added, "so varied are Canning's qualifications – such is his eloquence, wit, and humour – and so striking is his figure and manner, that I really must account him on the whole as perfect an orator as I have ever known."

Wilberforce enjoyed and greatly valued his long friendship with Edmund Burke. He often spoke "with great animation on the superior and lofty qualities of Burke's mind; but observed that the House of Commons was not the scene in which they were most advantageously displayed." Burke also had a quick temper, and there were those in Parliament who knew how to provoke him. Still, Wilberforce stated, "when [Burke] was in good humour ... the subject on which he spoke suited him, and the House was in a listening mood, he was delightful. On such occasions there was a depth of thought and a fervour and glow of eloquence which defied competition. He had only to scratch the ground and flowers sprang up."

For many years Wilberforce made it a point to dine at least once with Burke. "I had peculiar pleasure in his dinners with me," Wilberforce remembered, stating also that these convivial meetings were "an evidence of our perfect harmony."

Any mention of Burke, it seemed, called forth fond memories. "He was a great man," Wilberforce said. "I never could understand how he grew to be at one time so entirely neglected. In part undoubtedly it was, that, like [Sir James] Mackintosh afterwards, he was above his audience. He had come late into parliament, and had had time to lay in vast stores of knowledge. The field from which he drew his illustrations was magnificent. Like the fabled object of the fairy's favours, whenever he opened his mouth pearls and diamonds dropped from him."

On occasions such as their dinners together, Wilberforce recalled, Burke "was most delightful and instructive, and fairly let himself out. He was so good-natured and fond of talking that, whatever his engagements were, he was apt to commence conversation and then to forget time. He would give up an hour of his own time, or consume one of yours, without reflection on consequences." Their mutual friend William Windham agreed. "When I have business to transact," he said, "I avoid Burke as I would the plague."

Without question, the statesman for whom Wilberforce had the greatest admiration was Pitt. Yet, though one of Pitt's closest friends, Wilberforce stated that he "was by no means one of his partisans.... [I] even opposed him on some most important occasions." Their differences "arose commonly from a different view of facts, or a different estimate of contingencies and probabilities." Where there was a difference of political principles, it scarcely ever arose from moral considerations; still less by any distrust of Pitt's intention "to promote the well-being and prosperity of his country."

Because of their close friendship, Wilberforce "had an opportunity of seeing [Pitt] in all circumstances and situations, and of judging as much as any one could of his principles, dispositions, habits, and manners." In 1821, Wilberforce wrote *A Sketch of William Pitt*, describing many of his friend's ideas and achievements. This document provides a fascinating series of contrasts of Wilberforce's own ideas with those of Pitt, and at the same time reveals a great deal about the qualities Wilberforce admired and valued in a statesman.

On December 18, 1783, Pitt became prime minister at the incredible age of twenty-four. Wilberforce believed that Pitt's first administration, which endured for seventeen years "during times the most stormy and dangerous almost ever experienced by [Britain]," was a most valuable context in which to evaluate Pitt's character and to "specify the leading talents, dispositions, and qualifications by which he was distinguished."

Wilberforce was especially well qualified to do this. "Seldom has any man," he wrote, "had a better opportunity of knowing another than I have possessed of being thoroughly acquainted with ... Pitt. For weeks and months together I ... spent hours with him every morning while he was transacting his common business.... Hundreds of times, probably, I have ... seen him in every situation and in his most unreserved moments." Citing Rochefoucault, Wilberforce underscored his point. It was in a man's most unguarded and private moments that "character was subjected to its most severe test."

Wilberforce also admired Pitt's ability to "explain ... his sentiments [on] any complicated question and stat[e] the arguments on both sides." He took note of "the clearness of [Pitt's] conceptions,

[and] the precision with which he contemplated every particular object, and a variety of objects, without confusion."

The capacity to be a fair reasoner was in Wilberforce's judgment one of Pitt's great assets. Those who discussed political questions with Pitt in private, readily acknowledged that

> there never was a fairer reasoner, never any one more promptly recognising, and allowing its full weight to every consideration and argument which was urged against the opinion he had embraced. You always saw where you differed from him and why.... I never met with any man who combined in an equal degree this extraordinary precision of understanding, with the same intuitive apprehension of every shade of opinion, or of feeling, which might be indicated by those with whom he was conversant.

Pitt also possessed an extraordinary memory. Wilberforce particularly admired Pitt's ability to recall apt quotations from the great classical authors. He noted that "scarcely a passage could be quoted of their works, whether in verse or prose, with which [Pitt] was not so familiar as to be able to take up the cue and go on with what immediately followed. This was particularly the case in the works of Virgil, Horace, and Cicero, and I am assured that he was ... scarcely less familiar with Homer and Thucydides."

Though not a classicist of Pitt's abilities, Wilberforce worked hard throughout his life to retain what he had learned of Greek and Roman literature. From the original Greek and Latin, he read, reread, and memorized favorite or particularly instructive passages. On one occasion, he proposed "to read at least a hundred lines of Virgil daily – often more."

Epictetus was another favorite philosopher, but Horace was clearly the ancient writer whose works Wilberforce valued most. Wilberforce's sons wrote that a copy of Horace's *Satires* and *Epistles* abounded with "notes and references in his own hand" and testified to "the care and diligence with which he studied." References to learning "Horace by heart" occur again and again in his diaries.

During periods of recuperation in Bath from bouts of illness, he often had a pocket-sized copy of Horace with him. Other times he would carry a copy of the New Testament or Shakespeare. He would write notes reminding himself to "get these by heart," or "recapitulate [them] in walking or staying by myself." Other classical authors with whom he was well acquainted included Aristotle, Cicero, Juvenal, Lucan, Ovid, Sophocles, and Tacitus.

Wilberforce was also well acquainted with the teachings of contemporary or near-contemporary philosophers. These included Dugald Stewart (a leader of the Scottish Enlightenment) and John Locke. Indeed, Wilberforce had read Locke's writings for many years.

Then too, Wilberforce often read the writings of more than one Enlightenment philosopher at a time. A diary entry written on October 18, 1798 was typical: "[I am] engaged in reading Locke with my wife and sister, [along with] Coxe's *Life of [Sir Robert] Walpole*, [and] Montesquieu."

One year earlier, Wilberforce had written about Locke and other great intellects whom he admired in his book *A Practical View of Christianity*:

Christianity [has] been embraced, and that not blindly and implicitly, but upon full inquiry and deep consideration, by [Francis] Bacon, [John] Milton, [John] Locke, and [Isaac] Newton, and much the greater part of those, who, by the reach of their understandings, or the extent of their knowledge, and by the freedom of their minds, and their daring to combat existing prejudices, have called forth the respect and admiration of mankind.

Not surprisingly, there were similarities between Wilberforce's worldview and Locke's. Wilberforce believed that Christianity had an "obvious tendency to promote domestic comfort and general happiness." Likewise, Locke maintained, "God ... by an inseparable connexion, joined virtue and public happiness together, and made the practice thereof necessary to the preservation of society."

Wilberforce and Locke also shared a similar view on the nature of happiness. For Wilberforce, Christianity was "[the] system which is the only solid foundation of our present or future happiness." Locke wrote that it was "the Almighty, on whose good pleasure and acceptance [everyone's] eternal happiness depends."

⌒

Wilberforce was equally adept at discussing other intellectual pursuits. In one letter, written to his old friend Henry Bankes in September 1802, he donned the cap of both a literary critic and a political theorist. "I have," he told Bankes, "been running over Gibbon's Decline [and Fall of the Roman Empire].... He is an extraordinary man. Coxcomb all over ... of great learning as well as [the] very great show of it. He has the merit also of never declining a difficulty. But his style is abominably affected ..."

In the next sentence, he gave a considered opinion of the new French constitution written by Napoleon. "I saw," he said, "the same cause for admiration as in a former instance – I mean admiration of the genius of the deviser, who could create so many orders, and give so much apparatus, and yet part with so little power."

Wilberforce's facility in forming cogent intellectual critiques extended to apologetics and philosophy. His reading in 1803 of William Paley's widely influential Natural Theology – a work that purported to find proof of the existence of God in the design apparent in natural phenomena – gave rise to an important exchange of letters with Ralph Creyke, the learned friend whose home had afforded Wilberforce much needed "peace and rationality" after his difficult reelection contest of 1796.

Though he found much to admire about Paley's book, Wilberforce told Creyke that Paley's thinking had to his mind some serious flaws. "[N]o one could with more pleasure pour forth Dr. Paley's copious eulogy," he wrote, "yet – must I say it? – He appears to me a most dangerous writer, likely to head his readers into errors concerning the essential nature, genius, and design of Christianity. I cannot now go at large into this important discussion, but we will take it [up] when we can have a little quiet domestic chat."

As things turned out, Wilberforce did much more than have a quiet discussion with Creyke about Paley's philosophy. He wrote a lengthy and erudite review of Paley's *Natural Theology* that ran to thirty-three columns in an influential periodical, the *Christian Observer*.

In this piece, Wilberforce criticized many aspects of Paley's *Natural Theology*, stating his preference for the philosophical ideas set forth in Bishop Joseph Butler's famous *Analogy of Religion* (first published in 1736). Scholars today have concluded that Wilberforce's review of Paley's *Natural Theology* is one of the more important statements of evangelical philosophy and theology written in the early nineteenth century.

Wilberforce was the most important leader of the evangelical wing of the Anglican Church in his lifetime, but his philosophical and theological views have not received the attention they merit. The Butler/Paley debate concerning intelligent design was an important one. It is also worth bearing in mind that Wilberforce's review of Paley's *Natural Theology* was written several decades before the celebrated debates on Darwin's theory of evolution.

Equally important is the fact that Wilberforce sided with Butler over Paley in this ongoing debate. He believed that Butler's *Analogy* confirmed the fundamental doctrines of natural and revealed

228 ⁓ WILLIAM WILBERFORCE

religion. The reasoning advanced in it had, in his estimation, "resisted every attempt to weaken or overturn it."

Wilberforce's misgivings about Paley were later set out in a letter he wrote to his close friend Lord Muncaster. For the Christian, Wilberforce believed that Paley was very helpful in that he described in great detail how the hand of the Creator was discernable in the creation of humanity and in all nature itself.

This said, Wilberforce detected many problems in Paley's book. It was true that God's wisdom, power, and goodness were enforced by many new proofs, but the book entirely overlooked important matters relating to God's justice and holiness. Wilberforce was convinced that these errors would lead people to falsely estimate their goodness and to discount the claims of God upon them. Thus they could wrongly assume there was no need for a Redeemer and Mediator between God and man.

⁓

In August 1825 Wilberforce became absorbed in the establishment of two educational institutions: the Mechanics' Institutes and London University. Wilberforce's involvement with these institutions recalls – in terms of the ardent interest he took in them – Thomas Jefferson's labors late in life to establish the University of Virginia.

This is not to say that Wilberforce was about to set on foot an architectural project like Jefferson's work in designing the University of Virginia, described by the American Institute of Architects as "the proudest achievement of American architecture in the past 200 years." Nor was it Wilberforce's intent to establish an academic village along the lines Jefferson envisioned. Rather, Wilberforce was deeply concerned with securing courses of instruction in Christian apologetics at the Mechanics' Institutes and London University. It was a matter about which he was as passionate as Jefferson was in establishing the premier American university.

Early in 1825 Wilberforce had learned that a plan was in progress to establish Mechanics' Institutes for "instructing our artisans in general in the various branches of philosophy." Friendly to this design, he now endeavored "to obtain ... lectures on the evidences of the Divine authority of Christianity." He explained his reasoning at some length in a letter:

> I cannot but entertain a strong persuasion, that to instruct any class of men, but especially our artisans of all sorts, in the various branches of philosophy, leaving them altogether ignorant of the grounds on which we rest the Divine authority of Christianity, will be but too sure an expedient for training up a race of self-conceited sceptics.
>
> Hitherto our religion has been taken on trust; but now there will be a boast that no opinions are to be received implicitly and by prescription. Indeed it is a Scriptural injunction, that we should be able to render a reason for our hope. And as it has pleased God to make ours a reasonable service, and to give us a religion which will stand the strictest scrutiny, surely we shall be unpardonable if we suffer our youth to be wholly uninstructed in this particular only.

Wilberforce felt so strongly about this that he nearly published a short piece about it. In the end he did not, but only because he felt dissatisfied with what he would have published. He satisfied himself instead with working behind the scenes.

The plan for the Mechanics' Institutes that he had criticized was soon followed by another similar plan to establish the institution that became London University. Wilberforce pressed its founders to include courses of instruction in Christian apologetics. They replied that instruction in religion was incompatible with their first principle of receiving alike men of all faiths or of none.

One founder had written to Wilberforce soliciting his support as a noted educational reformer and saying that approval "would be of the highest importance." Still, this founder had resisted

Wilberforce's call for a curriculum that included Christian apologetics. "If you reflect on the composition and plan of our London University," the founder had written,

> you will perceive how impossible it is to have our doors open to all, and yet teach even the most general system of Christianity. It will not bear near inspection, though it sounds easy enough to say in general terms, all sects agree as to the evidences. They do not so agree....
>
> But look to our plan, and you will at once see how inconsistent with it any necessity of religious instruction is. In Oxford and Cambridge it is far otherwise. Oxford and Cambridge take youths wholly under their wing, and away from their families. We, acting on a better and more natural and moral plan, leave them wholly under domestic superintendence. To teach religion is necessary in the former case, but not in the latter.

Wilberforce warmly combated this argument and tried to secure the establishment of a professorship in Christian apologetics. He told Zachary Macaulay he was grieved by "the very idea of keeping the most influential class, in the most influential position of our country, ignorant of the irrefragable arguments by which the truth of Christianity is established." The goal of higher education, Wilberforce ardently believed, was to broaden the mind. He questioned how this goal could be served by excluding a vital part of Britain's Judeo-Christian heritage. Exclusion in the name of toleration produced intolerance, as well as undereducated students. Ultimately, he succeeded in getting a lecture on the evidences of Christianity incorporated into the London University plan "for such as chose to attend it."

Following this, a friend in London ventured without Wilberforce's permission to put down his name as a supporter of London University. Instead of immediately having his name removed from the list of supporters, he left his name on the list for a while, in the hope that the course might eventually become a required part of the curriculum. When it had not by 1829, he withdrew his support, saying, "I retain my old opinion of the evil of such a system of education."

Wilberforce believed the culture of Britain had been immeasurably enriched by an educational system that cherished instruction in the Christian religion. Christianity had had a profound impact on the lives of men whom he deeply admired – Francis Bacon, John Milton, John Locke, and Isaac Newton – men of great intellect and achievements who had embraced Christianity "not blindly and implicitly, but upon full inquiry and deep consideration." They had, "by the reach of their understandings ... the extent of their knowledge [and] the freedom of their minds ... called forth the respect and admiration of mankind."

Wilberforce also believed that the advancement or decline of religion in any country was "so intimately connected with the temporal interests of society, as to render it the peculiar concern of a political man." Consequently, he took an active interest as well in the publication of works on "the evidences of Christianity" – that is, works of Christian apologetics. He was likewise devoted to educational institutions where students could become well versed in these evidences. This kind of training, he thought, strengthened individual Christian belief, for students could discover through rational inquiry that theirs was an intelligent faith. In turn, they could become apologists for Christianity, propagate the faith, and strengthen the moral and religious foundations of British society.

This kind of educational vision was needed as never before, he believed, because the spread of unbelief had undermined the moral consensus of France. This, in turn, had contributed greatly to the political unrest and violence that had devastated France during the French Revolution. Over Wilberforce's lifetime, political unrest had likewise threatened Britain, but he believed a cogent argument could be made that the spread of Christianity and the corresponding growth of Christian philanthropies had done

232 — WILLIAM WILBERFORCE

much to better the lives of the less fortunate and forestall an outbreak of revolution there.

Wilberforce referred to the recent history of France to make his
point. "Will you therefore discard Religion altogether?" he asked.
"The experiment was lately tried in [France, but] ... the effects
however with which it was attended, do not much encourage its
repetition." To those who placed all their faith in the writings of
the secularist French Enlightenment philosophers so heralded
during the French Revolution, Wilberforce offered a stern warning: "What light it throws upon the philosophy of the human mind
in its present fallen state, that while the writings of Rousseau, Voltaire, D'Alembert, &c. abounded in sentimentality and supposed
refinement, they actually prepared the way for all the horrors of
the Revolution. The guillotine was in perpetual operation at the
very time when these books were so read and admired."

Wilberforce felt that his faith had provided him with the moral
framework that served as the most potent and proper antidote to
the secularist worldview that had "prepared the way for all the
horrors of the Revolution." His faith had taught him that "there is,
and ever has been in the world, a great portion of vice and wickedness." Men and women have always been prone to "sensuality and
selfishness," he wrote, and this runs counter "to the more refined
and liberal principles of their nature. "In all ages and countries,"
he concluded,

> in public and in private life, innumerable instances have been
> afforded of oppression, of rapacity, of cruelty, of fraud, of envy,
> and of malice.... [It] is too often in vain that you inform the
> understanding, and convince the judgment.... You do not
> thereby reform the hearts of men. Though they know their
> duty, they will not practice it; no not even when you have
> forced them to acknowledge that the path of virtue is that also
> of real interest and of solid enjoyment.

Wilberforce believed the remedy was Christianity, which from her essential nature is "peculiarly and powerfully adapted to promote the preservation and healthfulness of political communities." What is in truth their grand malady? he asked. "The answer is short: Selfishness."

Wilberforce discussed the implications of the disease of selfishness in the sixth chapter of his book, *A Practical View of Christianity*. He considered the principles in this chapter to be a blueprint for the good society and earnestly commended them to William Pitt, telling the prime minister that they were "the basis for all politics and particularly addressed to such as you."

Selfishness, Wilberforce had written, was a disease received at the birth of political communities. It grew "with their growth, and strengthen[ed] with their strength." It also assumed different forms. Sometimes, it showed itself in "luxury, pomp and parade," at others in a "sick ... and depraved imagination, which seeks in vain its own gratification."

Despotism, or the love of power, was another symptom, as was pride and its kindred symptom, rebellion. These symptoms opposed "the generous and energetic pursuits of an enlarged heart," by which all political communities were blessed.

The external effects of selfishness may vary, Wilberforce argued, but the internal principle was the same: "a disposition in each individual to make self the grand center and end of ... desires and enjoyments." All are prone to overrate their own merits and importance and magnify their claims on others. All are prone as well to underrate the claims of others on themselves and disposed to undervalue the advantages and overstate the disadvantages of their condition in life.

All these conditions undermined the well-being of political communities. Those in power became enamored with it and fought over it. Those who did not participate in the government of a community too often charged the nature or administration of government with the evils common to all, not the governing class alone. They too often blamed government as well for the "results of their own vices and follies."

Public spirit was the mindset directly opposed to selfishness, Wilberforce argued. It was, he believed, "the grand principle of political vitality, the very life's breath of states, which tends to keep them active and vigorous, and to carry them to greatness and glory." The tendencies of public spirit and selfishness, Wilberforce also wrote, had not escaped the observation of the founders of states in history or writers on government. They had resorted to various expedients for cherishing and extolling public spirit, while repressing selfishness. Sparta had "flourished for more than seven hundred years under the civil institutions of Lycurgus; which guarded against the selfish principle, by prohibiting commerce, and imposing universal poverty and hardship." Wilberforce believed that the long-enduring Roman commonwealth, which deeply cherished public spirit, had checked selfishness by "the principle of the love of glory." Tragically, this principle had naturally "produced an unbounded spirit of conquest, which, like the ambition of [Julius Caesar,] the greatest of its own heroes, was never satisfied while any other kingdom was left it to subdue."

Britain could know the same fate, he warned, for such a "principle of political vitality, when kept alive only by means like these, merits the description once given [by Tacitus] of eloquence":

> Great oratory is like a flame: it needs fuel to feed it,
> movement to fan it, and it brightens as it burns.

Wilberforce argued that the principles for promoting the continuance of the state adopted by Sparta and Rome seemed "to be in some sort sacrificing the end to the means." Happiness was the end for which people united in civil society, he wrote, but in societies constituted like Sparta and Rome, "little happiness, comparatively speaking, is to be found."

To underscore this point, Wilberforce asserted that while "the expedient of preserving a state by the spirit of conquest ... has not wanted its admirers, [it] is not to be tolerated for a moment when considered on principles of universal justice." Such a state, he maintained, lives, grows, and thrives by the misery of others. It becomes the general enemy of its neighbors and the scourge of the human race. It is, he concluded, a state "full of contradictory principles and jarring movements."

In contrast, Wilberforce was struck by the degree to which "Christianity in every way sets herself in direct hostility to self-ishness, the mortal distemper of political communities." Conse-quently, "their welfare must be inseparable from her prevalence." Indeed, he wrote that "it might almost be stated that the main object and chief concern of Christianity [is] to root out our natural selfishness, and to rectify the false standard which it imposes on us ... to bring us to a just estimate of ourselves, and of all around us, and to a due impression of the various claims and obligations resulting from the different relations in which we stand."

To those "mistaken politicians" who admired and endeavored to obtain "extended dominion ... commanding power and un-rivaled affluence, rather than the more solid advantages of peace, and comfort, and security," Wilberforce took direct aim. "These men would barter comfort for greatness," he asserted. "In their vain reveries they forget that a nation consists of individuals, and that true national prosperity is no other than the multiplication of particular happiness."

After the completion of his Great Change in 1786, Wilberforce believed he had learned "the true secret of a life at the same time useful and happy." Christianity taught him to follow peace with all men, looking upon them as members of the same family. As such, his fellow citizens were "entitled not only to the debts of justice, but to the less definite and more liberal claims of frater-nal kindness." People who acted in this way, Christianity taught, "would naturally be respected and beloved by others and be in themselves free from the annoyance of those bad passions (namely selfishness) by which those motivated by worldly principles are so commonly corroded."

The heart of this vision lay in the "true duty of every man to promote the happiness of his fellow-creatures to the utmost of his power." Happiness would be the hallmark of any country filled with people diligently performing the duties of their stations in life without breaking in upon the rights of others. If in doing so these citizens forwarded, so far as they might be able, the views of others and sought to promote their happiness, "all would be active and harmonious in the goodly frame of human society. There would be no jarrings, no discord. The whole machine of civil life would work without obstruction or disorder, and the course of its movements would be like the harmony of the spheres."

This is why Wilberforce felt so strongly about the need for Britain's rising generation to be instructed in Christian faith. It had changed his life and set him on the path to building the good society. Christianity had immeasurably enriched British culture, because Britain as a nation had in the past cherished instruction in the Christian religion. The lives and writings of Bacon, Milton, Locke, and Newton were influential and powerful, he believed, because of Christianity.

Wilberforce was not advocating a theocracy where Christian values were imposed on his fellow Britons. He was asking that Christian teaching be a valued part of curriculums at all levels of education in Britain. It could then afford her citizens the same opportunity he had to choose, based on an informed decision, whether or not to embrace a faith that had so changed his own life – a faith that lay at the heart of the many philanthropies in which he had been privileged to take part. His purpose was to commend his faith, not command it.

And so, his desire to see a course of Christian apologetics begun at the Mechanics' Institutes and London University was very much of a piece with his lifelong work to promote moral and cultural renewal. In 1787 he had written that this work was "worthy of the labors of a lifetime." His work to see this course of study implemented showed how devoted he still remained to these labors, even in retirement.

⌣

Sir James Stephen (1789 – 1859) was yet another who had a chance to observe Wilberforce's character and qualities up close. Stephen was Wilberforce's nephew, the son of his abolitionist colleague James Stephen (by his first wife, Anna). The elder Stephen had been married for a second time in May 1800 to Wilberforce's widowed sister Sarah.

After the publication of the five-volume *Life of William Wilberforce* by Robert and Samuel Wilberforce in 1838, Stephen wrote a lengthy review essay about it for the prestigious *Edinburgh Review*. Several years later he published an expanded form of this essay in his book, *Essays in Ecclesiastical Biography*. Taken together with Harford's *Recollections of William Wilberforce*, Stephen's essay contains the most telling descriptions of Wilberforce's personality and interests.

Wilberforce came into the world, Stephen wrote, "predestined to be the centre of love for the circle of his associates in it." He had been endowed with "genial warmth and graciousness of temper." To all who approached him, kindnesses "expanded with such a happy promptitude, that ... he might have passed for the brother of every man, and for the lover of every woman with whom he conversed."

Stephen believed that the basis of Wilberforce's natural character lay in an "instinct of philanthropy." He had a restlessness and vivacity that reminded Stephen of Voltaire, and "a sensibility more profound than that of Rousseau." These "met in him and mutually controlled each other. His responsiveness to the joys and sorrows of his companions made the happy and the wretched his captives in their turns. But, though ready to weep with those who wept, he was still more prompt to rejoice with those that rejoiced."

Society was not a mere delight or passion for Wilberforce, Stephen explained, "it was the necessity of his existence." He could, and did, mix freely and on equal terms "with all the men and women of his age the most eminent in wit, in genius, and in learning. . . . [He] drank in, with the keenest relish, every variety of . . . eloquence."

Stephen also believed Wilberforce was one of the most gifted conversationalists of his era. He illustrated this by comparing Wilberforce's gifts with those of his most celebrated contemporaries, some members of the famous Literary Club led by Samuel Johnson. Only in this way, Stephen believed, could one obtain a true "image of the social William Wilberforce." Imagine the great Shakespearean actor David Garrick, he wrote, "talking . . . from the resources of his own mind, and the impulses of his own nature." Imagine a man

> uttering maxims of wisdom with Johnsonian dignity – then haranguing with a rapture like that of [Edmund] Burke – telling a good story with the unction of James Boswell – chuckling over a ludicrous jest with the childlike glee of Oliver Goldsmith – singing a ballad with all the taste of [Thomas] Percy – reciting poetry with the classical enthusiasm of [Richard] Cumberland – and, at each successive change in this interlude, exhibiting the amenities of Sir Joshua [Reynolds].

Wilberforce had many admirers as a conversationalist, including three of the best conversationalists of his day: the French novelist Madame de Stael, Sir James Mackintosh – described as "one of the most cultured men of his time," and Sydney Smith, perhaps the early nineteenth century's most celebrated wit and essayist. Wilberforce's conversations, it was said, were marked by "rapidity of conception," "intuitive insight into the characters of other[s]," "a sense of the ludicrous and of the tender," "wit vaulting . . . lightly across his whole visible horizon," and "so ardent a love for every form of beauty, as justified [their] enthusiasm."

John Harford also noted this side of Wilberforce's character: "When Wilberforce aimed at giving peculiar force to a sentiment or a maxim, the point and terseness of his language could not be surpassed." One day, the topic of conversation was the misery to which the poet William Cowper was exposed during his years at a public school. "Yes," Wilberforce exclaimed, "it was a sensitive plant grasped by a hand of iron."

⁓

Much as he loved society, Wilberforce reveled in the pleasures of home life. After morning prayers he often strolled along the terrace of his house or into the flower garden. Those who went with him were "sure to see him full of delight at the various beauties or wonders of nature."

Wilberforce was particularly fond of flowers. He delighted "to gaze upon their colours and to investigate their structure." The pages of the pocket-sized books he so often carried "were thickly set with them in a dried state." It was with great reluctance that he could be persuaded "to quit the garden for the breakfast table and when he made his appearance it was generally with a flower in his hand."

Once he had joined his family and guests for breakfast, Wilberforce was the life of the party. Breakfast was a meal in which he took particular pleasure. He was "ready for conversation and discussion and . . . frequently forgot time when thus engaged." He was fond of observing that "it was one of the distinctions between us and animals, that the latter sat munching their food by themselves but that men have the faculty of exercising their mental powers while they satisfy the requirements of nature."

After breakfast Wilberforce retired to his dressing room and worked with his secretary answering letters. He would read or, if his eyes were troubling him, have books read to him. Important letters, or those to particular friends, were written in his own hand when his eyes permitted him to do so. Others were dictated to his secretary.

About two or three o'clock in the day, Wilberforce generally came downstairs and was ready for a carriage drive or a walk. Long walks were his particular delight, especially in the company of a friend. John Harford recalled that possessing "an unceasing fund of delightful conversation" and having spent his life "among many of the greatest men of his time," Wilberforce's walking conversations were deeply interesting. "Every previous sentiment of affection and veneration towards him," Harford wrote, "was deepened by being admitted to his company."

Wilberforce liked an early dinner, and throughout the whole course of it his mind was actively at work. While staying with him, Harford was often amused "to observe him carrying on a discussion while in the act of carving a large joint [of meat] – often addressed by others, and often interlacing his subject with exclamations at the bluntness of the knife, or paying little attentions to his guests, and then taking up the broken thread of his subject and pursuing it amidst the same sort of interruptions."

Similarly, when Wilberforce had owned his house across from the House of Commons, Number 4 Old Palace Yard, he and his cousin Henry Thornton "kept an almost open house for Parliament." About three o'clock daily their friends began to drop in on their way to the House. They partook of a light dinner, and as many as seventeen or twenty might appear. "It delighted us," Wilberforce said, "to see our friends in this way, especially as it gave us the opportunity of talking upon any important points of public business without any great sacrifice of time."

Wilberforce never lost his love for entertaining friends and guests. But during the last eight to ten years of his life, he began to feel the demands of having so many people around. In order to keep himself refreshed, he started taking what he referred to as his siesta in the early afternoons, retiring to his room and then reappearing for afternoon tea. Having had his siesta, he was ready to indulge his fondness for sitting up late with a friend either for reading or talking. Visitors and friends soon discovered, if they did not already know it, that his years in political life had made late hours so familiar that he was often reluctant to retire.

During such late-night sessions Wilberforce's conversation sparkled. Sometimes the writings of Francis Bacon would provide the topic for discussion, at others an idea advanced in the rather pedestrian writings of agriculturist Sir John Sinclair. It did not matter. Wilberforce's observations were always "irresistibly charming, though no memory could retain the glowing, picturesque, or comic language in which it was delivered."

Those who longed for examples of Wilberforce's table talk, Sir James Stephen suggested, would be best satisfied by referring to his letters. His letters to Hannah More were marked by brilliant language. His letters to Lord Muncaster showed how playfully he could rally his old friend, while those to William Hey were full of deep meaning. Affection was the hallmark of Wilberforce's letters to his sons. If one read these letters, Stephen concluded, Wilberforce's table talk could become "audible and visible to the imaginations of those who never heard or saw him, very much as he was to ... those who lived with him in familiar intimacy."

Wilberforce's letters possessed many literary merits. He was a discerning reader, an insightful judge of political events and figures, and a student of fine oratory. Liveliness of fancy and the command of a wide vocabulary were other traits of his writing. All of his letters were "written in a pleasant, easy style, leading the reader on from page to page without weariness."

Wilberforce wrote during a period when letter writing occupied much time and thought, and was a contemporary of two masters of the letter-writing art: William Cowper and John Newton. Readers then and now have noted "the charm of Cowper's letters – their perfect ease, their light and sweetness and their play of humour." Newton's letters combined wisdom with sprightliness, and he could illustrate points of Christian experience in vivid, readily understood ways.

Comparing Wilberforce's letters with those of Cowper and Newton, the nineteenth century writer John Stoughton provided some important insights: "One misses," he said, "the indescribable sort of charm which invests [the letters] of [Cowper and Newton], but in other respects – such as knowledge of the world – large experience gathered from varied [relations], a comprehensive and many-sided sympathy, and a peculiar habit of rapidly passing from one subject to another, as graceful as it is characteristic of his extraordinary versatility – Wilberforce is superior to [Cowper and Newton]."

Despite Wilberforce's gifts as correspondent, and for all the care that he put into his speaking, he was not one who was able to keep his papers in good order. He was so often deluged with correspondence that freeing himself from notes and letters was a constant chore.

It would have presented a formidable challenge to even the most organized. Sometimes, despite Wilberforce's best efforts, letters went missing or remained unanswered for colorful reasons. He once wrote an apology to John Quincy Adams for not sending a prompt reply. It seems that Adams' letter had been discovered several weeks later, stuck to the top of a desk drawer. Another correspondent heard from an embarrassed Wilberforce that he had not received a reply because Wilberforce, upon opening a several-weeks-old newspaper, saw this correspondent's unanswered letter flutter to the floor.

Wilberforce reproached himself for so often being "a universal defaulter" when trying to keep up with his voluminous correspondence. But then, he was perhaps too hard on himself.

If not always "up to the knees in papers," as he had been during his dash to Yorkshire in Pitt's carriage in 1795, he was not often far from it. Biographer Robin Furneaux has noted: "Wilberforce spent much of his life writing.... His correspondence alone would have buried most men. He often wrote and received as many as twenty letters a day and few of them were short." Add to this that Wilberforce was a member of Parliament for nearly forty-five years, and one begins to get a sense of the sheer volume of his correspondence.

His fertile imagination lent itself to memorable descriptions of the reasons for his "epistolary arrears." Zachary Macaulay received a letter that said: "Alps upon Alps arise [before me]." It was Lord Mornington, however, then serving as governor-general of India, who received what was perhaps the most inventive excuse Wilberforce ever wrote. "Were you ever unfortunate enough to have put yourself into the power of that foul fiend Procrastination? If so you will not hesitate to compare its tyrannical hold to the firm grasp of that cow-like old fellow who bestrode poor Sinbad the Sailor in the *Arabian Nights*, and could not be shaken off by his utmost efforts."

⌐

One of the keys to Wilberforce's effectiveness and longevity in political life was his observance of a sabbatical day every week and a sabbatical hour every day. These days and hours, Stephen wrote, "gave him back to the world, not merely with recruited strength, but in a spirit the most favourable to the right discharge of his ... duties."

Wilberforce was often beset with trivial, wearisome, and at times offensive tasks. Though often tempted to say "I've had enough," his weekly and daily sabbaticals reminded him of "the great ends for which life is given and the immortal hopes by which it should be sustained." Devotional retirements soothed him when he felt most harassed with the conflicts and the vexations that dog the steps of those who serve in public life.

There was no way a man like Wilberforce, so obviously pressed for time, could actively supervise all the complicated affairs in which he was immersed. Sir James Stephen believed that Wilber-force's real position in British society

> was that of a *minister of public charity*, holding his office by popular acclamation, and delegating the more toilsome de-tails of that laborious administration to the friends ... who rejoiced to co-operate with him. He maintained his authority over them by their affectionate reverence, by his own unfail-ing bounty, and by the spell which he exercised over every one whom he employed and trusted. No department in the state was ever so zealously served, or so well administered.

Though active in so many practical plans to promote virtue and the welfare of his fellow citizens, Wilberforce believed that true philanthropy could not flourish in an immoral society. His think-ing in this respect was similar to that of John Adams regarding the U.S. Constitution: it was designed for a moral citizenry and wholly unfit for any other.

For his part, Wilberforce believed that we deceive ourselves if we think we can detect within us the full amount of moral good or evil. We should "tremble to admit the slightest speck [or] the smallest seed of moral evil to pollute our country's soil." This rec-ognition, he said, should encourage us "to activity in all good."

Wilberforce set forth his vision for the good society in his book, *A Practical View of Christianity*, published in 1797. It was an apologia as well for his evangelical Anglican faith.

Sir James Stephen eloquently described the content of this work, one which Wilberforce came in time to call his "manifesto." Stephen quoted philosopher Abraham Tucker, who had written, "Philosophy may be styled the art of marshalling the ideas in the understanding, and religion that of disciplining the imagination." The task Wilberforce set before himself in *A Practical View* was to

> mark distinctly the departure of the luxurious, busy, careworn, and ambitious age to which he belonged, from the theory and the practice of Christian morality.... Never were the sensual-

ity, the gloom, and the selfishness which fester below the polished surface of society, brought into more vivid contrast with the faith, and hope, and charity, which in their combination form the Christian character ... never was that contrast drawn with a firmer hand, with a more tender spirit, or with a purer aspiration for the happiness of mankind.

Because Wilberforce was such a conspicuous member of the House of Commons, *A Practical View* excited great interest. Well-known literary critics like the satirist Thomas Matthias praised Wilberforce's book. Edmund Burke gratefully acknowledged the solace *A Practical View* gave him when it was read to him during the last two days of his life. Shortly before he died, Burke stated: "If I live, I shall thank Wilberforce for having sent such a book into the world."

The agriculturalist and travel writer Arthur Young traced his conversion to reading *A Practical View*, as did the Scottish philosopher and theologian Thomas Chalmers. "About the year 1811," Chalmers remembered, "I had Wilberforce's *View* put into my hands, and, as I got on in reading it, felt myself on the eve of a great revolution in all my opinions about Christianity."

The two men became close friends, and when Chalmers began to focus his energies on addressing the needs of the poor in Scotland, it was to Wilberforce's ideas and example that he turned. When in 1821 he published the first installments of his celebrated three-volume treatise on *Civic Economy*, he wrote to Wilberforce: "I took the liberty of inscribing for you some weeks ago two numbers of my ... *Civic Economy* ... in which I have ... attempted to sketch what I conceive to have been just your own line of politics in Parliament."

When writing *A Pracitical View*, Wilberforce had initially thought to write a tract that would set forth the first principles of his faith and his vision of the good society. He thought to do so for the sake of his friends and contemporaries – most of whom, he knew, he might never have the opportunity of speaking with individually.

What was intended as a tract grew into a book; and its influence far exceeded Wilberforce's most sanguine hopes that it might find an audience. In 1828 Chalmers spoke for many among the tens of thousands in Britain and America and on the continent whose lives had been shaped by *A Practical View*: "May that book, which spoke so powerfully to myself, and has spoken powerfully to thousands, represent you to future generations, and be the instrument of converting many who are yet unborn."

Chalmers was more right than he knew, for a copy of *A Practical View* had made its way some years before to a young curate just assuming his ministerial duties on the Isle of Wight. The year was 1798, and the curate Legh Richmond. It seems that one of Richmond's friends was on the eve of taking Holy Orders. Knowing this, a relative sent this friend a copy of Wilberforce's book. Richmond's friend didn't know what to make of the work, so he forwarded it to Richmond, asking him to look it over and write back with his thoughts. Richmond received the unexpected package, and his life thereafter was never the same. Beginning to read *A Practical View*, he found he could not put it down. All night he poured over its pages, and when he had finished, he wrote "[I] sought mercy at the cross of the Saviour."

During his years on the Isle of Wight, Richmond served the curacies of the adjoining parishes of Brading and Yaverland. He traveled to many homes visiting parishioners who would not otherwise have received spiritual comfort. Richmond later crafted three tales of village life, based upon his experiences. He sent them to the *Christian Guardian*, which printed them between 1809 and 1814. "Their simple pathos and piety," it was said, "won for them instant popularity." The demand for the most popular of these tales, *The Dairyman's Daughter*, was wholly without precedent. It told the story of Elizabeth Wallbridge, a young woman of deep faith who faced the prospect of death from consumption with great trust and fortitude.

Richmond greatly enlarged *The Dairyman's Daughter* after its first publication, and printers found they could not print copies fast enough to meet the demand. Translated into French, Italian, German, Danish, and Swedish, *The Dairyman's Daughter* also had a very wide circulation in America. It was calculated that in Richmond's lifetime 2 million copies in English alone were sold – by 1849, over 4 million copies, in a total of nineteen languages.

One day, about the year 1830, a tourist stopped by the village of Brading during his visit to the Isle of Wight. One afternoon he sought out the grave of Elizabeth Wallbridge in the old churchyard. As he neared the spot, he saw "seated beside the mound a lady and a young girl – the latter reading aloud, in a full, melodious voice," from *The Dairyman's Daughter*. Not wishing to disturb them, he turned away and decided to visit the site another time. Before leaving, however, he chanced upon the sexton of the church, who informed him that the visitors to the grave were the Duchess of Kent and the Princess (later Queen) Victoria.

⁓

As it turned out, writing *A Practical View* had been quite a challenge for Wilberforce. Over eight years, from 1789 until early 1797, he struggled to carve out time from his busy parliamentary schedule to write.

A debt is also owed to two of Wilberforce's dearest and wisest friends, Thomas and Mary Gisborne, under whose roof *A Practical View* was for the most part written. The Gisbornes understood how important a book it might be. They also knew that Wilberforce needed encouragement to steadily pursue the hard work of writing a book. Because he could be easily distracted, they resorted to clever ways of focusing the "concentration of his discursive thoughts."

Many of Wilberforce's best thoughts were voiced in conversation. Mary Gisborne, knowing this, became his secretary "when passages of peculiar energy burst, in all their native warmth, from his lips." At other times she would collect the scattered pages of Wilberforce's rough drafts that lay strewn throughout his drawing room or conservatory. When Wilberforce sat down again to write, he would find these scattered pages neatly ordered and ready for his use. At such times, the Gisbornes wisely made sure that the social Wilberforce was left in undisturbed solitude.

When Mary Gisborne saw *A Practical View* in its final published form, she was amazed at the result of such an unconventional method of writing. Wilberforce's ideas and reflections had been spread across so many notes and odd pieces of paper that his finished book appeared to be nothing less than a marvel. It was as though, she wrote, "a fortuitous concourse of atoms might, by some felicitous chance, combine themselves into the most perfect of forms, a moss rose, or a bird of paradise."

A major reason for the success of *A Practical View* was Wilberforce's high visibility as a politician. He was widely known as one of the prime minister's closest friends, and he had a growing reputation that stemmed from his commitment to principled politics – most notably his ten-year leadership of the fight to end the slave trade. Many wondered what motivated him.

Sir James Stephen explored the basis upon which Wilberforce's reputation in Parliament rested in his essay for the *Edinburgh Review*. In that legislative assembly, Stephen wrote, "anyone speaks with immense advantage whose character, station, or presumed knowledge is such as to give importance to his opinions.... No member, except the leaders of the great contending parties, addressed the House with an authority equal to that of Mr. Wilberforce."

Stephen believed Wilberforce's words and actions in Parliament were accorded such influence because of his personal character,

Wilberforce's close friend Thomas Gisborne (1758–1846), at whose home Wilberforce wrote most of his Practical View of Christianity

his independent neutrality, and the confidence he enjoyed among the great religious bodies in every part of England.

Yet he also believed Wilberforce's effectiveness in political life could be accounted for in another way. For his speeches most closely resembled his familiar conversation and thus possessed many of the same qualities that endeared him to friends and family. His comments in debate were marked by "natural and varied cadences … animation and ease … and … affectionate, lively, and graceful talk."

Then too, Wilberforce's long tenure in the House of Commons gave an increasing weight to his opinions and strengthened his moral authority as the years passed. Over his long career, Wilberforce's character was displayed in many different ways. During the long war against Napoleon's France and serious period of political unrest in Britain, Wilberforce articulated and acted upon the sacred principles he so cherished. "That he acted up to his opinions," wrote J. B. S. Morritt on a blank page of his copy of Wilberforce's *A Practical View*, "as nearly as is consistent with the inevitable weakness of our nature, is a praise so high that it seems like exaggeration; yet, in my conscience, I believe it, and I knew him well for at least forty years."

John Harford stressed the profound impact Wilberforce's Great Change had on his political philosophy. Wilberforce's politics, he observed, "were Conservative, yet Liberal, and whatever was the subject ... he spoke upon, his moral courage and independence of spirit never failed him. These were qualities which made it impossible for him to be a party man, and it was precisely because he was not such that there was scarcely any man who exercised so extensive an influence for good as himself throughout the length and breadth of the land."

James Stephen agreed: "Wilberforce was not to be drawn into the support or the rejection of any measure by arguments, however plausible or popular, which he considered to be erroneously deduced from the great laws of public morality.... [His] determination [was] fearlessly to pursue the right, into whatever consequences it might conduct him."

Wilberforce himself affirmed this most strongly when he wrote, "The author of all moral obligation has enjoined us to renounce certain actions without an inquiry as to reasons or consequences." Wilberforce practiced what he preached. His deep loyalty to the throne did not prevent him from opposing increased financial grants to the princes of the royal family. Still later, when many looked upon Australia only as a convict colony, Wilberforce used his parliamentary influence to lay the foundation of a church community that came in time to occupy every inhabited district of New South Wales.

Though such principled stands often cost Wilberforce a great deal when they occurred, they later provided him with an ample fund of object lessons for his children. While taking a sheltered walk among the trees with his children, he shared recollections, anecdotes, and reflections with them – many stemming from his long service in political life. He described what he had observed of the lives of others, passages of Scripture, and favorite or well-remembered poems. The time he spent with them buttressed and ornamented, as they saw it, "the two main pillars of his creed – the first, that God is love; the second, that God is truth."

Humility also marked Wilberforce's relations with his children. As an older man, he listened to his sons quietly and patiently. When they were grown, he "courted their advice, and deferred to their judgment with the same kindly confidence with which he stayed his feeble steps by leaning on their more vigorous arms." One family member affirmed, "Friendship never assumed a more touching form."

When Wilberforce's three younger sons (Robert, Samuel, and Henry) became ordained ministers in the Church of England, he took his seat "with a solemn and delighted complacency" among the congregation to which one of them was to minister. It was then that "he rejoiced to gather ... the harvest of the seeds which, in earlier days, he had himself sowed in their minds." He often accompanied his sons on their pastoral visits, joining in the prayers they offered by the beds of sick or dying parishioners.

During the last two years of his life, Wilberforce stayed with his sons Robert and Samuel for long periods of time. There "surrounded by his wife, his children, and his grandchildren, he yielded himself to the current of each successive desire ... the conflict between inclination and duty [was] over, and virtue and self-indulgence ... the same."

In the evenings, Wilberforce might walk along the downs and seashore skirting the rectory where Samuel lived in Brighstone on the Isle of Wight, or walk beneath the holly hedges that bordered the hop-gardens adjacent to Robert's home in East Farleigh, a village in the northern district of Kent. James Stephen, who had seen so many sides of Wilberforce's character, recalled that when one saw him in such settings, "it was difficult not to recall and (silently at least) to apply to him" lines written by the poet Abraham Cowley:

> *Nor can the snows which now cold age hath shed*
> *Upon thy reverend head,*
> *Quench or allay, the noble fires within:*
> *For all that thou hast been, and all that youth can be,*
> *Thou'rt yet – so fully still dost thou*
> *Possess the manhood and the bloom of wit …*
> *To things immortal time can do no wrong,*
> *And that which never is to die, for ever must be young.*

CHAPTER 8

HOME AND HEARTH

[Our father] was beloved in general society;
but if he sparkled there, he shone at home.
None but his own family could fully know the warmth
of his heart ... the full sunshine of his kindliest affections.
ROBERT AND SAMUEL WILBERFORCE

In an essay written for *The Dictionary of National Biography* Leslie Stephen, Sir James' third son, said of Wilberforce: "His relations to his family seem to have been perfect."

This may be overstated praise, but it is a very telling description of the home life of a man so devoted to his family. And it also shows that Wilberforce's influence on the Victorian era extended to home life, not just to politics or morals – for Leslie Stephen was one of the most eminent of eminent Victorians.

Wilberforce's relations with his wife and family reveal several important sides of his character. Many aspects of his relationship with them were progressive for their era. His understanding of what it meant to be a husband and father flowed from his understanding of faith, duty, and wisdom as described in the Scriptures.

It must also be said that Wilberforce's family life contrasted starkly with prevailing modes of the day, and certainly his own disruptive childhood. His home life also revealed colorful eccentricities – disorganized and funny habits that underscore his humanity. No matter what many of his critics believed, he was no statue or stodgy icon. His family life shows him in his fullness – a man of caring heart, ever-present humor, and committed love.

For many, Wilberforce's life was one characterized largely by perseverance and sacrifice. These were important sides to his personality, but they were not all that there was. He saw marriage as one of the crowning glories of his life, though the prospects for marriage proved elusive for many years.

Wilberforce wed within a year of the grievous defeat of his bill to abolish the slave trade in 1796. In some respects he was as surprised as his friends by this turn of events. He never intended to marry, and to all appearances he was a confirmed bachelor.

After a decision in 1789 not to propose marriage to a certain Miss Hammond, the sister-in-law of the Speaker of the House, Henry Addington, Wilberforce had written: "It is very likely I shall never change my condition; nor do I feel solicitous whether I do or not." He had, apparently, been in love but felt that the "difference of views and Plans of Life" between himself and "Miss H." were such that they "could not have been happy together."

A few years later, in February 1796, Wilberforce's cousin Henry Thornton married one of his best childhood friends, Marianne Sykes. Their evident happiness made Wilberforce take stock of his life. Quoting the poet William Cowper in a letter to a friend, he said that he "began to wish 'not to finish my journey alone.'"

In the spring of 1797 (the exact date is unknown) Wilberforce shared his thoughts with another of his friends, Thomas Babington. Babington knew of a beautiful young woman, Barbara Spooner, who had recently become an ardent evangelical. He urged her to write to Wilberforce. She did, and her letter charmed him.

Wilberforce talked further with Babington about Miss Spooner on April 13. Two days later he met her for the first time. Any further thoughts of confirmed bachelorhood were instantly banished. The two fell deeply in love.

A whirlwind courtship ensued. On April 23 Wilberforce proposed by letter. They became formally engaged when he received her letter that night. Overjoyed, he found it difficult to sleep.

"She is admirably suited to me," he wrote in his diary, "a real Christian, affectionate, sensible, rational in habits, moderate in desires and pursuits, capable of bearing prosperity without intoxication, and adversity without repining." Later he wrote to his friend Matthew Montagu: "Above all the women I ever knew, I believe she is qualified in all respects to make me a good wife."

The intensity of Wilberforce's sudden capitulation to matrimony was rather surprising, but it was not out of character. Though the notion of marriage dawned on him rather slowly, he had been longing, conscious or not, for a loving family all his life. He had lost his father at eight, nearly lost his mother to a fever at the same time, and moved around between friends and relatives for many years as a boy. Once he had met Barbara, it seems very likely that this intense longing for a happy, stable family came to the fore in a headlong rush. Once it did, he did not try to fight it.

Wilberforce married his Barbara on May 30, 1797, one and a half months after their first meeting. He was thirty-eight, she twenty. He had found the friend of his heart, and she fulfilled a deep need within him. He wanted to include her in everything he did, and within a few months he described their life together in a letter to James Stephen (the father of Sir James).

> My plan of life is every where the same. The morning I spend in some sort of reading and writing, taking Mrs. Wilberforce along with me as much as I can in my studies and employments. We carry our business out of doors, and muse or read whilst taking the air and exercise. Dinner and supper are the seasons when I enjoy the company of my friends.... I can willingly prolong the dinner conversation till it sometimes almost meets the beginning of our supper *conversazione*.

For the next thirty-six years they would walk together happily, hand in hand. "A more tender, excellent wife," Wilberforce said, "no man ever received [as a] gift from the Lord."

Within ten years they had six children, four boys and two girls. The eldest, William, was born in 1798. Barbara followed in 1799, Elizabeth in 1801, Robert in 1802, Samuel in 1805, and Henry William in 1807. "I delight in little children," Wilberforce once told a friend. "I could spend hours in watching them."

It was true enough. But the irrepressible, boyish side of his nature was not content with merely watching children: he loved to play with them. In 1820 he paid a visit to the Duchess of Kent, the mother of Queen Victoria. "The duchess," he recalled, "received me with her fine, animated child on the floor by her with its playthings, of which I soon became one."

This, the only meeting of the future queen and the man who had done so much to influence the nature of her reign, was a wonderful piece of symbolism. It would be easy to think that their meeting was nothing more than an interesting story. But in a very real way it was more than that. The picture of "the conscience of the nation," as Wilberforce was known, at play with the future sovereign of the nation underscores one of Wilberforce's most important bequests to the Victorian era. His family life was emulated by households of every class throughout Britain. That they increasingly ceased to be places where children were seen and not heard and instead became places where parents spent more time with their children – educating them, praying with them, reading with them, and playing with them – was due in no small measure to Wilberforce's example.

The widely read five-volume *Life of William Wilberforce* was published in 1838, one year after Victoria assumed the throne. The story of Wilberforce playing with her as a child appeared in it. As Victoria's reign continued, other memoirs about Wilberforce appeared, describing his happy relations with his family.

Broomfield, Wilberforce's home in Clapham. (Image provided through the kind permission of Lady Kate Davson.)

Perhaps the most telling tribute to this side of Wilberforce's life was the publication of his son Samuel's beloved series of children's stories in the 1840s, *Agathos, the Rocky Island and Other Sunday Stories*. Reprinted in scores of editions, these tales reflected the storytelling childhood Samuel had known when he sat at his father's feet. Some, in fact, were based on letters written by Wilberforce to Samuel.

Through these tales, the world learned more about Wilberforce as a father, for his sons and friends had already recorded many stories of Wilberforce family life. At any given moment one might, for example, visit his home and find the master of the house ("as restless and volatile as a child himself") refreshing himself by throwing a ball or excusing himself from important deliberations with fellow MPs to go out on the lawn and have a race with the children "to warm his feet."

Marianne Thornton, the eldest daughter of Henry Thornton, once remembered: "I know one of my first lessons was I must never disturb Papa when he was talking or reading, but no such prohibition existed with Mr. Wilberforce. His love for, and enjoyment in all children was remarkable."

This enjoyment assumed many forms. Wilberforce was once "irresistibly summoned to a contest at marbles" in the midst of writing a letter and left it unfinished to answer the summons. Having not had a chance to play cricket with his eldest son for some time, he joined William and his friends and played with gusto – too much gusto in fact – for he sustained a severe injury when the "ball struck my foot with great violence." He told his friend Lord Muncaster: "You will laugh heartily when you hear the story.... By the positive injunctions of my surgeon I have been ever since sentenced to a sofa. It will lessen the marvel and render the tale less laughable to hear that my son William was ... in the *dramatis personae* of the cricket players and I have not played with him at cricket before for I know not how long."

One senses that the injury was worth it all in the end. Wilberforce's love of cricket continued unabated. In July 1821 he provided "ale and cricket to the servants, and all the family, in honor of the coronation" of King George IV.

Festive scenes were commonplace in the Wilberforce home, for he loved his children's "holyday amusements." In 1815 he described a Twelfth Night party that must have been filled with the kind of hilarity that marked Fezziwig's Christmas party in Dickens' *A Christmas Carol*. Heeding the earnest entreaties of his children, he and his invited guests "all played blind-man's buff for two hours or more." Then too, it was not uncommon for him to "run ... races with [the children] in the garden" or collect them, as he did one day in 1817, and take them "to see some jugglers" or for a visit to a toyshop.

In more quiet intervals, he would play chess with them or read to them. He made it a priority to "set apart some time in the afternoon for lighter and more entertaining books," such as *The Arabian Nights*. In the evening, he often read to them from Shakespeare. One day might find Wilberforce taking his children, as he did over the Christmas holidays in 1812, "to the British Museum" – on another "to see the great fish."

One year earlier Wilberforce engaged his Quaker friend William Allen (an eminent chemist and lecturer) "to show my family some experiments – philosophical and chemical." The following morning he had planned to take his children (and those of his friend John Venn) "to the Liverpool Museum or to see Mr. Parker's glass manufactory or something of the kind."

Such pursuits yielded gratifying, if at times surprising results. Wilberforce once noted in his diary that one of his sons (whose name was omitted in the text) was "showing at times much thought – [he] used ... in play yesterday Euclid's axiom, 'Things that are equal to the same are equal to one another.'"

During the sessions of Parliament, Wilberforce was often so busy that he could see little of his children through the week. But, as his sons wrote, "Sunday was his own and he spent it in the midst of his family."

His children met him when he had concluded his morning prayers and went with him to church, repeating in the carriage hymns or passages from poems by William Cowper. Returning home, they walked with him in the garden and each had "the valued privilege of bringing him a Sunday nosegay for which the flowers of their little gardens had been hoarded all the week." Everyone would then dine together at an early hour.

One of Wilberforce's Sunday commonplace expressions was: "Better says the wise man, 'is a dinner of herbs where love is than a stalled ox and hatred therewith.' But, my children, how good is God to us! He gives us the stalled ox and love too."

Some among Wilberforce's friends and family grudged the expenditure of time and the sacrifice of privacy his lifestyle required. It was once suggested that he withdraw to a greater distance from London in order to escape it. To this his brother-in-law James Stephen made a telling reply, which says much about Wilberforce's ability to make goodness fashionable.

There was, Stephen said, "a peculiar and very important species of usefulness to friends and acquaintances for which Wilberforce's character and manners fit him in an extraordinary degree." Nowhere could his talents be better employed than at Kensington Gore, his home from 1808 to 1820.

To those who thought "so respectable a mansion" ostentatious Stephen said that at Kensington Gore Wilberforce was "in the eye of the great and fashionable world ... in Hyde Park with appearances that proclaim he might live like them if he would [and] that it is not for want of fortune Wilberforce has not like others sunk his name in a [peerage]." Moreover, while Wilberforce "abstains from fashionable luxuries, he indulges himself in those congruities to his station and fortune which best become the English gentleman and the Christian in the means of family comfort and extensive, though simple hospitality."

To exclude guests from Wilberforce's home in any significant degree, Stephen believed, "would not only be to impair Wilberforce's usefulness but to change his nature.... Witnessing his domestic life is one of the best cures I know for prepossessions against religion, best human incentives to the practice of it, and best guards against those errors and excesses into which misdirected zeal is apt to run."

Stephen was aware that too much stress could be laid on this kind of usefulness. Still, he argued, "there is something peculiar in Wilberforce's character and situation that seem to point it out as the design of Providence that he should serve his Master in this high and special walk, and should have, so to speak, a kind of domestic publicity – that he should be at home a candle set on a candlestick as well as abroad a city built upon a hill."

Stephen also drew attention to Wilberforce's responsibilities as a parent. "If Wilberforce were less hospitable," he maintained,

> sure I am his children would see less of what may be most
> useful to them in his example. They would have less of that

important and difficult lesson, how to live with the world, and yet not be of the world. They would be less likely to learn how ... to please both friends and strangers without any sacrifice of Christian character. Besides it is of unspeakable importance that they will thus gain a taste for the ... conversation which distinguishes their father's table and their father's fireside.... The trash, the trifles, the insipidities, that make up conversation in general ... contrast [greatly] with even the worst table-talk that one generally meets at his house. Wilberforce himself does not see a tenth part so much of this as I have done because he knows how to lead conversation wherever he goes.... Rest assured his home parties are in this respect useful schools for his children.

Wilberforce's sons confirmed this assessment of their home life. There was, they wrote, "nothing costly or luxurious in his style of living; these were banished on principle and none of his guests missed them." One friend, known for the excellence of the dinners he hosted, complimented Wilberforce: "You can do what you please, people go to you to hear you talk, not for a good dinner."

During the sitting of Parliament, Wilberforce felt he could never spend sufficient time at Kensington Gore each day to witness the progress of spring. When he could, and weather permitting, he sat for long periods in his beloved garden "under a spreading walnut-tree" known among his children as his study. The grounds, Wilberforce told a friend, consisted of "about three acres ... around my house (or rather behind it) and several old trees – walnut and mulberry – of thick foliage. I can sit and read under their shade, which I delight in doing, with as much admiration of the beauties of nature (remembering at the same time the words of [Cowper], my favourite poet, "Nature is but a name for an effect whose cause is God") as if I were 200 miles from the great city."

Kensington Gore was in many ways an ideal home. But as Wilberforce's sons pointed out, in other respects their father was less favorably circumstanced. "My situation near town produces numerous visitors," Wilberforce wrote, "and frequent invitations, difficult and painful to resist."

These interruptions lasted as long as he remained near London, and he found that he could often only write his letters by stealing to a den at the "Nuisance" (a small adjoining house which he had purchased). "And even there," he said, "I should be no more safe, if it were known that I had such a lurking-hole, than a fox would be near Mr. Meynell's kennel [of foxhounds]."

Stolen hours in the Nuisance notwithstanding, Wilberforce cherished long walks with his children, "examining them in the books which they are reading, and talking them over together." One favorite book was William Robertson's *History of America*, which he would have his children read to him if his eyes were proving particularly troublesome. If they were not, he would read to them. In either case, "his efforts were aimed at opening the mind and creating a spirit of inquiry."

One of his sons remembered how effective these times of instruction could be.

> I shall never forget the happy expedient by which he impressed on me the characters of the several Spanish chieftains [while we were reading Robertson's *History*]. When the prayer bell cut short our [daily] reading, he would bid me mark how its heavy tones chimed in with the epithets by which he had distinguished the [chieftains]. To this hour, the sound of a bell irresistibly reminds me of his exclamation, "There it is again, cruel Cortes, perfidious Pizarro."

During these walks and discussions of literature, Wilberforce sometimes learned as he taught. "Children," he once concluded, "are very sagacious and attentive observers." Picnics were a regular occurrence. Daily excursions would be made, for example, to "Caesar's camp [a favorite picnic destination] and the cherry orchards." No hint of pressing parliamentary business could be

detected at such times. A friend who accompanied the Wilberforces on one picnic recalled: "We took our dinner with us upon
Saturday, and were fourteen in number. Mr. Wilberforce made us
all very happy. He read, and talked, and carved [the meat], and
reminded us of the benevolence of God in making the avenues
of innocent pleasure so numerous, and forming us for so many
enjoyments."

One interest Wilberforce bequeathed to his third son, Samuel,
was a love of birds. Nightingales were a particular favorite. One
of Wilberforce's diary entries ran: "A very fine day, after excessive
rain. All the trees are in leaf. The Lilacs have come out. I heard
the nightingale a little for the first time this year." Warming to
his description of his many "domestic comforts," he continued:
"My children are around me, my wife is in good health, and all is
most beautiful and comfortable about me. What cause have I for
thankfulness!"

To Lord Muncaster he wrote at another time:

> I am staying today in the country, enjoying the first greet-
> ings of summer – the nightingales are abundant and, my dear
> friend, while through nature I look up to nature's God, and
> still more, when from regarding the Author of nature, I fur-
> ther contemplate Him in the still more endearing character
> of the God of grace and consolation; my heart is warmed and
> thankful for the unequalled blessings I enjoy. I look down
> with unaffected superiority on the contentious sparrings of
> our political parties.

Samuel Wilberforce's diary picked up where his father's left off
when it came to describing the pleasures afforded by birds – indeed
by animals of all kinds. "The first swallows of the year, the first
nightingale [and] the first cuckoo" were almost always recorded
in it. This love of nature continued into adulthood when he wrote
reviews of Arthur Knox's *Ornithological Rambles in Sussex* and his
Autumns on the Spey, both published in the *Quarterly Review*.

The Wilberforce home, like Winston Churchill's or Theodore Roosevelt's in a later time, was filled with pets of every description. Among them was a tame hare, about which Wilberforce wrote to a guest due soon to arrive: "How can you ask such a Question, will you receive my tame hare? Are you so bad at analogy? and if '[Love me], Love my dog' is an established axiom, much more 'Love me, Love my Hare' holds true in this House, where among some of us, Dogs have not their due estimation."

Samuel Wilberforce's household, not to be outdone, included a tame fox. Like his father, Samuel had a penchant for interrupting a letter on a serious subject with odd bits of news. Two times at least, the fox's adventures prompted an abrupt departure from the subject at hand: once when the fox was lost, and second, when everyone felt great relief because the hungry fox returned.

If Kensington Gore was at times a zoo in everything but name, and if Wilberforce's fondness for excusing himself from important deliberations to play with children left an impression that his household had a certain happy eccentricity about it, the impression was accurate. His household was not always so chaotic, but neither was life there correct in every detail. The shrubs were not always carefully trimmed, the servants were not always efficient, but it was a loving and nurturing home.

At times, there was a decidedly comical element to the way the Wilberforce household was managed. Dinners, for example, could be an adventure. Barbara would make sure Wilberforce's needs were attended to – she doted on him and he on her – but she often did so to the detriment of other guests, such as Wilberforce's old friend Isaac Milner, who had a prodigious appetite.

Wilberforce's poor eyesight made it difficult for him to be attentive to the needs of guests. On one occasion Milner waited patiently for sustenance to arrive, but to no avail. Realizing he would have to fend for himself, he shouted to no one in particular: "There is nothing on earth to eat!" He called in the servants and told them to bring bread and butter – "plenty without limit" – to which Wilberforce replied: "Thank you, thank you kindly Milner, for seeing to these things. Mrs. Wilberforce" – whose health was often a concern – "is not strong enough to meddle much in domestic matters."

Family prayers – though intended to be a daily time of devotion and instruction – could at times produce an unintended result. Usually everyone, family, friends, and servants, knelt while Wilberforce read a prayer from *The Book of Common Prayer.*

On one occasion all was proceeding according to custom, when the pockets of Wilberforce's coat – filled to capacity with small books and other oddments – burst. Still kneeling, still perhaps trying to read the prayer, he tried to gather up his now widely scattered possessions.

Then too, there were times when things were not much, if at all, better managed when the Wilberforce clan set out on vacation. A stay at Stansted Park, a home lent to him by a friend, was a case in point. Things started off promisingly, as Wilberforce wrote to a friend: Mr. Smith, the steward, was all that could be desired – "extremely obliging; in short, justly representing his master. He, dear kind man, had endeavoured in every way to render me comfortable, had left me wine, and even china, plates, &c.; and the key of all his libraries. . . . We of course tried to do as little harm as possible. Though at first I thought we must have gone away on account of the housekeeper's bad temper, which sadly effervesced."

The vexatious housekeeper provided the inspiration for one of Wilberforce's more descriptive (and funny) asides: "Our kind host . . . left me a case of port [wine], and an order for half a [deer]; but you would really be amused as much as by any part of Smollett or Fielding to witness an interview between the housekeeper, for I put her first, and Mrs. W. You know the Indians have a way of setting oddly contrasted animals to fight with each other, and I really long to set our [cantankerous] old coachman and this fine lady in single combat."

Barbara Wilberforce may have had to contend on occasion with a truculent housekeeper, but she could always count on her husband's unalloyed devotion. That he treasured her, despite any shortcomings in the management of household affairs (he knew he was not blameless on that score), is reinforced time and again in his letters to her. "My dearest Love," he once wrote,

> I have resolved to take up my pen ... and send this Letter to London, that it may go by the stage and convey to Thee the tender love of Thy Wilber.... I shall admit no needless delay [in coming to you] and I shall not be surprised on this day [if, two weeks from now] I am by my love's side, beholding that look of affection with my bodily eyes which is now distinctly visible to my mental.... I am most tenderly Thine, William Wilberforce. [P.S.] I hope I haven't scribbled so fast as to be illegible. The truth is I did not think of writing above a few lines when I began but I was drawn by my desire to spend a few minutes on the stay with my beloved.

Given Wilberforce's love and devotion to his family, it is not surprising that it was his family more than his always precarious health that prompted him to resign in 1812 his powerful seat in the House of Commons as MP for the county of Yorkshire. He had always been an attentive husband and father, even if called away much more often and for longer than he liked to attend to political concerns. But his return on one occasion from a trip on parliamentary business brought the matter to a very uncomfortable head.

Arriving home and having one of his small children placed on his lap, Wilberforce was chagrined to find that the child began to cry. The nursemaid said by way of explanation, "He always is afraid of strangers." Wilberforce, ever sensitive, was hurt to think that he might in any way be a stranger to his children. His sons summed up his reaction succinctly: "This he could not suffer to continue."

And he didn't. Altering what he called his "plan of life," he wrote: "I conceive that my chief objects should be First; My children. Secondly; Parliament." He then wrote round to his friends, constituents, and colleagues in government and told them that he was resigning his seat for Yorkshire to take a more active role in educating and rearing his children.

Wilberforce was as good as his word. Interviewing prospective tutors, traveling with his children to the homes of tutors who had secured his approval, writing letters to his children, and seeing to their needs while at school – all of these tasks he now took upon himself. He planned extracurricular activities to enrich their time at home. Reading aloud to them through the long evenings continued to be a favorite holiday pastime. Walter Scott's novel *Rokeby* was particularly enjoyable: "All [are] earnest for reading it," Wilberforce wrote in his diary, "and interested in it beyond measure."

Though he had resigned his seat for Yorkshire, Wilberforce was not done politically. His brother-in-law Lord Calthorpe offered a so-called safe seat in Parliament that Wilberforce accepted right away. He would become MP for Bramber in West Sussex, a smaller and much less demanding constituency. He could now be useful in politics and spend the time he wished with his family.

Wilberforce's letters to his children, as with those of C. S. Lewis, were entertaining, instructive, loving – and treasured. Many of his letters to his children were posthumously published, most of them written to his third son, Samuel, the others to his youngest daughter, Elizabeth.

Wilberforce's letters to Samuel appear to have had a particularly profound and lasting impact. No fewer than six hundred letters are still extant. Each was carefully numbered and kept by Samuel as long as he lived. Canon A. R. Ashwell, Samuel's biographer, said that these letters

> must have exercised the most powerful influence on the formation of [Samuel's] character. Compare these letters with

his subsequent career, and it will at once be seen that Samuel Wilberforce was indeed his father's son. Nascent faults carefully marked and checked, personal habits of upright conduct strenuously enforced, shrewd practical counsels as to social duties and conduct ... constantly suggested, and all these strung upon the one thread of ever-repeated inculcation of the duty of private prayer as the one holdfast of life, – these remarkable letters exhibit the influences which formed the solid ... character which underlay the brilliant gifts and striking career of Samuel Wilberforce.

Ashwell notes that these letters are no less significant when considering that Wilberforce was forty-six when Samuel was born, fifty-seven when he began writing letters to his son. He had little leisure time, and Samuel was neither an only nor an eldest son that he could lay claim to a large share of his father's time. Add to this the fact that Wilberforce's health and eyesight were often poor, so poor in the case of his eyesight that there are many letters in which he tells Samuel that he was writing with closed eyes.

The Private Papers of William Wilberforce, published in 1897, contain several letters written by Wilberforce to his daughter Elizabeth. The correspondence began when she was fifteen. "When I do address my dear girl," the first letter ran, "I ought to consider how I can best testify my friendship: for friendship let there be between us; never can you have a friend more warmly attached to you or more interested in your well-doing and happiness than myself."

This letter and ones that follow contain wise advice on living the Christian life ("keeping the heart with all diligence"), candid admissions about his own failings ("I have often detected my own self-partiality and self-deceit"), and advice on reading: "I understand you are reading Philip Doddridge's *Rise and Progress of Religion in the Soul*. You cannot read a better book. I hope it was one of the means of turning my heart to God. Certainly, there are few books which have been so extensively useful."

Samuel Wilberforce (1805–1873), third son and biographer of William Wilberforce

Wilberforce wrote an enchanting and inventive letter on July 13, 1830, in which he describes the system of philosopher George Berkeley by way of an apology for not writing sooner. "My Dear Lizzy," he began,

> if many intentions to write could be admitted as making up one letter, you would have to thank me for being so good a correspondent. But I fear that this is a mode of calculation that will only come into use, when the system of good Bishop Berkeley has become established.
>
> I cannot explain what this is so well as [your brother] Robert could, but its distinctive principle is that there are no such things as substances. You may suppose that you have had the pleasure of re-visiting a very dear friend, called Miss Palmer, and you probably could assure me, if I asked you whether they

still continued at the Hall any such vulgar practice as that of eating, that the turkies and fowls were as good and as freely bestowed as when I used to partake of them in earlier years. All mere delusion. All imagination. All ideal. There is no Elizabeth (she only appeared to occupy an ideal place in an ideal carriage, when she travelled down to Mosely and Elmdon), there is no Miss Palmer, nor are the fowls and turkies a whit more substantial than the supposed eaters of them.

I really am serious – such is the system of one of the ablest and best of men (he was spoken of by [Alexander] Pope as "Having every virtue under heaven"); he held that the Almighty formed us so as to have impressions produced on as if these were realities, but that this was all. [However,] I little intended when I took up my pen to give you such a lecture in metaphysics.

Wilberforce's sprightliness as a writer notwithstanding, he always urged his daughter to "open … your heart to me without disguise." And she did. After receiving one letter from her in which she confessed to feeling a "solitariness of spirit," he wrote back: "I wish you could have seen the whole interior of mine when I had read through it: I am not ashamed to say that I melted into tears of affectionate sympathy." Lizzy deeply appreciated the love, wisdom, and constant affection interlaced in these letters.

Death brought the only great sorrows that touched Wilberforce's family life. Lizzy died in 1831 of complications resulting from a chest infection, shortly after her marriage to the Rev. John James. Ten years earlier, her older sister Barbara had died of consumption, or tuberculosis of the lungs.

Death also claimed the life of a grandchild to which Wilberforce touchingly referred in a letter written to his son Robert on July 22, 1827: "Yesterday [was] the birthday of our beloved and, I confidently hope, sainted Barbara – already joined by our sweet little grandchild."

These losses were devastating. As a boy, Wilberforce had lost two sisters. He had now outlived his two daughters. His faith was strong and had so often sustained him – his letters reveal as much – but it was grievously painful to see history repeating itself in the loss of two daughters within successive generations of his family. After his daughter Barbara's death, he found himself referring to it in his correspondence: "How striking is the change of fifty years [since 1776] when Samuel Smith and I travelled as bachelors.... Now he has a house full of descendants; and I also have five children and a grandchild living, besides a daughter and sweet little grandson gone, I humbly trust, to a better world."

Wilberforce's surviving children and the birth of more grand-children were the great joy of his remaining years. He rejoiced, too, in the birth of grandchildren to old friends. To Lord Muncaster he wrote:

> It is one of my first occupations after my return to send you our best congratulations and kindest wishes. I can conceive grandchildren to be sources of more unmixed pleasure than children themselves, because in their case we feel less responsibility, and consequently less anxiety. I can see you dancing the bantling in your arms, and being as young [at heart] as old Agesilaus [the King of Sparta in Plutarch's story] is reported to have been.

It was a source of never-ending amazement to Wilberforce that he had lived long enough to see his children grown and having children of their own. In 1788, he had been told that he didn't have the strength to last two weeks. Against all hope, he had recovered. More than that, he had married and his family had flourished.

After spending some time with Henry Thornton in Clapham at Battersea Rise in 1809, he had reflected: "I carried Mrs. Wilberforce and my six children to the same house in which were now contained his own wife and eight but which he and I once inhabited as chums for several years when we were solitary bachelors. How naturally I was led to adopt the old patriarch's declaration, 'With my staff I passed over, &c. and now I am become two bands!'"

As he grew older, he rejoiced too that his sons were "living in much harmony." He particularly loved seeing his children, their wives, and his grandchildren all around his table. "Praise the Lord, O my Soul," he would say.

Wilberforce had much to be thankful for. He lived long enough to see that, for the most part, his surviving children responded well to the parenting they had received. Samuel won a First in Classics at Oxford. A gifted preacher who inherited his father's natural eloquence, he became the bishop of Oxford many years later and chaplain to Prince Albert. Robert won a Double First at Oxford in Classics and Mathematics, became a Fellow and Tutor at Oriel College, and later a distinguished clergyman. Henry, the youngest son, also won a First in Classics at Oxford.

When news of Henry's accomplishment reached him, Wilberforce proudly (if somewhat uncharacteristically) exclaimed, "I have had three sons at Oxford, and all of them first-class [honors] men. Show me the man who can make the same boast!"

Wilberforce's one great disappointment was his eldest son, William, a ne'er-do-well who was often irresponsible with his time and money. He never took to religion as his younger brothers had done, and he failed to mend his profligate ways despite his father's repeated attempts to reach out to him and help him.

Wilberforce didn't live to see his grandchildren emerge beyond their childhood years. But one very representative story illustrates how his life and example influenced them. When biographer John Pollock was conducting research in the 1970s, he met Wilberforce's last surviving great-grandson, then over one hundred and blind. He told Pollock that his father, when a small boy, had been walking with Wilberforce one day on a hill near Bath. While walking, they encountered a shocking scene: a carthorse being cruelly whipped by a carter, while struggling to haul a heavy load of stone up the hill. Wilberforce pleaded with the carter to cease beating the animal.

The carter turned, and began to curse him. Somehow, however, he recognized Wilberforce. "Are you Mr. Wilberforce?" he asked, his anger giving way to shame, "Then I shall never beat my horse again!"

Near the end of his life Wilberforce (weakened by what would prove to be his final illness) spoke at length of the delight he took in the affection and care of his wife and children. "Think what I should have done had I been left, as one hears, [amidst] people quarrelling and separating. 'In sickness and in health' was the burden, and well has it been kept." Just as he said this, his beloved Barbara entered the room. Turning to her tenderly he said, "I was just praising you."

Three days before he died, Wilberforce's thoughts turned once more to his domestic comforts. He had endured a disruptive and, at times, sad, lonely childhood. Now, near the end of his pilgrimage, he spoke with a profound sense of gratitude for the blessings of home and hearth he had known for so many years.

"I do declare," he said, "that the delight I have in feeling that there are a few people whose hearts are really attached to me, is the very highest I have in this world. What more could any man wish at the close of life, than to be attended by his own children, and his own wife, and all treating him with such uniform kindness and affection?"

CHAPTER 9

FINISHING WELL

Where could there have been found a leader more humane,
more accomplished, or more determined?
[Wilberforce] foresaw and aimed at the ultimate
emancipation of [slaves in] the British colonies. . . .
He laid the foundation by annihilating the commerce in man.

BENJAMIN HUGHES,
AFRICAN-AMERICAN EDUCATOR AND ABOLITIONIST

As 1823 began, freedom for the slaves in Britain's West Indian colonies was uppermost in Wilberforce's mind. He now launched a campaign to secure their emancipation that he hoped would be the culmination of all his years in public life. He began by writing an *Appeal in Behalf of the Negro Slaves in the West Indies*, a work intended to be the opening salvo for the final push to secure emancipation.

He plunged into the work. His worsening eyesight, however, a symptom of a slow buildup of opium poisoning, made his progress slow and difficult. At this time, doctors did not understand that opium could slowly poison a patient's system. Wilberforce had been taking the drug in small doses since 1788 to prevent or mitigate any recurrences of ulcerative colitis, and over time his eyesight, never good, had steadily worsened. He also had to contend with frequent interruptions, the incessant visits and letters that always required his attention, and a discouraging inability at times to focus his thoughts adequately for the research and writing of his book. He thought it a sign of age, though he was only sixty-three, but it was in reality another symptom of opium poisoning.

His diary entries reflect his frustration. "Jan. 26th. At work on my Manifesto, but I cannot please myself.... I am become heavy and lumbering, and not able at once to start into a canter, as I could twenty years ago. Happily, it is a good road, and in a right direction."

"[Jan.] 29th. I get on slowly. [We had] music in the evening. To have friends in the house sadly consumes time, though no one loves music better than I do.... Yet the time is short with me, I must husband it."

In March 1823 Wilberforce's *Appeal* was published. It had a profound effect in Britain and throughout Europe. "My pamphlet is well liked," he told his diary, "thank God." Perhaps the most gratifying response he received was from a West Indian plantation owner who wrote to say that the tract "had so affected me, that should it cost me my whole property, I [would] surrender it willingly, that my poor negroes may be brought not only to the liberty of Europeans, but especially to the liberty of Christians."

Baron de Stael, the son of abolitionist Madame de Stael – one of Wilberforce's old friends, wrote from the continent expressing his "unqualified admiration." The rootedness of Wilberforce's *Appeal* in his Christian faith particularly impressed de Stael. "There are few stronger arguments," he said, "in favour of the immortality of the soul (setting aside revelation), than the constant rise ... in the mental powers of those who direct their course towards heaven. Indeed I cannot conceive how public opinion could resist an attack led on by you, and I hope that having begun the holy struggle, you will witness the ultimate victory."

In Britain, Archbishop Magee affirmed: "This addition to the noble exertions which you have persevered in making for the relief of that cruelly injured portion of the common children of the one great Father, will be followed with the blessing which belongs to such labours of Christian love."

Wilberforce's tract was written in the spirit of the golden rule. As with his first speech calling for the abolition of the slave trade in 1789, he had infused his pamphlet with kindness and forbearance toward those he hoped to persuade that the institution of slavery was a great moral evil. He condemned the institution without appearing to condemn those who owned slaves.

This, in combination with his vivid descriptions of the various abuses associated with slavery, made his book doubly powerful and effective. As terrible as slavery was, and no one was more firmly convinced of this, he knew that his task was to persuade his fellow citizens every bit as much as it was to decry a great moral evil. It was a harder task than merely condemning, for he hoped to recruit to the abolitionist ranks the very people who were slaveholders themselves. The response he received from the West Indian slave owner shows just how effective he could be in this regard.

In this pamphlet Wilberforce made it clear that people of conscience were obligated to seek social justice even though they might face great opposition. Alongside this, they should also remember that the West Indian slave owners were not necessarily evil; the practice of slavery was. Wilberforce stated his sincere belief that many West Indian slave owners were "men of more than common kindness and liberality." He had found many of them "utterly unacquainted with the true nature and practical character of the system with which they have the misfortune to be connected." He closed his tract by saying,

> Justice, humanity, and sound policy prescribe our course, and will animate our efforts. Stimulated by a consciousness of what we owe to the laws of God, and the rights and happiness of man, our exertions will be ardent, and our perseverance invincible. Our ultimate success is sure; and ere long we shall rejoice in the consciousness of having delivered our country from the greatest of her crimes, and rescued her character from the deepest stain of dishonour.

As ever, Wilberforce had his opponents. One slave-owning visitor to Britain from America wrote dismissively of abolition as that "old fool ... Wilberforce's infatuation."

Wilberforce knew only too well that despite the good done by his tract, the British nation would be slow to forsake a system it had so long maintained – one linked with such considerable wealth and private interests. However, the campaign of public persuasion culminating in the abolition of the slave trade proved that securing the abolition of slavery throughout the British Empire was possible. This was underscored in a letter written to Wilberforce by an American correspondent: "It tasks our historical faith to believe that you should have been almost singular not very many years ago in supporting opinions on the subject of the Slave Trade, which at the present period are common throughout the civilized world."

Wilberforce's efforts to lead the fight for emancipation were hampered further by increasing bouts of poor health. On April 15, 1823, an inflammation of the lungs severely weakened his voice during a key debate on the issue in the House of Commons. He realized that he might soon have to leave public life. "I must accustom myself to be willing to retire," he wrote. "A Christian, considering himself the servant of God, does his Master's business ... by action ... no less by retiring. I hope I have been acting on this principle (applying 'he must increase, but I must decrease') to other and younger men.... May I be enabled to walk by faith, not sight.... How cheering is the consideration that all events are under the guidance of infinite wisdom and goodness."

Two years before, Wilberforce had acted on this principle and formally committed the leadership of the antislavery crusade to Thomas Fowell Buxton, a young Quaker MP whose efforts to secure prison reforms he greatly admired. He had something of a father's affection for Buxton, writing to him on one occasion to suggest a meeting: "We are almost on a meridian. I sincerely say ... that it would greatly gratify me to be able to join our [traveling] parties. Our high west wind would this very day carry us to you in a balloon in a few hours."

The letter in which Wilberforce solicited Buxton's leadership was powerful. It was also marked by great humility and pathos. Wilberforce spoke movingly of the years he had devoted to abolitionist labors.

My dear Buxton, It is now more than thirty years since, after having given notice in the House of Commons that I should bring forward, for the first time, the question concerning the Slave Trade, it pleased God to visit me with a severe [illness]....

I was so exhausted that the ablest physician in London of that day declared that I had not the stamina to last above a very few weeks.... I went to Mr. Pitt and begged of him a promise, which he kindly and readily gave me, to take upon himself the conduct of that great cause.

I thank God I am now free from any indisposition; but from my time of life, and much more for the sake of my constitution, and my inability to bear inclemencies of weather and irregularities, which close attendance on the House of Commons often requires, I am reminded ... that I ought not to look confidently to my being able to carry through any business of importance in the House of Commons.

Now for many, many years I have been longing to bring forward that great subject, the condition of the negro slaves in our Trans-Atlantic colonies, and their advancement to the rank of a free peasantry; a cause ... recommended to me, or rather enforced on me, by every consideration of religion, justice, and humanity. I have been waiting ... for a proper time and suitable circumstances for ... introducing this great business; and ... for some Member of Parliament, who, if I were to retire or to be laid by, would be an eligible leader in this holy enterprise.

I have for some time been viewing you in this connection; and ... I can no longer forbear resorting to you, as I formerly did to Pitt.... Let me then entreat you to form an alliance with me, that ... should [I] be unable to finish [this work] ... you would continue to prosecute it.

Your assurance to this effect would give me the greatest ... peace and consolation.... Alas! my friend, I feel but too deeply how little I have been duly assiduous and faithful in employing the talents committed to my stewardship.... [I]n forming a partnership of this sort with you, I cannot doubt that I should be doing an act highly pleasing to God, and beneficial to my fellow creatures.

Both my heart and head are quite full to overflowing, [and] I must conclude.... May it please God to bless you.... If it be His will, may he render you an instrument of extensive influence ... but above all, may He give the disposition to say at all times, "Lord, what wouldest thou have me to do or suffer?" looking to Him, through Christ, for wisdom and strength.

Wilberforce was saddened by the prospect of retirement, but he took heart that support for emancipation appeared to be steadily gaining throughout Britain. The work of moral reform begun in 1787 had also taken root in British life. Scores of voluntary societies were now in existence, many of which were run by evangelicals of all denominations. Their cumulative effect helped a great deal to push the public toward the abolition of slavery. The moral apathy that had marked Wilberforce's early years in political life was giving way, increasingly, to a spirit of philanthropy.

So while Wilberforce was seriously ill with an inflammation of the lungs, he could rejoice about the progress of abolition: "It is wonderful how people accord with us about the slaves; both government and West Indians.... The country takes up our cause surprisingly. The petitions, considering the little effort [we have made as yet, are] very numerous."

On May 15 Buxton introduced his antislavery motion in the House of Commons. It declared slavery "repugnant to Christianity and the British constitution." During the long debate that ensued,

Wilberforce also spoke. His remarks struck a bittersweet chord of symmetry with the events that occurred on the night the slave trade had been abolished in 1807. Even as Sir Samuel Romilly had contrasted Wilberforce with Napoleon on that night, Wilberforce now paid tribute to Romilly's humanitarianism. Tragically, Romilly had committed suicide in November 1818, grief-stricken over the death of his wife.

"Let it never be forgotten," Wilberforce began, "as Sir Samuel Romilly used to exclaim, 'these poor negroes, destitute, miserable, degraded as they are, are nevertheless his Majesty's liege subjects,' and are entitled to as much, aye ... by the principles of our holy religion, to more of the protection of the British constitution, because they are deserted, destitute, and degraded." Looking to the day when emancipation would become a reality, Wilberforce expressed his confidence that "we shall this night lay the foundation of what will ultimately prove a great and glorious superstructure."

Throughout the remainder of this parliamentary session, Wilberforce's meager physical reserves were taxed further. His breakfast table was often crowded by "a consultation on our slave cause," and by other variously assorted guests. It all reminded him of "the old bustle of a Kensington Gore breakfast."

But these heady days would become difficult. In the discussions of bettering the condition of the West Indian slaves, confusion was about to break out. The British government was receiving conflicting information about the cruel use of whips on slaves. Without fully investigating the matter, the government ordered the disuse of whips in crown colonies.

When copies of this order arrived in Britain's West Indian colonies, it caused great alarm among the white settlers. Local governors refused to publish or obey it. Meanwhile the slaves gathered that some great measure concerning them was being resisted by their masters. Rumors ran riot. It was said that their masters alone stood between them and freedom. In the Caribbean island of Demerara, these rumors led to open insurrection. Many whites were killed, and the rebellion was violently suppressed.

Wilberforce had dreaded such a turn of events. As soon as he heard of the government's order, he exclaimed: "What, have they given such an order without preparation, and without explaining their purpose to the slaves – why it is positive madness!"

Wilberforce and his abolitionist colleagues were now charged with being behind the insurrection. Zachary Macaulay told Wilberforce of news he had received from foreign secretary George Canning, whose private secretary had stated that "the insurrection in Demerara had been instigated by Wilberforce, Buxton, and Co." Soon after, a letter was sent to Wilberforce with only three words on it "Thou vile hypocrite!" He told his diary: "I should have been thirty or forty years in public life to little purpose if this discomposed me."

To Zachary Macaulay, Wilberforce expressed concern that this kind of political vitriol would deter people from coming forward in public life. Many people, he knew, were not willing to risk their reputation or aspirations in a great cause, especially if they or their families had to endure constant venom and vitriol on the long road to victory.

One critic, George Wilson Bridges, had written a proslavery pamphlet in reply to Wilberforce's *Appeal*. Wilberforce had it read to him. He judged it "below criticism [and] shamefully discreditable in some parts." Seeking to defend slavery in his tract, Bridges had cited the conduct of the apostle Paul in sending back the fugitive slave Onesimus. "St. Paul," Wilberforce stated, "directed Philemon to regard [Onesimus] as a brother. He did not rend the civil tie that bound him to his master by [arbitrary] individual power" – as with the charge that Wilberforce and his friends were fomenting insurrection – "No more do we; but by directing him to be treated as a brother, did he not substantially claim for him even more than [the freedom that] we ask for negro slaves? And Onesimus had been a thief as well as a runaway. Yet to these gentlemen

I would reply, in [Samuel] Johnson's language, 'I am glad they read the Scriptures at all, and for any purpose.'"

In the end, the charges of hypocrisy and falsehood brought against Wilberforce and his colleagues furthered the cause they were intended to obstruct. The charges forced the abolitionists to conduct a painstaking investigation of the colonial slave system, which eventually resulted in much more widespread knowledge of the abuses connected with slavery. As Wilberforce's sons phrased it: "Then was laid open that prison-house abhorred by God and man, and those secrets were revealed which posterity will view with equal wonder and abhorrence."

Age and increasing physical infirmity now prevented Wilberforce from taking the leading part he had occupied in the twenty-year fight to abolish the slave trade. Then he had supervised the gathering of evidence, monitored changes in public opinion, procured and circulated abolitionist information, and delegated various responsibilities to those abolitionists with whom he worked. Such tasks had often cost more labor and care than fighting the cause through Parliament. Now he had to assign these tasks to others, most notably Zachary Macaulay, whose encyclopedic knowledge on so many subjects was so extensive that whenever Wilberforce or another colleague needed to know something they simply said, "Let us look it up in Macaulay."

"I am almost good for nothing," Wilberforce wrote to Macaulay, "and I rejoice that there are younger and better labourers." To James Stephen he said: "The decay of my memory is enforced on me continually, and indeed, I perceived it ... before I resigned the representation of Yorkshire [in 1812]. It powerfully strengthened my determination to relinquish that honourable and useful station, though I did not talk much about it at the time."

Still, Wilberforce exerted himself as much as he could. He returned to London in December 1823 to take part in discussions about future strategies aimed at securing emancipation. Parliament reassembled in February 1824 and Wilberforce was at his post. A daunting array of meetings and consultations awaited him. On February 3 he met with Buxton and several others to discuss abolition strategies. The next day was devoted to consultations on the Demerara insurrection.

Ten days later, he attended a meeting of the African Institution, the group most directly responsible for pursuing the emancipation of the slaves in the British West Indies. After this he met with foreign secretary George Canning for several hours, then went to the Duke of Gloucester's, where he consulted with the Duke, Lord Lansdown, James Stephen, and Henry Brougham for another two hours. Dinner followed with a party that included the Duke, Lord and Lady Rosebery (the grandparents of the future prime minister), Lord and Lady Lansdown, Brougham, and Sir James Mackintosh.

One unexpected reward for diligently pursuing the business of the day, as Wilberforce recorded in his diary later, was a lengthy and "most pleasant conversation" with Sir James Mackintosh. "I drew," he said, "the highest prize in the lottery."

On March 1 Wilberforce went to the House of Commons for the debate on a bill decrying cruelty to animals. It was, he wrote,

> opposed on the ground of the rich having their own amusements, and that it would be hard to rob the poor of theirs – a most fallacious argument, and one which has its root in a contempt for the poor.
>
> I would zealously promote the real comfort of the poor. I love the idea of having comfortable causeway walks for them along the public roads. This is most strictly congenial to the British constitution, which, in its political as well as its religious regulation, takes special care of the convenience of the poorer classes. The great distinction between our constitution and that of the ancient republics is, that with them the general advantage was the object, without particular regard to individual comfort: whereas in England individual comfort has been the object, and the general advantage has been sought through it.

As Wilberforce renewed his efforts to secure emancipation, "to come forward again as an advocate for ... the most despised portion of his fellow-subjects," he was harassed by two new developments.

On March 3, he heard of a pamphlet written against him by a Dominican planter that charged him with "the grossest false-hoods, and [made] the most unfounded assertions." Wilberforce also discovered that the home where he now resided in Bromp-ton Grove needed some serious repairs. He was, he wrote, "busy with [an] architect and builder about the great nuisance we have discovered."

Other members of Wilberforce's family were greatly bothered by this, but not him. "It is in little things that men are seen," he wrote. "It is only as if I had lost £4,000 or £5,000. These are the things that are to season the insipidity of life. [Samuel] Johnson says, 'All men have their troubles and annoyances, but the man of the world is too wise to talk about them.' I am sure an old man should be too wise to feel them."

It was at this time Wilberforce received a letter from a gentle-man in want, asking for £100. "Ah," he said, "these are the things which go to my heart."

On March 5 Wilberforce consulted with Buxton and Zachary Macaulay about their united reaction to George Canning's plan for instituting reforms for the treatment of slaves in the British West Indies. The debate on Canning's plan took place on March 16. Wilberforce spoke and felt good about his long, powerful speech, saying, "I was better voiced and better heard than usual."

He was greatly disturbed by the thought that the government was trifling with the hopes of the slaves. He spoke freely, strongly condemning the government's uncertain tone about which policy to pursue. He believed that this tone was detrimental to the safety of slaves and slave owners alike, and he warned any inclined to push for colony-based reforms that they were pursuing a fool's errand. He stated, "I fear that despairing of relief from the British parliament, the negroes will take the cause into their own hands and endeavour to effect their own liberation. No man living would more sincerely lament such conduct than myself." Wilberforce mourned the bloodshed accompanying any armed conflict. He continued:

> I can most solemnly declare that the subject of my daily and nightly prayer – the hope and desire which I feel from the very bottom of my soul is that so dreadful an event may not happen. Still, it is a consequence which I cannot but apprehend; and as an honest man I feel it my duty to state that apprehension.

> Let the House only consider what a terrible thing it is for men who have long been strangers to the light, when the bright beams of day have begun to break in upon their gloom, to have the boon suddenly withdrawn, and be afresh consigned to darkness. Whatever Parliament may do, I implore them to do it speedily and firmly. Let them not proceed with hesitating steps; let them not tamper with the feelings and the passions which they have themselves excited. "For hope deferred maketh the heart sick."

Following this noble effort, Wilberforce became seriously ill, though the onset of his illness was somewhat slow. Feeling unwell on March 19, he had gone to the House of Commons for the debate on Lord John Russell's motion about the French evacuating Spain. Despite feeling sick, Wilberforce was always appreciative of fine oratory and noted in his diary that Canning on this occasion had been "invincibly comic."

Wilberforce had in fact been so enchanted by Canning's humor that he returned home full of it. He described to his family what he had witnessed. Canning's droll voice and manner were inimitable, he said. A master of the memorable one-liner, Canning was equally adept at refuting the arguments of opponents through satire.

Canning's gift for comic sarcasm was in fact very similar to Wilberforce's own, though in the years since his Great Change he had seldom, if ever, used this debate tactic. Still, as Thomas Fowell Buxton recalled, he could still demonstrate this ability – though in a discreet way. "Often during a debate," Buxton stated, Wilberforce "would whisper to me hints and witticisms which would have filled the House with merriment, and overwhelmed his opponent. But when he rose to speak, though he went close to the very thoughts he had poured into my ear, he restrained himself from uttering them, nor would he ever give vent to any one allusion which could give another pain."

In his later years Wilberforce seldom allowed himself to be provoked in debate, but when he was, his response could astound those who heard him. Once, during a debate on the suspension of Habeas Corpus in the spring of 1817, the radical reformer Sir Francis Burdett (once imprisoned in the Tower of London for supporting violent political agitation) attacked Wilberforce. Burdett said he was "astonished at the concurrence in this measure of an honourable and religious gentleman who lays claim to a superior piety." In a voice dripping with sarcasm, Burdett repeatedly taunted Wilberforce. Over and over again, he used the phrase "honourable and *religious*" – quite contrary to the rules of order for the House of Commons. This prompted cries of "order, order!" throughout the legislative chamber.

Wilberforce had not planned to speak, but he had heard enough. He rose, was called upon by the Speaker, and, according to Henry Brougham, unleashed a "strain of sarcasm which none who heard it can ever forget."

Facing Burdett, Wilberforce turned the tables in an instant, a feat which both surprised and delighted most of the members then present. He told Burdett that he was deceiving himself if he thought that in censuring religion he was morally superior – when, in fact, his conduct showed him to be a man of small character. As a parting shot, he said that those who talked loudest in their professions of love and admiration for the British constitution were often driven by ulterior motives if not a true contempt for it.

That Wilberforce had so quickly and so completely over-matched Burdett amazed everyone. Sir Thomas Acland stated that when the diminutive Wilberforce turned and spoke directly to Burdett (who was much taller), a complete role reversal ensued. Wilberforce looked like "a giant dangling a dwarf."

One MP whispered in astonishment to Samuel Romilly that Wilberforce's display surpassed even Pitt, who when living was the acknowledged master of sarcasm in debate. In reply, Romilly said: "It is the most striking thing I ever heard. But I look upon it as a more singular proof of Wilberforce's virtue than his genius, for who but he was ever possessed of such a formidable weapon and never used it!"

After hearing Canning's impressive performance, Wilberforce had returned home and gone to bed, feeling ill. At first no one thought it particularly serious, but it was soon clear that he had suffered a recurrence of the inflammation of the lungs that had threatened him the previous year. Despite the deep anxiety of his family and a very slow recovery, Wilberforce felt a remarkable measure of peace and even gratitude under these trying circumstances. He kept saying to those who watched by his bedside: "No man has been more favoured than I, for even when I am ill, my complaints occasion little suffering."

Touchingly, he called one of his young sons to him. Scarcely able to speak he whispered, "At this moment I have your face before me when I left you [as a boy] at school in Leicestershire."

Wilberforce would not return to the House of Commons for eight weeks. Before being confined to his sickbed, Wilberforce had heard of the death of John Smith. Smith, a methodist missionary to slaves, had died in prison in Demerara after a trial during which he had been wrongfully charged with inciting an insurrection. Wilberforce was not the only one to be greatly grieved by Smith's death. In the eyes of many, Smith became an antislavery martyr.

Once he was well, Wilberforce resolved to take up Smith's case in Parliament. Though he did not know it, this would be the last major issue he would take up in the House of Commons. At the same time, he ardently supported three other important legislative initiatives: the establishment of the National Gallery (of art), the formation of Trustee Savings Banks, and the birth of the organization that eventually became the Royal Society for the Prevention of Cruelty to Animals – or RSPCA.

On June 1, 1824, Wilberforce went to the House of Commons for the debate on the Smith case. Expectations ran high among those who thronged the Visitor's Gallery. Perhaps this would be the last time he ever spoke in the House and the last time as well that he would plead the cause of the slaves. This proved not to be true on both counts, as things turned out. Many MPs were out watching a balloonist named Graham make an ascent. There were not enough members present in the House for a quorum, and it was adjourned.

On the day of the adjourned debate, Wilberforce had gone to his brother-in-law James Stephen's house for three or four hours' rest. He hoped to be quiet and reflect on the topics of his intended speech. He was deeply frustrated when he experienced difficulty remembering his topics; and when he spoke, he made what he described as "sad work" of his speech. Upon further reflection, he wrote, "I greatly doubt if I had not better give up taking part in the House of Commons."

Ten days later Wilberforce spoke again when debate on the Smith case recommenced. In a brief speech he appealed to the government not to trust that colonial governments in the British West Indies would take steps to alleviate slavery. The government's plan would call upon the colonial assemblies to imitate a model to be set up in Trinidad. Wilberforce considered this "hopeless and dangerous.... If mischief happens, as I fear, it will not be chargeable on me." He spoke directly to this concern:

The West Indians abhor … the end we have in view, and the means by which we hope to reach it. They frankly avow that from the emancipation of their slaves they look for inevitable ruin; whilst all their prejudices are revolted by each of our remedial measures.

If they agreed with us as to our grand object, we might hope to lessen by degrees their aversion to our several steps.… Were those measures singly acceptable to them, we might hope gradually and almost insensibly to lead them to our end. But what can we hope, when they abhor alike both means and end? It is with reluctance and pain I come forward, but I esteem it my bounden duty to protest against the policy on which we are now acting.

These were the last words Wilberforce uttered in the House of Commons. Ten days later, after attending a meeting, he became gravely ill once more. Upon reaching Lord Gambier's, he was "but just able to be helped upstairs to bed."

His health was so shattered that absolute rest was prescribed, and he remained in bed for almost a month. As soon as he could be moved safely, Wilberforce and his family took possession of a new home on Uxbridge Common, called "the Chestnuts."

Built in the early 1700s this "gentleman's residence" – with its ivy-covered walls and Greek-columned entrance – was situated on about five and a half acres of grounds.* These included an ornamental woodland and a walled kitchen garden with a "fernery" at one end. The house itself was of Georgian design and commanded fine views of Hillingdon House Park. Within was a handsome entrance hall and library, a double drawing-room and dining room, eight principal bedrooms, and quarters for resident housekeepers and other servants.

---

*The descriptive information about the Chestnuts has been supplied by London archivist John Fricker.

Elsewhere on the grounds were the stables, comprised of four stalls, a loose box and two coach houses. The coachman's quarters "over" included a kitchen, three bedrooms and large loft.

At the Chestnuts, Wilberforce lived in entire seclusion, a great trial for a man who so loved company. Some nights he would have family readings after tea, and William Robertson's *History of America* (long a favorite text) would be read. Wilberforce also confessed to his diary that he longed to write another religious book. "I have also a wish," he wrote, "to write something political; my own life, and Pitt's too, coming into the discussion."

Wilberforce did later dictate an autobiographical manuscript (apparently to one of his daughters) that covered the years from his birth to 1793. He also dictated other, relatively brief recollections to his sons Robert and Samuel and to his friends Joseph John Gurney and John Harford. He wrote a few brief memoranda about his early life and other significant events of his political career, but these were all he was able to produce.

He was more successful in writing *A Sketch of William Pitt* – an important, albeit unfinished essay, which was discovered in an unused cupboard more than sixty years after his death. It featured brief but important discussions of some tenets of Wilberforce's political philosophy and firsthand accounts of significant events that occurred during the early years of Pitt's premiership.

At the request of his physician, Dr. William Chambers, Wilberforce and his wife journeyed to Bath to rest and receive whatever medicinal benefits the city's celebrated mineral waters could afford. The Wilberforces remained there until late November. For the Christmas holidays, the Wilberforces returned to the Chestnuts.

Here Wilberforce looked forward to having his children around him "according to the good old English custom." "I lay no little stress," he said, "on the bringing together at Christmas all the members of the family if it can be effected. Such an anniversary, annually observed, tends to heal any little divisions, and to cherish mutual attachment."

Everyone stayed through the New Year, and Wilberforce delighted in seeing "our dear boys living in much harmony. What cause have I for gratitude, seeing my five children, my [eldest] son's wife, and two grandchildren all round my table!"

No man, Wilberforce's sons later wrote, lived "in more perpetual sunshine" than their father, yet there was, nonetheless, "a deep vein of pathos which mingled with his [happy] temper, not perceived perhaps by the superficial eye, but discernible to close observers in his great tenderness of spirit."

Wilberforce once spoke of this to his old friend Thomas Babington (the uncle of Thomas Babington, Lord Macaulay): "I sometimes think that I have the art (though I am sure undesignedly) of concealing from my most intimate associates my real character. One particular I doubt if you have ever observed. I ought ... to say that it is not constant: *but I am at times much more disposed to melancholy* than you would imagine."

Wilberforce was subject to emotional and physical duress in times of great strain. One example was his dark night of the soul, when he was first forced to begin taking opium in 1788. Another was his great grief and serious sickness following the devastating defeat of his slave trade abolition bill in 1796. Babington and Wilberforce's other close friends, however, were probably aware of this periodic tendency to melancholy. Certainly Isaac Milner was, who had so often treated him in times of illness.

Throughout his autumn sojourn in Bath, Wilberforce had been seriously reflecting about the question of his retirement. The severe attacks of the previous spring and summer had weakened him considerably. Still, he found the idea of retiring, especially from the fight to secure emancipation, very painful.

He did not wish to be in action for its own sake, however. Three years previously he had written in this vein to the noted philosopher Thomas Chalmers. "To express my sentiments briefly," he said, "I may say that I more and more enter into the spirit of that beautiful sonnet of Milton's on his blindness, ending,

Who best
Bear his mild yoke, they serve him best –
They also serve who only stand and wait.

⁓

During that same autumn of 1824, Sir John Sinclair, the eminent agriculturist, suggested an arrangement to Wilberforce that might make it easier for him to continue in public life: the prospect of accepting a peerage and taking his place as a member of the House of Lords. Sinclair knew that Wilberforce would resist the idea of a peerage in the traditional sense, for his eldest son, William, was unsteady at best (he would later lose most of the family fortune). A traditional peerage would mean that William Wilberforce Jr. would inherit a title with duties for which he was not prepared and could not responsibly discharge.

Sinclair came up with a wise and appealing alternative. The remainder associated with Wilberforce's title, should he choose to take it, would pass to heirs born after the date it was given. Because Wilberforce would have no more children, he would in essence be receiving a life peerage, though the patent granting it would not in fact say so.

Wilberforce was moved by Sinclair's gesture, but gently refused it.

To your friendly suggestion respecting changing the field of my parliamentary labours, I must say a word or two, premising that I do not intend to continue in public life longer than the present parliament.

I will not deny that there have been periods in my life, when on worldly principles the attainment of a permanent, easy, and quiet seat in the legislature, would have been a pretty strong temptation to me. But, I thank God, I was strengthened against yielding to it. For (understand me rightly) as I had done nothing to make it naturally come to me, I must have endeavoured to go to it; and this would have been carving for myself – if I may use the expression, much more than a Christian ought to do.

Sinclair could not have known it, but Wilberforce was being extremely forthright with him in this letter. As early as 1782, four years before Wilberforce's Great Change, there had been rumors that he would be granted a peerage. Hopes for a peerage at that time had died along with Lord Rockingham, the prime minister who would have obtained it for him. As Wilberforce himself later admitted, however, it would have been an easy thing for him to obtain a peerage had he ever wanted one.

The rejection of a peerage shows the importance Wilberforce placed on keeping promises. Early in his political career, he had joined a group called the Independents, a club of about forty members of the House of Commons, most of whom were opponents of the Fox-North coalition ministry, whose principle of union was a resolution not to accept a plum appointment to political office, a government pension, or the offer of hereditary peerage. Yet, as Wilberforce's sons report, "in a few years so far had the fierceness of their independence yielded to various temptations, that [our father] and [Henry] Bankes alone of all the party retained their early simplicity of station. [Our father] was the only county member [of Parliament] who was not raised to the peerage."

Wilberforce had explained this some years before in a letter to his friend and constituent Samuel Roberts. He felt he had acted most faithfully as an MP for Yorkshire by not using his high position to benefit his relatives. It would have been tempting to do so, for among his relatives were several with large families "reduced from great affluence to entire destitution by commercial misfortunes." In fact, Wilberforce had once angered his mother, who had written to him asking favors for relatives on her side of his family. Lastly, he had never used his position as "a means of aggrandizing myself or my [immediate] family."

Wilberforce then explained why this prospect had at times appealed so strongly to him. "When you consider on the one hand, that more than half of the present House of Lords has been created or gifted with their tides ... since I came into Parliament, and on the other that my intimacy with Mr. Pitt for so many years [would] have rendered it not difficult for me to obtain such an elevation, you may assign more weight to this circumstance than at first sight might appear to you to be due to it."

He continued:

> I remember [William] Cobbett (commenting on this subject with his usual fairness) observed that my pride was more gratified by being MP for Yorkshire than by receiving a peerage from any minister....
>
> I will not deny all force to the remark; but I can assure him that this pride would never have had the effect of preventing my accepting a seat in the House of Lords – they were principles of a very different and far higher order which produced that operation.

Wilberforce discussed these principles in subsequent correspondence with two of his Clapham circle colleagues, James Stephen and Thomas Babington. To Stephen he said: "I have always thought that it would be an instance of conduct truly Christian [and] suited to our times for a man to retire voluntarily from such a situation as mine without a peerage.... You reckon little of this of which I think very much." To Babington he wrote, "It appears to me to be a consideration of no small moment [that] ... a Christian ... should determine the remainder of his life without being biased by a great worldly situation.... Quietly retiring to a private life instead of a peerage does seem an action which ... it is right to do in such a manner and at such a time that it may not be misconstrued."

Wilberforce wished, as he had always done, to retain his political independence. But he also wished to set an example by making it perfectly clear that a peerage was not why he had remained in political life.

Neither was it what he expected as a reward for his service on behalf of the county of Yorkshire. He had done so because he believed that God had called him to use the talents, gifts, and opportunities with which he had been blessed. He had tried to dedicate his life to the ideal that it was "the true duty of every man to promote the happiness of his fellow-creatures to the utmost of his power." Wilberforce could do so most effectively, he believed, in the House of Commons, not the House of Lords.

Wilberforce summed up how he felt about being given a hereditary peerage following a visit with the Prince of Wales at the Royal Pavilion in Brighton in 1815. Stephen had playfully taunted him saying, "You will live to be a peer at last." Wilberforce replied:

> No, my dear Stephen, I ... shall go out of the world plain William Wilberforce.... I seldom have had less reason to be dissatisfied with that less dignified style: I mean in the degree of civility or even respect to which even plain W.W. may be deemed entitled. For really, had I been covered with titles and ribbons, I could not have been treated [while at the pavilion] with more real, unaffected, unapparently condescending, and therefore more unostentatious civility.

～

Wilberforce's reluctance to retire completely from Parliament in 1824, as with his reluctance to accept a peerage, also stemmed from motives of humility. His sons wrote, "It was not so much that he wished to do more, as that he regretted he had done so little."

Wilberforce spoke of this in a letter to his young friend John Harford.

> When I consider that my public life is nearly expired ... I am filled with the deepest compunction from the consciousness of my having made so poor a use of the talents committed to

my stewardship. The heart knows its own bitterness. We alone know ourselves the opportunities we have enjoyed, and the comparative use we have made of them....

To your friendly ear ... I breathe out my secret sorrows. I might be supposed by others to be fishing for a compliment. Well, it is an unspeakable consolation that we serve a gracious Master, who giveth liberally and upbraideth not.

This sense of sadness over missed opportunities lingered. A year later, in October 1825, Wilberforce spoke of it in a letter to his Quaker friend and fellow abolitionist Joseph John Gurney. His eyes were troubling him, he wrote,

but were they ever so strong I should wear them out, were I to attempt to give expression to [my] sentiments and feelings.... Let us rejoice and bless God that we live in a land in which we are able to exert our faculties in mitigating the sufferings, redressing the wrongs, and above all, promoting the best interests of our fellow-creatures.

I sometimes fear we are not sufficiently thankful for this most gratifying and honourable distinction.... I feel this the more strongly ... for ... so far as I can recollect ... I always spoke and voted according to the dictates of my conscience, for the public and not for my own private interest.... Yet I am but too conscious of numerous and great sins of omission, many opportunities of doing good either not at all or very inadequately improved.

Wilberforce's great sense of responsibility was once observed by Lord Clarendon, who told Wilberforce's sons,

I was with [your father] once when he was preparing to make an important motion in the House of Commons. While he was most deeply engaged, a poor man called, I think his name was Simkins, who was in danger of being imprisoned for a small debt. He could find no one to [vouch] for him.

[Your father] did not like to become [Simkins' benefactor] without inquiry; it was contrary to a rule which he had made; but nothing could induce him to send the man away. "His goods," [your father] said, "will be sold, and the poor fellow will be totally ruined." I believe, at last, [your father] paid the debt himself; but I remember well the interruption which it gave to his business, which he would not resume till the case was provided for.

Wilberforce later told Sir Thomas Fowell Buxton "that public men ... should consider it one of the duties imposed on them by Providence, to receive and inquire into the case of distressed persons." Wilberforce's colleague Lord Erskine later affirmed that throughout his political career Wilberforce faithfully acted upon this principle. Erskine wrote that through his many daily charities, as much as by his public conduct, Wilberforce had "urged on the lingering progress of the human mind."

Wilberforce's decision to retire became final when he learned that while his physician, Dr. William Chambers, would not absolutely prohibit him from attending the House of Commons, he nonetheless asserted that if Wilberforce were to suffer another attack of inflammation of the lungs, he might not have the strength to survive it.

Wilberforce then wrote to Buxton "as my parliamentary executor," asking him to move the writ of abdication through which he would resign his seat in Parliament. Buxton was deeply touched and responded in a manner that showed how wisely Wilberforce had chosen his successor.

"I feel it just about the highest honour I could have," Buxton wrote to a friend, "and yet it gives me unaffected pain, from a consciousness of my inability to be his successor. I must, however, labour hard, and [see] how far labour [might replace] his talents and reputation.... Well, only one thing is absolutely necessary to do some good, and that is pure and fervent determination to do my duty in private and in public."

Wilberforce announced his retirement from politics on February 22, 1825. On that day his sense of melancholy had lifted, even as the morning fog had given way to a warm, sunny day that hinted at the promise of spring. His diary captured his feelings: "Foggy in the morning, but it cleared up and became delightful. The sun [was] full out all day. The bees [were] seduced to fly about into the crocus cups. The blackbirds [were] singing."

The news of Wilberforce's retirement was received with mixed feelings. The Poet Laureate Robert Southey, long a Wilberforce friend, spoke for many when he wrote: "I will not say that I am sorry for it, because I hope you have retired in time, and will therefore live the longer as well as more for yourself ... [the] House 'will not look upon your like again.'"

Others lamented the loss of Wilberforce's authority on moral and religious questions. His parliamentary colleague Joseph Butterworth had written:

> After the arduous services in which you have been engaged for so many years, a little repose must be very desirable for the sake of your health, for the comfort of your family, and for the tranquillity of your own mind.... Lord Coke says, "every man is a debtor to his profession," yet I do not think you are now any debtor to the public whom you have so long, so faithfully, so disinterestedly, so beneficially served.
>
> It must be a satisfaction to you to have observed, that the moral tone of the House of Commons, as well as of the nation at large, is much higher than when you first entered upon public life.... There can be no doubt that God has made you the honoured instrument of contributing much to this great improvement. There are, I hope, some young men of promise coming forward, but ... would that there were many Elishas on whom your mantle might fall.

⌐

One of Wilberforce's American friends, William Buell Sprague, was an early American author of note. In 1855 Sprague published a book called *Visits to European Celebrities*, a series of detailed vignettes about many of Europe's most distinguished men and women. Included was a chapter describing a memorable visit to Wilberforce at his home, Highwood Hill, near Hendon, not long after Wilberforce's retirement from Parliament in 1825.

Sprague had very nearly missed the opportunity for a visit, as he was ready to leave London for America. But when he learned that Wilberforce's home was only about ten miles distant from his lodgings, "it took me but a moment to decide that I would not leave without doing my utmost to obtain an interview with him."

Sprague's impressions afford a rare glimpse of Wilberforce's domestic life. He described Highwood Hill as "a large stone building, situated on a delightful eminence, overlooking a fine valley beneath.... Everything around it, though perfectly simple, showed exquisite taste and the very perfection of culture. The place seemed ... quite in keeping with the character of its illustrious occupant."

After delivering his letter of introduction to Wilberforce's servant, Sprague and his friend Joshua Wilson were taken through the drawing room into the library until Wilberforce could receive them. Upon receiving permission to look into some of the books, they discovered that each one they picked up contained "notes which Mr. Wilberforce had made with his pen and pencil [while] reading them." Sprague noted that not a few books had been presented to Wilberforce by the authors themselves.

When Wilberforce entered the room, Sprague was struck by his personal appearance. "Being very near-sighted, [Mr. Wilberforce] took his [eye] glass, which was suspended from his neck, and looking me in the face, asked if I was the gentleman from America.... On being answered in the affirmative, he gave me his hand in the most affectionate manner, and welcomed me to the country and his house."

Wilberforce immediately revealed his own excitement at receiving a visitor from America by asking Sprague if he had made arrangements to stay for the entire day. Wilberforce had long considered Britain and America to be "members of the same family" and throughout his life was most grateful for any visitors from the United States or news from there.

When Sprague informed Wilberforce that he was obliged to dine later that day in London, Wilberforce urged him to come and pass another day with him before leaving the neighborhood. Sprague regretfully told him this would be impossible as he was leaving the country in two days. Wilberforce then "expressed great astonishment that I should go so soon, and went into quite an argument with me to induce me to change my purpose."

Sprague was so taken with Wilberforce's appearance that he described it for a second time at greater length.

> Mr. Wilberforce's personal appearance was altogether peculiar. He was small in stature, extremely rapid in his movements, very nearsighted, and crooked almost to deformity. I can hardly say what his countenance would have been in a state of repose, for I think I had no opportunity of seeing it in that state; but in conversation it seemed perfectly radiant with intelligence and benignity. He soon took us to the window and pointed out the beauties of the surrounding scenery, in which nature and art seemed both to have done their utmost.

After several minutes, Wilberforce said, "I am wronging my family in the other room by monopolizing your company." He immediately took Sprague and Wilson into the drawing room where he introduced them to one of his sons and one of his daughters.

While sitting in the drawing room, Sprague's attention was drawn "to the most splendid set of china that I ever saw." Wilberforce noticed his fascination and, taking up several pieces, pointed out some of their features. Sprague then asked from what country the china came. Wilberforce replied modestly, "Why, to tell the truth, it is a present to me from the King of Prussia." What he did not tell Sprague was that the King of Prussia had sent him this splendid set of Dresden china in gratitude for his unremitting efforts to provide relief for Prussians suffering from the hunger and destruction brought on during the long war against Napoleon, during which Prussia and Britain had been allies.

At one point, Sprague remarked that Wilberforce's health "seemed more vigorous than I had expected." Wilberforce said that he had "great reason to be thankful that he had such a measure of health; for his life had been little else but a struggle with disease and debility; and Dr. [Richard] Warren, one of the most eminent physicians in London, had told him, more than forty years before, that he had not stamina enough to last a fortnight."

Wilberforce then mentioned several American religious writers "in terms of very high respect," in particular Dr. Timothy Dwight, the much-regarded president of Yale who was a grandson of Jonathan Edwards. Sprague noted that Dwight's "writings seemed to be familiar to Wilberforce." Sprague was "glad to tell him that his regard for Dr. Dwight was most fully reciprocated," as he had "more than once heard the Doctor mention him with most affectionate respect in his lectures to his pupils."

Wilberforce then presented Sprague with a copy of *A Practical View of Christianity*, "splendidly bound, and containing a very kind inscription with his own hand.... As he gave it to me, he remarked that it was a book which he wrote many years before – soon after it pleased God to open his eyes, and bring him to a knowledge of the truth."

Wilberforce also told Sprague that he "had great reason to be thankful that [his book] had been in some degree useful; that soon after it was published he sent a copy of it to [Edmund] Burke, who, in acknowledging it, said that he approved it most cordially."

Sprague had enjoyed his visit that morning with Wilberforce greatly. "I can truly say," he wrote, "that I never parted with a human being with my mind more filled with grateful and reverential recollections. I had a long letter from [Wilberforce] after my return home, which I treasure as a precious memorial of one of the noblest spirits of his own or any other age."

⌐

Wilberforce's retirement commenced with the most pleasant of dilemmas: how to gratify the wishes of "the multitude of friends who affectionately claimed a share of his first year of leisure." He decided to pay a series of "touch-and-go visits" to his friends, including one to Dropmore, where he was received very kindly by his old abolitionist colleague Lord Grenville.

The two old friends walked together for an hour before and after dinner. Wilberforce was grieved to see that Grenville had become rather feeble, but their conversation was animated enough. They discussed philosophy, a favorite subject for both. Grenville said he had profited more from Aristotle's *Rhetoric* than any other work. This Wilberforce knew, for some years before he had written an appreciative "Review of Lord Chatham's *Letters to a Nephew*," a work Grenville had edited and introduced. Aristotle's *Rhetoric* had been discussed prominently in this book.

As the visit continued, Grenville also critiqued the ideas of human understanding advocated by John Locke, who taught that objects of knowledge are ideas. Grenville supported instead the views of Common Sense school philosopher Thomas Reid and his disciple Dugald Stewart, who taught that objects of perception, not unrelated ideas, are those that really exist. It must have been a fascinating dialogue.

Wilberforce was well acquainted with the teachings of Stewart, and Locke was an author he had known and read for many years. Indeed, Wilberforce often read the writings of Enlightenment philosophers, sometimes more than one at a time. Many years before, on October 18, 1798, he had written in his diary "[I am] engaged in reading Locke with my wife and sister, Coxe's *Life of [Robert] Walpole* [and] Montesquieu."

After leaving Grenville's home at Dropmore, Wilberforce's brief visits continued. To Thomas Gisborne, his friend since their college days at Cambridge, he wrote apologizing for not being able to stay longer. Such visits were all too short, he wrote, but they were "better than not doing homage to [my friends'] lairs at all, especially in your instance, under whose roof I formerly spent months of tranquil, and ... friendly enjoyment, which can never be forgotten."

Each excursion prompted a similar reflection. It was with a grateful and cheerful spirit that Wilberforce visited friends and favorite locales of days long past.

In the early summer of 1825 he stayed for some time at his old seaside residence at Sandgate. He visited the cliffs of Dover and viewed the "wild beasts" kept there in a zoo. He returned with his old college friend Gerard Noel "and two of his daughters in his landau, [drawn by] little black Swiss horses – [sometimes] walking part of the way." It was a beautiful night for riding, with a "full moon and not a cloud – [the] sea-view magnificent."

By October 12 Wilberforce's delightful round of visits had ended and he now journeyed to Bath to receive mineral-water therapy treatments. Thankful for the treatments Bath afforded, he nonetheless chafed at the thought of the incessant callers he inevitably faced while there. Of "all places in the world" he wrote, Bath afforded him the least uninterrupted time. "You are required to second the influence of the waters before, between, and after the glasses, by a liberal quantity of air and exercise.... If in despite of the doctors, you go to your desk, you cannot write for five minutes without a rat-a-tat by the knocker, reminding you that you are in a large city.... [And in Bath] it is the practice to carry on most diligently an incessant system of calling."

One of the pleasures to which Wilberforce was now able to devote more time was reading novels. On October 17 he began having his friend Sir Walter Scott's *The Heart of Mid-Lothian* read to him in the afternoons and evenings. His interest in this "beautiful" work was such that he pronounced the book "much the best of [Scott's] novels that I have heard. Jeanie Deans [is] a truly Christian character."

Wilberforce had met Scott in February 1821. Those in attendance at this dinner party, hosted by Sir Robert Inglis, included former prime minister Lord Sidmouth (Henry Addington) as well as Wilberforce's friend and political protégé Sir Thomas Acland. Harford, with whom Wilberforce had taken a coach to attend this dinner, recalled that "Mr. Wilberforce much enjoyed this meeting with Sir Walter, and the pleasure appeared to be mutual."

Scott was arguably Wilberforce's favorite novelist – and a poet whose skill he greatly admired. He considered Scott's works "full of genius." He had been reading them for years prior to their meeting in 1821. More allusions to Scott's works appear in his diaries than to that of any other novelist. In July 1810 Wilberforce had written to his old friend Lord Muncaster:

> Have you read [Scott's poem] *The Lady of the Lake?* ... I did not think that I continued in such a degree subject to the fascination of poetry. I have been absolutely bewitched. I could not keep the imaginary personages out of my mind when I most wished to remove them. How wonderful is this dominion over the heart which genius exercises! There are some parts of the poem that are quite inimitable – all that precedes and follows [the line:] *"And Saxon, I am Roderick Dhu."*

Before being enchanted by *The Lady of the Lake*, Wilberforce had read Scott's epic poems *Marmion* and *Rokeby*. Other novels by Scott that captured his fancy included *Waverly*, *Peveril of the Peak*, *The Fortunes of Nigel*, *Old Mortality*, and *Rob Roy*.

After "running over" *The Fortunes of Nigel*, Wilberforce pronounced it

> the best, I mean the most moral in its tendency, of any of Walter Scott's stories which I have heard, illustrating the ways of Providence, the character of men of the world, and their

unfeeling selfishness.... It is strange how much Nigel has haunted me while reading it.... I am extremely interested by it ... partly because I consider it all as substantially true, giving the account of the manners and incidents of the day.... [It has] some admirable strokes of nature and character.

Wilberforce continued to visit friends he had not seen for a long time. On July 26, 1826, he dined with several Quaker friends and abolitionist colleagues at Samuel Hoare's in Hampstead. The party included Dr. and Mrs. Stephen Lushington and chemist William Allen. Wilberforce and Allen had known one another for many years, and Allen's philanthropies were considerable in their own right. Wilberforce rejoiced to hear that Allen "still goes on doing good."

That evening Joanna Baillie, author of the best-selling novel *Orra*, joined the party. As the conversation continued, Wilberforce was briefed on Lushington's efforts to improve conditions among West Indian slaves. Always able to be immediately stirred by a discussion of slavery, he later told his diary "what a glorious thing it is for a man to be a member of a free country!"

One other part of the evening's conversation stood out. Lushington and Baillie were asked if they believed in a particular providence. "Yes," they replied, "on great occasions."

This prompted one of Wilberforce's brief but cogent observations. Dipping his quill pen into the inkwell once again, he wrote that Lushington and Baillie's response was "as unphilosophical as (it is) unscriptural – must not the smallest links be as necessary for maintaining the continuity [of the world], as the greatest? Great and little belong to our littleness, but there is no great and little to God."

⌒

Early in 1827, Wilberforce found himself yearning to see the friends and places of childhood he so loved in Yorkshire. It had been almost twenty years since he had passed through his native county, and he felt that if he did not seize an opportunity now to return, he might never do so again. He decided to take a six-month tour of Yorkshire, visiting every part.

With great pleasure Wilberforce renewed his acquaintance with his early haunts, including Yoxall Lodge, the home of Gisborne. His remarks to Stephen on this visit revealed that his love of nature had only grown with the passing years.

> Well as I thought I knew this place, and much as I had admired it, I never saw its riches displayed in such overflowing profusion. I never was here before till late in the year, or saw the first foliage of the magnificent oak contrast with the dark holly, the flowering gorse, and the horse chestnut. A fine tree always seems to me like a community in itself with the countless insects which it shelters and nourishes in its roots and branches. It is quite a merciful ordination of Providence, that the forests of our country to which as a maritime nation we look for protection and commerce should be so admirable for their beauty.

As his travels continued, encompassing as well the county of Derbyshire, Wilberforce's recollections of the past were interwoven with bittersweet thoughts of long departed friends. He thought of Pitt, who had been dead for more than twenty-one years. "My friends are daily dropping around me," he wrote to Hannah More. "The companions of my youth, then far stronger and more healthy than I was, are worn out, while I still remain."

To Thomas Babington he wrote,

> When you last wrote to me, you were under the influence of a feeling that has of late been often called into exercise with me also; that which is excited by seeing our old friends dropping off one after another while we are left behind. [And here he quoted from the tenth *Satire* of Juvenal:]
>
>> *Haec data poena diu viventibus ut renovata*
>> *Semper clade domus, multisque in luctibus, inque*
>> *Perpetuo maerore et nigra ves te senescant.*

[This punishment (is) given for a long time to those living,
that they might grow old, always renewed by destroyed home,
in many sorrows, I say, perpetually mourning and in somber
clothing.]

But how different are the emotions with which we may regard
the deaths of our mends from those of the heathen poet! And it
is one of the indirect rewards of such religious principles and
habits as lead us to select our mends from the excellent ones
of the earth, that we are not compelled to seek for comfort by
forgetting the companions of our choice that are taken from
us, but may follow them in our thoughts and sympathies into
that paradise into which we trust they have been received, and
may hope at no distant period to see them once more.

Far too often Wilberforce would inquire after contemporaries
only to hear, "Oh, he has been long gone" or "He died years ago."
Wilberforce marveled that "many far stronger and healthier than
I, died early, while I still survive in spite of Dr. Warren's statement thirty-nine years ago [that I had not the stamina to last a
fortnight]!"

For most of his tour, however, Wilberforce thoroughly enjoyed
himself. At Huddersfield, he met with a gentleman named Smart,
"an honest, warm-hearted shopkeeper, originally from Hull."
Smart said he remembered Wilberforce when they both had been
boys, and that he vividly recalled the ox Wilberforce had roasted
whole in one of his fields for prospective voters when first seeking
office in 1780.

On July 12 Wilberforce stopped in the town on Keighley for
a four-day visit. He had come to see his friend Theodore Dury,
but his arrival and his stature as "the African's friend" were cause
for a celebration by the whole town. A pink flag flew from the
church tower, and church bells pealed. Patrick Brontë, the father of
novelist sisters Anne, Charlotte, and Emily, was a friend of Dury's
and very likely was one of those who received a prized invitation
to the Keighley vicarage to meet Wilberforce.

If so, this would only have been fitting. For in addition to being Dury's friend, Brontë had important connections to Wilberforce in his own right. Early in 1804 Wilberforce had learned through his friend Henry Martyn (the great missionary pioneer) that Brontë, who had gained admission to Wilberforce's alma mater, St. John's College, was in great financial need. Wilberforce, who for many years had seized virtually every opportunity to sponsor the education of deserving young men, agreed to cover Brontë's expenses. Henry Thornton joined him in this patronage.

In the autumn of 1810 Brontë repaid Wilberforce's kindness in a way that lay very close to Wilberforce's heart – aiding a young man who had been wrongfully imprisoned. William Nowell of Daw Green had been arrested as an army deserter, taken from his parents' home, and committed to Wakefield prison. Nowell was innocent, for the only prosecution witness claimed that he had enlisted Nowell at an annual fair in the Dewsbury area. Nowell's parents had been to the fair, but he himself had not. He had a number of witnesses who could support his alibi.

At Nowell's committal, the magistrate had refused to accept their evidence or to allow time for additional witnesses to be summoned. Nowell was sent to prison and stayed there for ten weeks. An outcry in Dewsbury ensued, and Brontë led the effort to secure his release.

When Brontë's initial efforts did not bear fruit, he sought Wilberforce's aid. One of Brontë's friends, John Halliley, was sent to London with a letter for Wilberforce. Wilberforce and Halliley then went to the War Office to see Lord Palmerston (the future prime minister) and secure Nowell's release. Palmerston was not in. Wilberforce personally requested that Mr. Dawson, the magistrate in this case, reexamine the evidence. Dawson refused. Wilberforce then sought and obtained a personal interview with Palmerston. Wilberforce was successful and in early December Nowell was set free.

This story, from Wilberforce's perspective, affords other insights into his character. He had described this affair in his diary in a terse summary that was indicative of his resolve to see justice done: "Off early to London to the War Office about the boy Nowell unlawfully recruited.... Lord Palmerston [had] not yet read the minutes of the second examination which [was] decisive.... Off again next morning after breakfast to the Horse Guards where [I] talked to Lord Palmerston about the poor boy and got the necessary orders sent down for his discharge."

Yet about this time, even as he was interceding on Nowell's behalf, Wilberforce had also written in his diary: "Alas! I feel my uselessness and unprofitableness; but I humbly hope I desire to employ my faculties so as may be most for God's glory and my fellow-creatures' benefit."

A few weeks later he received news from his constituents that afforded him an unexpected pleasure regarding the Nowell affair. "I hear that I am likely to be popular now [in Yorkshire] amongst the West Riding clothiers about poor Nowell – the boy falsely enlisted. How this shows that God can effect whatever He will by means the most circuitous and the least looked for."

Palmerston himself was so moved by the evidence with which Wilberforce had furnished him that he wrote to Brontë: "Sir, Referring to the correspondence relative to William Nowell, I am to acquaint you ... that if the indictment which the lad's friends are about to prefer against James Thackray they shall establish the fact of his having been guilty of perjury, I shall be ready to indemnify them for the reasonable and proper expenses which they shall incur."

In 1823 a further point of connection between Brontë and Wilberforce occurred concerning the patronage of a school for women. Some of the most eminent philanthropists of the day, including Wilberforce and More, had consented to sponsor the Clergy Daughters School, a school to which Brontë sent his daughters. Thus Wilberforce not only sponsored Patrick Brontë's education, he was a sponsor for Brontë's daughters, who later wrote many classic novels, including *Wuthering Heights* and *Jane Eyre.*

Given all of this, it seems strange indeed that Wilberforce should have feelings of uselessness and unprofitableness. The best explanation is that he was so often busy facilitating charities, either by funding them or using his influence to establish them, that he seldom had a chance to step back and take stock of the good that was being done. Not that he should or would have done so for its own sake – keeping score, as it were, regarding his good works – but it is a measure of his selflessness that he was so busy pursuing good works that he really had no way of knowing the true extent of the good that he was able to do.

Nearly the last and one of Wilberforce's most gratifying visits was to Wentworth House, the home of his old political opponent Lord Fitzwilliam. When Wilberforce had first been elected member of Parliament for Yorkshire in 1784, it had been in defiance of the hereditary political interest Fitzwilliam commanded. He had been used to having great say in who became the two county members, if not essentially appointing them outright. Wilberforce's victory had been so decisive that Fitzwilliam had not even been allowed the recommendation of one county member. In light of this, Wilberforce told Stephen, "Lord Fitzwilliam might well have been forgiven if he had conceived an unconquerable antipathy to me."

Instead, Lord Fitzwilliam received Wilberforce with a cordiality and kindness that moved him profoundly. Wilberforce marveled that "in spite of all repelling principles" that had formerly stood between them, Fitzwilliam "behaved to me with an unaffected, unassuming friendliness, that at times has brought tears into my eyes."

None of his election triumphs probably ever meant more to him. Reflecting on this singular visit, he wrote, "It has really brought powerfully to my feelings that better state in which all misconstructions will be done away, and all truly good men will love one another."

CHAPTER 10

ABIDING ELOQUENCE

And faith receives the prize.
WILLIAM COWPER

After leaving Wentworth House, Wilberforce's tour was nearly finished. He had made thirty-six visits, and he noted with particular pleasure the many indications of an improved religious character among the clergy he had seen. As a whole he found these clerics to be "solid and Scriptural, not fanatical or tinctured with partiality." Wilberforce was always committed to ecumenism, and he was happy to see the decline of sectarianism: "a fault, by the way, which I never so well understood as of late years."

Wilberforce finished his tour on October 3 by "looking into R. Ramsden's Museum, and dropping a sovereign into his missionary box." He then traveled on to Northampton. The weather was beautiful, and it was a fine day for a homecoming. He reached Highwood Hill safely at half-past nine in the evening and rejoiced to find his family well.

The morning after his return, Highwood Hill was "delightful, dewy like autumn, but the sun full out and warm as summer." The day was a reflection of his own feelings. His sons observed that their father had entered old age and retirement with "the elasticity of youth, and the simplicity of childhood." Busy, social, and affable, he was the delight of old and young and readily joined in the "animated talk amongst the young hands" or among surviving friends.

Wilberforce's days were regularly spent. He rose soon after seven in the morning and spent the first hour and a half closeted for personal prayer and devotions. Then he dressed and had a book read to him for three quarters of an hour. At half-past nine he gathered his household for family worship – "always a great thing in his esteem."

During this time, Wilberforce read a portion of the Scriptures, generally from the New Testament. He then "explained and enforced it … with a natural and glowing eloquence, always with affectionate earnestness, and an extraordinary knowledge of God's word." Family prayers lasted about half an hour, following which Wilberforce sallied forth for a few minutes "to take the air and hear the thrushes sing."

He enjoyed this stroll exceedingly. On the morning of October 23, 1827, he wrote in his diary: "A delightful morning. [I] walked out and saw the most abundant dew-drops sparkling in the sunbeams on the [hills]. How it calls forth the devotional feelings in the morning when the mind is vacant from worldly business, to see nature pour forth, as it were, its song of praise to the great Creator and Preserver of all things."

From long years in parliamentary life, Wilberforce had been used to observing a late breakfast hour. Part of his dedication to this habit was his belief that it tended to give others time for morning prayer and meditation. Breakfast itself was prolonged and animated by conversation with friends who ate with him. It was not unusual for such discussions to last until noon.

After breakfast Wilberforce went to his study until 3:00 p.m., when the post call came. He commonly spent several hours writing letters. If these were finished, he would spend free time during this period of the day reading. He also contemplated writing a work on the epistles of Paul and a supplementary chapter for a new edition of A Practical View of Christianity. This good intention was defeated by weak health and increasing periods of poor eyesight.

When the post was gone, Wilberforce strolled into the garden, often humming to himself some favorite tune. Sometimes he was alone, other times in the company of friends or with his reader.

Alone or with a companion, he took great delight in "pacing up and down some sheltered sunny walk."

As he walked round his garden for an hour of daily exercise, he would interrupt conversation to collect flowers for pressing in books. He was fond of standing before a favorite gum cistus and gazing upon it. At such times he would point out the plant's harmony of tints and coloring. "He loved flowers," his sons recalled, "with all the simple delight of childhood. He would hover from bed to bed over his favourites; and when he came in, even from his shortest walk, deposited a few that he had gathered, safely in his room."

The fragrance of various flowers enchanted him as well. "How good is God to us!" he was often prompted to say. "What should we think of a friend who had furnished us with a magnificent house and all we needed, and then – coming in to see that all had been provided according to his wishes, should be hurt to find that no scents had been placed in the rooms? Yet so has God dealt with us. Surely flowers are the smiles of His goodness."

While on his garden walks, Wilberforce stayed until just before dinner, which took place late in the afternoon. After his early evening nap, he was ready to entertain, astonishing those who expected to see an old man on the decline.

These evenings were not often spent solely in conversation. A book was commonly suggested for family reading, its text affording ample opportunities for digression and illustration. This time was cause for great contentment. Wilberforce described one such evening in a letter to his son Robert.

> We went to prayers, and after about half an hour, surely well spent, we returned to the common room and renewed our reading, which I now stopped, finding how late it was, and being in the singularly favoured circumstances of an old fellow, who is allowed to say "Come or go, do this or do that," without the appearance of fretfulness.... We have been reading an article ... on [Edward] Gibbon and Madame de Stael,

and latterly also on Voltaire. You remember, I doubt not, the last sentence in Gibbon's *Autobiography*; I have engaged my young friend to write under it [Isaac] Watts's beautiful hymn, ending with the line – "Foretells a bright rising again."

In old age the consolation of hope is reserved for the tenderness of parents, who commence a new life in their children.

EDWARD GIBBON

SUMMER'S EVENING

How fine has the day been! how bright was the sun!
How lovely and joyful the course that he run;
Though he rose in a mist when his race he begun,
And there followed some droppings of rain:
But now the fair traveller's come to the west,
His rays are all gold, and his beauties are best;
He paints the skies gay as he sinks to his rest,
And foretells a bright rising again.

"This is one of [Watts'] *Hymns for Children*," Wilberforce told his son, "but surely it is for the children of God, for the heirs of glory … [whether] you compare it either in point of good sense, or imagination, or sterling value, or sustaining hope, with the considerations and objects which feed the fancy, or exercise the understanding or affections."

In the evenings during these years, Wilberforce's thoughts "commonly took on this color." After prayers as he walked up and down the room, he "would have read to him missionary accounts, and journals of what was done by foreign Christians. His sons recalled: "The midnight hour was his zenith, and like the beautiful cereus with all her petals expanded, he was then in full bloom."

As a younger man, Wilberforce had placed a high premium on intellectual conversation. He still loved such talks, but now found much pleasure as well from the society of "the simplest person who fears God." His playful humor was often displayed at such times. After hearing one sermon, he said, "Good old Mr. C. preached uniformly rapid – like a watch hand when the spring chain broke."

Wilberforce's love for music was as strong as ever. While hearing a performance of Handel's "Hallelujah Chorus," he was overpowered and "a flood of tears ensued." He wrote in his diary that the impression produced on his mind "remained throughout the day."

The love of books was still a consuming passion. Though because of his eyesight he could not read much or for very long, he could quickly "pick out the pith of most works" by rapidly glancing through their pages. There were few modern works that he did not thus run through or have read to him. Within two days of visiting a friend's house, he commonly knew "the full amount of its literary stores." His one great lament was that his "feeble eyesight prevented him from maintaining an accurate acquaintance with the great writers of antiquity."

Daniel Wilson, the Bishop of Calcutta, was one of many who recalled what Wilberforce was like during his last years.

> The nearer you observed him the more [he] appeared ... to be modest and lowly.... It required some management to draw him out in conversation, and therefore some of those who saw him only once, might go away disappointed. But if he was lighted up, and in a small circle, where he was entirely at his ease, his powers of conversation were prodigious.... [A] natural eloquence was poured out, strokes of gentle playfulness and satire fell on all sides, and the company were soon absorbed in admiration. It commonly took only one visit to gain over the most prejudiced stranger.

One writer came to Highwood Hill prejudiced against Wilberforce by some who had maligned his character. After spending two days at the house, she wrote to her sister:

No one could see him as I have done without being charmed. I wish I could send you something of what I have heard in the beautifully simple explanations that he gives every day of a chapter that he reads from the [New] Testament [or that] you could hear him reading, as he does, the poems in [Keble's] *Christian Year*. [His] sentiments and ideas [are] all so beautiful, and so true.... I think nothing more striking in him than that spirit of general benevolence which governs all that he says; joined to the extreme beauty of his voice, it does indeed make him appear to love whatever he speaks of ... he is a dear, good, admirable old man. I have been praying that I may be enabled to imitate whatever is imitable in this excellent being; his talents and attractions are not to be acquired, but is it not a cheering reflection that such principles as his may be gained by all?

In many ways, Wilberforce's years at Highwood Hill were happy, but even in retirement he encountered some trials. Upon settling there in 1825, he found that the parish church of Hendon (the one nearest his home) was too far away for him to easily attend or to adequately minister to the needs of the farmers and cottagers of Mill Hill – whose homes were adjacent to his own. Wilberforce described his feelings upon learning of this to Hannah More: "I could not lay my head on my pillow with a quiet conscience, if I were not to have done my best to secure for all my poor neighbours the blessings of Christian instruction, and ... pastoral care."

Together with his near neighbor and fellow evangelical Sir Stamford Raffles (a former governor of Singapore), Wilberforce planned to build a church. He then consulted with the Hendon parish vicar, Theodore Williams, who seemed supportive of the plan and would allow Raffles and Wilberforce to appoint a minister of their choosing.

There were warning signs, however, though these were not initially apparent. For Williams harbored a suspicion of evangelicals, even highly respected evangelical Anglicans like Raffles and Wilberforce.

Shortly before his death in 1826 Raffles learned more troubling news. Williams was heartily disliked by his parishioners, prone to violent outbursts, and deeply in debt. In 1823, during a dispute over burial fees, Williams had demolished a new tomb in the Hendon parish churchyard and scattered the materials in the road outside.

It was a highly offensive act. What is worse, and what Raffles probably also knew, this incident was part of a long-running dispute that involved the distribution of lucrative burial fees, which were supposed to be divided between the vicar and the parish. In 1814 Williams, who had maintained that the parish's share of this money was wasted at vestry meetings, refused to bury non-parishioners. An acrimonious suit followed, which was won by the vestry in consistory court.

One other piece of information about Williams provides a further window into his character: he kept a noted collection of potted coniferous trees in the handsome vicarage house where he resided on Parson Street. It was, in all likelihood, the only thing he was ever noted for.

Aside from this, it is clear that Williams was punctilious, combative, and uncharitable – jealous of his prerogatives and willing to suspect the worst in others. It is little wonder then, that Wilberforce took note of "the wretched spiritual state of the parish" after he took up residence at Highwood Hill.*

After Raffles' death, James Stephen's eldest son, James, took his place and worked with Wilberforce to build the church under an act that allowed the founder of a church the right to appoint the incumbent minister. As yet, there was no sign of trouble on the immediate horizon.

---

*This information about Hendon parish comes from T. F. T. Baker, ed., *A History of the County of Middlesex, Vol. 5*, (1976).

It was in 1829, however, that Williams turned his coat and became as thoroughly disagreeable in his dealings with Wilberforce as he had ever been in earlier years with the parishioners of Hendon. He was now violently opposed to the construction of Wilberforce's church at Mill Hill and the plan to appoint its first minister. He published a pamphlet falsely alleging that Wilberforce's purpose in building his church was in fact a scheme for his own and his family's financial gain – one launched under the guise of seeking to promote the spiritual welfare of his neighbors. Williams, always focused on money himself, imputed his own cupidity to others. He went still further. He began to preach against Wilberforce, saying Wilberforce was really disloyal to the Church of England and a promoter of dissent from it.

Wilberforce said that after forty-five years in public life, he was used to having false charges brought against him. "It would be strange," he wrote, "if I now regarded them." Still, he thought Williams' charges reckless enough to warrant a response in print, and on June 5, 1829, published an *Address to the Parish of Hendon*. Copies of this address are very scarce, but it was apparently a broadside or brief pamphlet.

As work on the church continued, John Sargent (whose daughter Emily had married Wilberforce's son Samuel) accidentally discovered that building costs were beginning to press somewhat heavily on his friend. He wrote to several of Wilberforce's old friends and members of his extended family asking for donations, a flood of which promptly rained down upon a grateful Wilberforce. These funds enabled the work to continue.

About the same time Wilberforce's family fortune sustained a heavy blow. In the spring of 1830 a large dairy farm run by his eldest son, William, failed. Wilberforce, trying to settle his unsteady son in a safe career as a gentleman farmer, had invested much of the family fortune in the project. William had chosen poor business partners, and Wilberforce soon learned that his son's debts were in excess of £50,000 – well over $13 million today.

Robert Wilberforce (1802–57), second son and biographer of William Wilberforce

The news could not have come at a worse time. Because he had invested so much of the family fortune, Wilberforce was in no position to provide further help for his son. It was also a time of great agricultural distress throughout Britain. In response, Wilberforce had reduced the rents of his Highwood Hill tenant-families (which had never been high), by 37 percent.

Several of Wilberforce's old friends now resolved to come together, combine contributions, and retire this enormous debt. Amazingly, Wilberforce's old political opponent Lord Fitzwilliam, with whom he had enjoyed such a cordial visit just three years before in 1827, offered to cover the entire debt himself. He discreetly approached a mutual friend with this offer. The friend, knowing Wilberforce only too well, told Lord Fitzwilliam that his munificent offer would be graciously declined. Wilberforce meanwhile, had already resolved to assume his son's debts, even if it meant leaving his beloved Highwood Hill.

This was in fact what happened. Early in 1831 Wilberforce, his family, and household servants – many of whom were almost family – left Highwood Hill. The estate and its great house would now be leased to generate income – a measure Wilberforce believed would allow him to leave his children "so much as to enable them to live in comfort." He now had no home of his own.

On March 16, 1831, Wilberforce described his feelings:

> I wished that you should receive from myself rather than from the tongue of rumour, tidings which sooner or later were sure to be conveyed to you, and which I know would give you pain. The loss [we have] incurred has been so heavy as to compel me to descend from my present level, and greatly to diminish my establishment.... The cup presented to me has some bitter ingredients.... What I shall most miss will be my books and my garden.... I own I do feel a little the not (for I know not how long, if ever) being able to ask my friends to take a dinner or a bed with me under my own roof.

Wilberforce also felt himself like the apostle Paul, who, among the many trials he endured in life, had "no certain dwelling place." Still the loss of his home was, he wrote, "not a great evil ... [as I have] so many kind friends who will be happy to receive [me]."

The kindness of friends notwithstanding, it was a bitter blow. As he prayed and reflected during walks along garden paths that were not his own, he arrived at the belief that this turn of events was in some way part of God's plan for his life. He had known chronic illness and difficulties of many kinds, but at this stage he could not think of why his life had been spared so long "except it be to show that a man can be as happy without a fortune, as with one."

Wilberforce saw it as a mercy that the loss of his home did not "take place till all my children were educated, and nearly all of

The village of East Farleigh, the second of Wilberforce's last residences after he lost his beloved home Highwood Hill, and where Robert Wilberforce served as rector

them [established in life] in one way or another." On another level, he felt that the timing of loss of his fortune had been providential. Before, he had been able for many years to support "charities of various kinds [which] were necessarily large." He believed there was "a special blessing on being liberal to the poor, and on the family of those who have been so." He concluded: "My children will fare better even in this world, for real happiness, than if I had been saving ... £20,000 or £30,000 of what has been given away."

The blessing was not long in coming. His second and third sons, Robert and Samuel offered Wilberforce "a delightful asylum" in their homes. He and Barbara would spend part of the year with Robert and his young family, the remainder of the year with Samuel and his. Samuel was then serving as a rector in the village of Brighstone on the Isle of Wight, while Robert served in the same capacity in the village of East Farleigh in Kent. "What better could we desire?" Wilberforce reflected. "A kind Providence has enabled me with truth to adopt the declaration of David, that goodness and mercy have followed me all my days."

Wilberforce described his feelings to his brother-in-law James Stephen. "We have now been here for about six weeks," he wrote from one of the rectories in which he resided. "How can I but rejoice rather than lament at a loss, which has produced such a result as that of bringing us to dwell under the roofs of our dear children, and witness their enjoyment of a large share of domestic comforts."

He wrote to Lady Olivia Sparrow in a similar vein:

[We have] great cause for thankfulness in being moored in our latter days in the peaceful haven which we enjoy, (after all my tossings during my long and stormy voyage in the sea of politics), under the roofs of our sons in Kent and in the Isle of Wight, relieved from all the worry of family cares, and witnessing the respectability, usefulness, and domestic happiness of those most dear to us.... It is really true ... that our heavy loss has led to the solid and great increase of our enjoyments.

⌐

Nearly one year earlier, on May 15, 1830, Wilberforce had faced a far more pleasant and satisfying task than contending with the loss of Highwood Hill: he was able once again to lend his voice to the cause of emancipation. He accepted an invitation to take part in a great meeting of the Anti-Slavery Society. It was the last time he was involved with any public abolitionist event in London. The meeting was held at the Freemason's Hall, where two thousand people crowded inside and hundreds had to be turned away at the door.

Thomas Clarkson, now one of the few surviving early champions of abolition, made a gracious speech nominating Wilberforce as chairman of the meeting: "I rise to make a proposition which I am sure will be agreeable to you all – it is, that my old friend and fellow-labourer, Mr. Wilberforce, be called to the chair. I may say that this chair is his natural and proper right in this Assembly. He

The rectory in the village of Brighstone, Isle of Wight, one of Wilberforce's last places of residence after leaving Highwood Hill

is entitled to it as the great Leader in our cause – as one who has always been foremost in its support."

Moved by Clarkson's great kindness, Wilberforce accepted the offer and paid tribute to his old friend. His voice had now grown weak, but his spirit and gratitude were undiminished.

Ladies and Gentlemen, I shall only remark to you ... that I could have been called to take this chair by no person more dear to me than my valued friend and fellow-labourer, for I wish to be known by no other name in this great cause.... The purpose for which we meet is great – it is urgent; and when I see those by whom I am surrounded – when I again meet my esteemed friend Mr. Clarkson in this cause – I cannot but look back to those happy days when we began our labours together; or rather when we worked together – (for he began before me) – and we made the first step towards that great object, the completion of which is the purpose of our assembling this day.

Wilberforce's brief but moving reentry into the public arena helped to set the stage for the general election of 1830. Yorkshire was now entitled to four members of Parliament; and four abolitionists, including Henry Brougham (a future Lord chancellor of England), were elected. Brougham wrote to tell Wilberforce that the election had "turned very much upon slavery; your name was in every mouth, and [toasts to] your health the most enthusiastically received."

In 1831 Wilberforce had decided that he would never again speak in public, as he considered himself truly retired. Two years later he was, however, persuaded to propose a petition against slavery at a public meeting while staying with his son Robert in Maidstone. Wilberforce did this on April 12, 1833.

Often considered his last significant act associated with redressing the wrongs suffered by African slaves, in reality it was his second-to-last act of this kind. "It was," wrote Wilberforce's sons, "an affecting sight to see the old man who had been so long the champion of this cause come forth once more ... and with an unquenched spirit, though with a weakened voice and failing body ... maintain for the last time the cause of truth and justice."

In this, his last public speech, Wilberforce declared: "I say, and say honestly and fearlessly, that the same Being who commands us to love mercy, says also, 'Do justice.'" His conclusion was moving. "I trust [I] now approach the very end of [my] career," he began. Suddenly, a ray of sunshine broke into the hall. He seized the moment. "The object [of emancipation] is bright before us, the light of heaven beams on it, and is an earnest of success."

In mid-May 1833 the recurrence of yet another chest ailment prompted Wilberforce and Barbara to travel to Bath for the mineral-water therapy that had in the past helped him regain his health. A week after their arrival Wilberforce learned from Zachary Macaulay that Lord Stanley, the new colonial secretary, had introduced a set of resolutions by which the British government hoped to end slavery in Britain's colonies. "Last night [slavery's] death-blow was struck," Macaulay wrote. "Stanley's allusion to you was quite overpowering and electrified the House."

Stanley had movingly quoted the words spoken in the New Testament by Simeon, who after years of faithful service in the temple of God had at last seen Christ: "Now lettest thou thy servant depart in peace ... for mine eyes have [finally] seen thy salvation" (Luke 2:29–30).

One month later, on June 19, Wilberforce received a visit from a young American abolitionist whose admiration for him bordered on hero worship: William Lloyd Garrison. Garrison had journeyed to England to inform Wilberforce that the American Colonization Society was a racist institution, unlike Wilberforce's earlier efforts to repatriate former slaves to Sierra Leone to right the injustice of slavery. Garrison's meeting with the grand old man of abolition would lead to the last act Wilberforce performed on behalf of African slaves.

Garrison had two interviews with Wilberforce, the first of which lasted three hours. When he was introduced, Garrison was greatly surprised at the smallness and frailty of his host. At the same time, he wrote that he had "instantly been struck with admiration to think that so small a body could contain so large a mind!" The moment made him think of a quatrain written by Isaac Watts:

> Were I so tall to reach the pole,
> Or grasp the ocean with my span,
> I must be measured by my soul;
> The mind's the standard of the man.

Wilberforce's head, Garrison recalled, "hung droopingly upon his breast, so as to require an effort of the body to raise it when he spoke.... His back had an appearance of crookedness; hence, in walking, he looked exceedingly diminutive." In earlier years, Garrison speculated, Wilberforce "was probably erect and agile;

but feeble health, long continued, has thus marred his person in the vale of time."

During their time together, Garrison related to Wilberforce all the prominent facts relating to a great controversy that had arisen concerning the American Colonization Society. American abolitionists and freed slaves in particular, he said, were grieved by seeing Wilberforce's name listed "among the friends of the Colonization Society."

Wilberforce explained that his commendation of the American Colonization Society was restricted to the colony at Liberia. Based on information he had received from another American, Elliott Cresson, he had been induced to believe that the colony was much like Sierra Leone, a British colony where former slaves had been accorded the rights and privileges of British subjects. Wilberforce explained that he had never regarded the American Colonization Society "as providing a remedy for slavery." Indeed, he "viewed with abhorrence the doctrine of the Society that slaves or former slaves could never be accorded equality with white Americans. He had "repeatedly contested that wicked position with Mr. Cresson, and told him that he considered it fundamentally false and unchristian."

Wilberforce was grieved to learn that Cresson had used his name (and restricted commendation of the Liberia colony) to endorse other goals of the American Colonization Society. Immediately he asked one of his sons to write down a series of questions to put to Cresson.

1. How far has Mr. Elliott Cresson made use of Mr. Wilberforce's name? Has he merely stated that Mr. Wilberforce approved of the colony as calculated to benefit Africa; or has he said that Mr. Wilberforce approves of the principle of the SOCIETY – namely, that the blacks ought to be removed for the advantage of America, as well as for their own?

2. Did Mr. Cresson (aware that it must be considered as the fundamental principle of the American Colonization Society,

that there is a difficulty, amounting to a moral impossibility, in the blacks and whites living together in prosperity and harmony, as members of the same free community) make it clear to these to whom he professed to state Mr. Wilberforce's sentiments, that the two classes MIGHT AND OUGHT TO LIVE TOGETHER, as one mutually connected and happy society?

3. Has Mr. Elliott Cresson made it publicly known in England, that the American Colonization Society has declared that it considers that colonization ought to be a *sine qua non* of emancipation?

Wilberforce then gave Garrison these questions "to make such use of them as [he] might think proper."

At Wilberforce's urgent request, Garrison visited him again the next morning. He ate a breakfast meal with Wilberforce and his family, which "was served in patriarchal simplicity." Afterward, Wilberforce showed that his intellect was as keen as ever. For between four and five hours, he and Garrison again discussed American slavery and the American Colonization Society. Wilberforce's mind, "seemed to be wholly unaffected by his bodily depression: it was ... studded with starry thoughts, in beautiful and opulent profusion."

Like so many others, Garrison was struck by Wilberforce's voice. It had, he wrote, "a silvery cadence." Describing other aspects of Wilberforce's appearance, Garrison noted that his face had "a benevolently pleasing smile, and his eye a fine intellectual expression. In his conversation he was fluent, yet modest; remarkably exact and elegant in his diction; cautious in forming conclusions; searching in his interrogations; and skillful in weighing testimony."

Other aspects of Wilberforce's character also captured Garrison's imagination. Four traits impressed him: dovelike gentleness, amazing energy, deep humility, and adventurous daring. "These," he wrote, "were mingled in the soul of Wilberforce."

Wilberforce's love for his wife was also clearly evident. He was deferentially attentive to her, and Garrison observed that "she could not drop her thimble or her cotton on the carpet but he would stoop down to find it, in spite of her entreaties [that he not do so]."

Another thing, Garrison wrote, "which [I] remarked with surprise and delight was, the youthful freshness and almost romantic admiration which [Wilberforce] cherished for natural scenery." During their interview, Wilberforce had been lying on a sofa, but toward its close he called for his shoes and proposed walking up and down a portion of his residence called the South Parade, in order "to point out some of the beauties of the landscape" in view from there. Garrison entreated Wilberforce not to make the effort, satisfying his desire by taking him to a front window from which Wilberforce pointed out "with considerable pleasure the house which [Alexander] Pope the poet occasionally occupied, and other interesting and beautiful objects."

Before leaving, Garrison sought to "tenderly and solemnly" impress Wilberforce with "the importance of his bearing public testimony against the American Colonization Society, if he was satisfied that its claims to the confidence and patronage of the British nation were preposterous and illusory; especially as he was constantly quoted as the friend and advocate of the Society." He left Wilberforce with copies of the fifteenth and sixteenth Reports of the American Colonization Society that he might "form an opinion of its true character."

Wilberforce read these reports and wasted no time in obtaining signatures for a written protest against British support of the American Colonization Society. It was made public in England and signed by a long list of abolitionists and members of Parliament that included Wilberforce, William Smith, Zachary Macaulay, William Evans, Samuel Gurney, George Stephen, Stephen Lushington, Thomas Fowell Buxton, William Allen, and Daniel O'Connell. Thus, Wilberforce completed his last act on behalf of the sons and daughters of Africa – an act on behalf of those enslaved in the United States – though he had never been there.

Later Garrison reflected on his interview with Wilberforce. It was, he wrote, "too delightful and too important ever to be forgotten by me – I bade him farewell, expressing my fervent wishes for a long continuance of his valuable life, and my hope to meet him in that world of glory where change, and decay, and separation are unknown."

⁓

On July 11, Wilberforce received a visit from an old and dear friend, the Quaker Joseph John Gurney. During the last two decades of his life, Wilberforce and his family had often visited the Gurneys, who were related by marriage to Wilberforce's parliamentary successor in the fight to end slavery, Thomas Fowell Buxton. This meeting would be their last.

Entering Wilberforce's upstairs apartment in Bath, Gurney found him reclining on a sofa, with his feet wrapped in flannel. They talked about matters of faith. Wilberforce told Gurney that the biblical text on which he was then most prone to dwell, and from which he was deriving peculiar comfort, was a passage in the epistle to the Philippians: "Be careful for nothing, but in every thing by prayer and supplication, with thanksgiving, let your requests be made known unto God; and the peace of God which passeth all understanding shall keep your hearts and minds through Jesus Christ."

As he said this, Gurney noticed that Wilberforce was shaking, and that "his mortal tabernacle seemed ready to be dissolved." Still, Gurney observed, his old friend seemed to be at peace. In fact, the mention of the text in Philippians immediately called forth, Gurney recalled, "one of his bright ideas, and led to a display, as in days of old, of ... [the] peculiar versatility of mind."

Wilberforce expressed his admiration for "the harmony and variety of St. Paul's smaller epistles." Recalling that Gurney had recently published a book on the evidences of Christianity, he stated that Gurney might well have included a section on the harmony and variety of the smaller Pauline epistles in it. Warming to this idea, Wilberforce observed, "The epistle to the Galatians contains a noble exhibition of doctrine. That to the Colossians, is a union of doctrine and precept, showing their mutual connexion and dependence; that to the Ephesians, is seraphic; that to the Philippians, is all love."

Wilberforce's humility had only grown with the years, Gurney noted, for speaking of himself Wilberforce said that he had "nothing whatsoever to urge, but the poor publican's plea, 'God be merciful to me a sinner.'" Wilberforce had spoken these words with "peculiar feeling and emphasis" and later reminded Gurney of Wilberforce's definition of the word *mercy*: "Kindness to those that deserve punishment."

It was, Gurney felt, a powerful lesson. "If Wilberforce," he wrote, "who had been labouring for these fifty years in the cause of virtue, religion, and humanity, could feel himself to be a poor criminal, with no hope of happiness, except through the pardoning love of God in Christ Jesus, surely we all ought to be bowed down and broken under similar feelings!"

Wilberforce also spoke of the loss of his fortune. He was, he said, almost "afraid of telling you what I feel about it, lest it should appear to you like affectation, but rest assured that the event ... has only increased my happiness, for I have in consequence been spending the winter with my son – [I have known] the joyful witness of his gospel labours."

The meeting had been moving for both men. Gurney was reluctant to leave Wilberforce, but it was obvious his old friend was very weak, and he knew it was time to go. He grasped Wilberforce's hand and bid him farewell. He expressed "the humble and reverent hope that ... we shall meet again where pain and parting, sorrow, sin, and death, are no more."

On July 15 Wilberforce's wife, Barbara, wrote to the Reverend William Jay, one of Wilberforce's old and nearby friends. Jay was the long-time pastor of Argyle Chapel in Bath, a dissenting chapel of great prominence. He was also the author of a widely read devotional work, *Morning and Evening Exercises*, which he had dedicated to Wilberforce. Barbara urged Jay to come, as Wilberforce's health appeared to be failing, and Jay might not see him again otherwise.

Their brief visit revealed much of the wisdom and compassion that so many had seen in Wilberforce in his last years. Always seeking to promote good relations between the Church of England and other Christian traditions, Wilberforce told Jay: "The best way to reduce an undue attachment to the subordinate things in religion ... is to keep up a supreme regard to the more important ones.... For then we shall have little time and less inclination to engage in the strivings and strifes of bigots."

Agreement on the basic orthodox tenets of the Christian faith was what mattered most to Wilberforce. Denominational distinctives meant little to him, for they too often precluded any possibility of mutual cooperation and edification. "Though I am an Episcopalian by education and conviction," he once said, "I yet feel such a oneness and sympathy with the cause of God at large, that nothing would be more delightful than my communing once every year with every Church that holds the Head, even Christ."

There was, Wilberforce confessed, "much in the state of the world and church which I deplore, yet I am not among the croakers. I think real religion is spreading; and, I am persuaded, will increasingly spread, till the earth is filled with the knowledge of the Lord, as the waters cover the sea."

When they parted, Wilberforce took Jay's hand and said earnestly, "I am glad you have not turned aside after any of the 'Lo! heres' and 'Lo! theres,' many of which you must have witnessed; but have kept to the common, plain, and important truths, in which all Christians are nearly agreed; and I hope you will never leave the good old way – God bless you!"

Increasing concern over Wilberforce's declining health prompted a move to London so that his physician, Dr. William Chambers, might be consulted. They arrived at the home of Wilberforce's cousin Lucy Smith, 44 Cadogan Place, on July 19, 1833.

Initially Dr. Chambers believed Wilberforce was not gravely ill. After some rest, it was thought that he could go into the country to continue his convalescence. Things began to appear more hopeful. In the morning Wilberforce could be taken outside in a wheelchair for ten minutes to get some air, later in the day, visitors would find him lying propped up on sofa. Still, he tired easily and these visits were short.

On July 25 Wilberforce received a visit from a young member of Parliament named William Gladstone. Gladstone would later become one of Britain's greatest prime ministers, but he was at this time just entering upon his six-decade career in political life. The two breakfasted together, and Gladstone stayed to hear Wilberforce pray with his family. "Blessing and honour are upon his head," Gladstone observed.

Wilberforce seemed to be improving, and he was greatly encouraged to receive word on July 26 that a bill for the abolition of slavery throughout the British colonies was now assured of becoming law. His work and the work of those who had taken up his mantle had done the job of winning the hearts and minds of the nation. "Thank God," he said, "that I should have lived to witness a day in which England is willing to give £20,000,000 for the Abolition of Slavery."

The £20,000,000 was a sum set aside to essentially purchase the freedom of the roughly 800,000 slaves in Britain's colonies. Thomas Babington Macaulay was present when Wilberforce received the news. Wilberforce, he wrote, "excelled in the success which we obtained ... as much as the youngest and most ardent [of us] could have done."

Two days later, on July 28, Wilberforce fell victim to a series of fainting spells and took a decided turn for the worse. Fading in and out of consciousness, he was briefly lucid long enough to whisper, "I am in a very distressed state."

His youngest son, Henry, sought to comfort him, saying, "Yes, but you have your feet on the Rock." Wilberforce's last words were ones of humility and hope. "I do not venture to speak so positively," he told his son. "But I hope I have." He died at three the next morning, a little less than one month before his seventy-fourth birthday.

As soon as Wilberforce's death became known, his family received a letter from his old friend Henry Brougham, now chancellor of the exchequer and second only to the prime minister in the political leadership of Britain. "We the undersigned members of both Houses of Parliament," it read, "being anxious upon public grounds to show our respect for the memory of the late William Wilberforce, and being also satisfied that public honours can never be more fitly bestowed than upon such benefactors of mankind, earnestly request that he may be buried in Westminster Abbey; and that we, and others who may agree with us in these sentiments, may have permission to attend his funeral."

Brougham had been authorized to add that "nearly all the members of both Houses of Parliament would have [signed the letter], had the time allowed." Shortly thereafter, another application arrived signed by almost one hundred members of all parties in the House of Commons.

Wilberforce's family gratefully acceded to Brougham's request, for burial in Westminster Abbey was an honor reserved for the greatest of Britain's citizens. His funeral was attended by the highest-ranking bishops of the Church of England, by royal princes, and by the Duke of Wellington. Wilberforce's sons wrote, "Whatever England had most renowned for talent and greatness ... assemble[d] ... around his unpretending bier. His simple name was its noblest decoration."

St. Paul's Church, Mill Hill, the church Wilberforce built with his own funds during the last years of his life

The pallbearers included the Speaker of the House of Commons, Lord Chancellor Brougham, and Prince William of Gloucester. Wilberforce's body was laid in the north transept of the abbey, close to the tombs of William Pitt, Charles Fox, and George Canning. One bishop observed that this most moving tribute to Wilberforce's memory was all the more remarkable considering that Wilberforce had been out of public life for eight years. This "unequalled mark of public approbation" was a fitting testimony to Wilberforce's character, which could only be known by many of the younger mourners in attendance by tradition and not personal experience.

The nation grieved. One friend wrote to tell Wilberforce's family, "You will like to know, that as I came towards [the funeral procession] down the Strand, every third person I met going about their ordinary business was in mourning."

A few days after Wilberforce's death, the first service at St. Paul's Chapel at Mill Hill was held. His cherished project after the purchase of his home at Highwood Hill had taken eight years of arduous struggle to see through to completion. It stands today as a vibrant legacy of faith.

Other memorials for Wilberforce followed. Within a short time, donations were taken among his surviving friends in London for the purpose of erecting a memorial statue in Westminster Abbey. A charitable endowment was established in his memory to fund projects in keeping with his philanthropic legacy. Decades later, this endowment still funded good works. A county asylum for the blind was also founded in his honor, and the people of Hull, his birthplace, later raised a memorial column to his memory.

Among the many tributes paid to Wilberforce, the one given by William Jay was particularly fitting. Wilberforce, he wrote, was a man who was "great among the good and good among the great.... His disinterested, self-denying, laborious [and unceasing] efforts in [the] cause of justice and humanity ... will call down the blessings of millions; and ages yet to come will glory in his memory."

AFTERWORD: WHAT REMAINS

As much as any writer, Thomas Babington, Lord Macaulay, was representative of the age that followed Wilberforce's death. No one was more Victorian. And yet Macaulay's reaction to Wilberforce's passing was both personal and representative of what Britain had lost. He had known Wilberforce all his life, and he knew what Wilberforce had meant to the nation. Two days after Wilberforce's death, Macaulay wrote to his sister Hannah. His letter clearly shows that Wilberforce's passing had prompted much reflection about his own mortality, and what remains when a great soul has departed.

> So Wilberforce is gone! We talk of burying him in Westminster Abbey; and many eminent men, both Whigs and Tories, are desirous to join in paying him this honor ... Wilberforce kept his faculties, and ... his spirits, to the very last. He was cheerful and full of anecdote only last Saturday. He owned that he enjoyed life much, and that he had a great desire to live longer. Strange in a man who had, I should have said, so little to attach him to this world, and so firm a belief in another: in a man with an impaired fortune, a weak spine, and a worn-out stomach!

One night before writing his letter Macaulay had called at 44 Cadogan Place, where Wilberforce's body lay, to pay his respects. "I was truly fond of him," he told Hannah. As he walked back from Cadogan Place to his own lodgings, Macaulay became lost in thought. He shared those thoughts with his sister. "How very little one human being generally cares for another!" he wrote. "How very little the world misses anybody! How soon the chasm left by the best and wisest of men closes! ... There are not ten people in the world whose deaths would spoil my dinner; but there are one or two whose deaths would break my heart."

Macaulay was one of the solemn procession that had attended Wilberforce's funeral in Westminster Abbey. "We laid him side by side with Canning," he wrote, "at the feet of Pitt, and within two steps of Fox and Grattan."

Macaulay's nephew and biographer, George Trevelyan, was an heir to his uncle's legacy. Like his uncle, he was also an heir to the legacy bequeathed by Wilberforce. He offered his own tribute. "[Wilberforce] died with the promised land full in view. Before the end of August Parliament abolished slavery, and the last touch was put to a work that had consumed so many pure and noble lives."

Macaulay penned other tributes to Wilberforce. He remembered "the sweetest and most exquisitely modulated of human voices, [his] affectionate heart, caressing manners, and brilliant wit." All these, had "made him the most delightful of companions." One sentence seemed to capture all that Macaulay felt: "[Wilberforce] was a very kind friend to me, and I loved him much."

Other eminent and equally representative Victorians retained lasting impressions. Many years after Wilberforce's passing, William Gladstone wrote again about his one and only meeting with him. Small kindnesses that showed the young heart of a frail and elderly man stood out. "In 1833 I had the honour of breakfasting with Mr. Wilberforce a few days before his death, and when I entered the house, immediately after the salutation, he said to me in his silvery tones, 'How is your sweet mother?' He had been a guest in my father's house some twelve years before."

Another story from Wilberforce's funeral survived, passed down for years. As the Duke of Wellington, the great hero of the age, walked in the procession that accompanied Wilberforce's coffin to Westminster Abbey, he was recognized by some who watched it pass. When they saw him, they made as though they were going to cheer him. The Duke saw it, and before they could, raised his finger to his lips in a silent but firm admonition. It was, said one who witnessed it, as though the great man were saying: "You are not here to honour me, but him whom I have come to honour."

Time renders memory in curious ways. We are separated by many years from the age of Wilberforce and Wellington, or that of Gladstone and Macaulay. Many of the homes where Wilberforce once lived are gone; fields and forests he knew well are no more. Lord Rosebery, the near kinsman of Pitt and future prime minister, reflected on the passing of the age that Pitt and Wilberforce knew. His eloquent words, written in 1891, are a fitting epitaph for that friendship and that age – and what they offer still to our living memory: "The Holwood of Pitt has long disappeared. The house he built has been demolished, and the woods he planted can no more be traced. There remains, however, an ancient, memorable oak; stretched under which, Wilberforce and he resolved on that campaign for the abolition of the slave trade, which gave honour to the one and immortality to the other."

APPENDIX:
AN ORIGINAL ACCOUNT OF
WILBERFORCE'S FUNERAL

Here is the most detailed and moving account of Wilberforce's funeral we have. It affords rich, moving detail. It is taken from the Appendix of the second American edition of Thomas Price's *Memoir of William Wilberforce*, (Boston: 1836).

> The following account of the last honors rendered to the remains of Wilberforce, is taken from a London paper. It will be considered an appropriate sequel to the history of his life and services, contained in the preceding pages of this volume.

FUNERAL OF MR. WILBERFORCE

The funeral of that most excellent man, Mr. Wilberforce, eminent through the course of his long life for his public and private virtues, for his sterling patriotism, his Christian piety, and his universal feeling of philanthropy, took place on Saturday. It was at first intended, in conformity to the wish of the deceased, to conduct his funeral with the utmost privacy, and to inter his remains in Newington church yard; but a very considerable number of the most distinguished members of the Houses of Peers and Commons, anxious to pay a last tribute of respect to the memory of a man who, through a long series of years, had been so honorably distinguished in the British senate, prevailed on his sons and immediate friends to allow the funeral to be a public one, and the place of interment to be Westminster Abbey, that solemn habitation of "the departed great;" thus conferring the highest possible honor on the memory of Mr. Wilberforce, and giving to the world (for of Mr. Wilberforce it may be said, that he was not the property of a nook, but of the world) an exalted testimony of the country, and of the friendship which his mild manners and noble qualities had won him.

At about half past twelve o'clock, the Order of the Procession having been arranged, the coffin containing the remains of the deceased was placed in the hearse, and the procession began to move in the following order:

> Horsemen, two and two abreast, wearing black scarves and hat bands, and proceeded by Mr. Birch, the Family Undertaker
> Two Mutes abreast
> (One attendant) Plume of Feathers (One attendant)
> Two Mutes Abreast
> (Attendants) Horsemen, two and two abreast (Attendants)
> Hearse, (bearing the Coffin,)
> Richly studded with black plumes, and
> (Pall supporters) Drawn by six jet horses, richly (Pall supporters)
> Caparisoned, with black velvet trappings,
> And adorned with nodding plumes.
> Eight mourning coaches,
> The first bearing the Deceased's Son
> (Attendants) As Chief Mourners; (Attendants)
> The others containing the Mourners.
> Noblemen and Gentlemen's Carriages,
> To the number of nearly fifty, being chiefly those of the members of both Houses of Parliament.

In this manner the procession moved slowly from Cadogan place towards Westminster Abbey, forming a very lengthened train, accompanied by immense crowds of people, who flanked it in moving columns, on either side; and a little after one o'clock, the signal that it was approaching the Abbey was given by Mr. Lee, the High Constable of Westminster, to the Peers and Commoners, who had assembled in their relative Houses of Parliament for the purpose of following the body in procession through the aisles of the Abbey. The Peers, amounting to a considerable number, all dressed in deep black, having put on scarves and hat bands, proceeded from the Jerusalem Chamber of the House of Lords into the Abbey, entering at Poets' Corner; while the members of the House of Commons, numbering between one and two hundred, in full mourning, proceeded two abreast to the west door of the Abbey, by which they entered.

The coffin, at this period, having arrived at the western door, was moved from the hearse and placed on the shoulders of six men, the pall of rich black velvet with a deep border of white satin, having been thrown over it. When inside the door the bearers were ordered to halt; it was here a proud sight to see the royalty, the high station, rank and greatest talent of the country, become the pall bearers of a virtuous citizen, which was at once a compliment to the memory of the man, a credit to their own hearts and understandings, and an honor of which the people of this great country may proudly boast to other nations. The following are the names of the distinguished individuals who supported the pall: — The Lord Chancellor [Henry Brougham], Speaker of the House of Commons, Lord Bexley, and the Marquis of Westminster, on the one side; The Right Honorable Charles Grant, Sir Robert Inglis, Mr. W[illiam]. Smith [grandfather of Florence Nightingale] (as we are informed) and his Royal Highness the Duke of Gloucester, on the other. His Royal Highness was the last on the extreme right, it being a rule, according to the etiquette of such occasions, for royalty to be last among the pall bearers: the Lord Chancellor was first on the extreme left.

A solemn stillness now prevailed, amid which the order of the procession through the aisles was formed, and the sight was altogether a most impressive one. The King's Boys, in their uniforms, and the Westminster School Boys, in their white surplices, two and two abreast, formed the van of the procession. The Abbey Choristers, robed in their robes of white and scarlet, together with the Choristers of St. Paul's Cathedral, Whitehall Chapel, and the various other important places of public worship throughout the metropolis, next followed; then followed the Peers, at the head of whom was his Royal Highness the Duke of Sussex, and his Grace the Duke of Wellington, both in deep black, and exhibiting a star on the left breast; next in order were the Archbishop of Canterbury, the Bishop of Chichester, and various other Bishops; after them followed the Dean and Chapter of Westminster, then the Rev. Dr. Holcombe, accompanied by the Rev. Dr. Deakins; next to them the coffin and distinguished pall bearers; and lastly, the members of the House of Commons, two and two abreast. During all this time, the Abbey bell tolled slowly and solemnly; and the procession having been arranged, the signal to advance was given. The organ here commenced its melancholy and devotional funeral notes, the Choristers chiming in with a sweetness and solemnity of voice, producing, as the sounds travelled from aisle to aisle, the deepest feeling that the presence of man's mortality and immortality can inspire. The Choristers, as the procession moved towards the north transept of the Abbey; where the grave was formed, close to the tombs of Canning, Fox and Pitt, chanted the funeral dirge composed by Croft. Having arrived at the grave, the coffin was lowered into it, and the funeral service was most impressively read by the Rev. Dr. Holcombe, the Choristers, King's Boys, &c. chanting in occasionally, with the accompaniment of the organ. During this most solemn part of the service, their Royal Highnesses the Dukes of Sussex and Gloucester, the Duke of Wellington, the Archbishop of Canterbury, the Bishop of Chichester, and the various other Bishops, the Lord Chancellor, the Speaker of the House of Commons, and the other Pall Bearers, the Marquis of

Lansdowne, Lord Rosslyn, Lord Althorp, Lord Auckland, &c. formed a circle around the grave.

Among the most distinguished Commoners present, besides those already mentioned, we observed Sir James Graham, Sir Robert Peel, Lord Morpeth, Mr. Fowell Buxton, Dr. Lushington, Mr. Stanley, Mr. Lyttleton, Sir Robert Grant, Mr. Spring Rice, the Messrs. Attwood, Messrs. James and Henry Grattan, Mr. Tynte, Mr. Carew O'Dwyer, &c. &c.

Besides the above, the Abbey was crowded by persons of distinction, among whom were many ladies.

After the funeral service was over, the numerous persons pressed eagerly towards the grave, to get a sight of the coffin, which was covered with rich black velvet, and ornamented with gilt moulding, heading, &c. In the centre of the lid was a splendid brass plate of considerable dimensions, with the following simple inscription:

WILLIAM WILBERFORCE, Esq.
Born 24th of August, 1759;
Died 29th of July, 1833.

Thus terminated the mortal career of as pure and virtuous a public man as ever lived—of "a man whom (in the words of Ben Jonson) no sordid hope of gain, or frosty apprehension of danger, could make a parasite to time, or place, or opinion."

Mr. Wilberforce's public life forms one of the brightest pages in the annals of this country, so long renowned among the nations of the earth. By his exertions in the Senate, the heart of the nation was first impressed with the horror and degradation of its long-cherished traffic in human beings. His glowing eloquence inspired in others the feelings of humanity in which it had its source, and he had the glory of witnessing the triumph of that holy cause to which he had devoted all the energies of his gifted mind, in the deliverance of his country from the abomination of the slave trade—a consummation well characterized by one of his ablest coadjutors as "the saving of the soul of the nation." A delicate constitution compelled him to retire from parliament and public life some years ago, which deprived the cause of humanity of his personal exertions in the total extinction of slavery; but the feelings he mainly contributed to inspire can never die; and the people of this country, while they honor the name of Wilberforce, will feel their own highest honor in imitating the conduct of him whose benevolence, founded on the sincerest piety, regarded the whole human race as friends and brothers.

The funeral ceremony did not terminate before three o'clock. We may here mention that we saw two gentlemen of color in the procession, who appeared to feel a deep interest in the solemnity of the passing scene.

A NOTE ON SOURCES

For a complete documentation of all sources consulted for this book, readers should consult the first edition (published by NavPress in 2002). Suffice it to say, I have drawn a great deal on the massive five-volume *Life of William Wilberforce* (1838), written by Robert Isaac and Samuel Wilberforce. John Harford's classic work, *Recollections of William Wilberforce* (1864), has also been of great utility, as has Sir James Stephen's most valuable *Edinburgh Review* essay.

For other books that have been helpful in the writing of this book, refer to the list in the bibliography that follows.

Lastly, I wish to acknowledge my indebtedness to John Pollock, who allowed me permission to quote extensively from his authoritative biography, *Wilberforce* (London: John Constable, 1977). I am honored by this mark of friendship and kindness.

BIBLIOGRAPHY

Belmonte, Kevin. *Travel with William Wilberforce: The Friend of Humanity.* Leominster, England: Day One Publications, 2006.

Belmonte, Kevin, ed. *365 Days with Wilberforce: A Collection of Daily Readings from the Writings of William Wilberforce.* Leominster, England: Day One Publications, 2006.

Colquhoun, John Campbell. *Wilberforce: His Friends and Times.* London: Longmans, Green, Reader and Dyer, 1866.

Cormack, Patrick. *Wilberforce: The Nation's Conscience.* London: Pickering, 1983.

Coupland, Reginald. *Wilberforce: A Narrative.* Oxford: Clarendon Press, 1923.

Furneaux, Robin. *William Wilberforce.* London: Hamish Hamilton, 1974.

Gurney, Joseph John. *Familiar Sketch of the Late William Wilberforce.* Norwich: Josiah Fletcher, 1838.

Harford, John Scandrett. *Recollections of William Wilberforce.* London: Longman, Green, Longman, Roberts, and Green, 1864.

Hague, William. *William Wilberforce.* (Forthcoming, June 2007).

Lean, Garth. *God's Politician.* Colorado Springs: Helmers & Howard, 1987.

Newsome, David. *The Parting of Friends: The Wilberforces and Henry Manning.* Grand Rapids, Mich.: Eerdmans, 1993.

Patten, John A. *These Remarkable Men: The Beginnings of a World Enterprise.* London: Lutterworth Press, 1945.

Pollock, John. *Wilberforce.* New York: St. Martin's, 1977.

Stephen, Sir James. "William Wilberforce" and "The Clapham Sect," in *Essays in Ecclesiastical Biography*, 2 vols. London: Longman, Brown, Green, and Longmans, 1850.

Stephen, Sir Leslie. "William Wilberforce," in *The Dictionary of National Biography*.

Stoughton, John. *William Wilberforce*. London: Hodder and Stoughton, 1880.

Warner, Oliver. *William Wilberforce and His Times*. London: B.T. Batsford Ltd., 1962.

Wilberforce, A. M. ed. *Private Papers of William Wilberforce*. London: T. Fisher Unwin, 1897.

Wilberforce, Robert and Samuel. *The Life of William Wilberforce*, 5 vols. London: John Murray, 1838.

Wilberforce, Samuel. *The Life of William Wilberforce*. London: John Murray, 1868. A one-volume abridgement of the five-volume *Life*.

Wilberforce, William. *A Practical View of Christianity*, ed. by Kevin Belmonte. Peabody, Mass.: Hendrickson, 2006.

Wilberforce, William. *The Correspondence of William Wilberforce*, ed. Robert and Samuel Wilberforce, 2 vols. London: John Murray, 1840.

Wilberforce, Yvette. *William Wilberforce: An Essay*. Foreword by C.E. Wrangham. Privately printed, 1967.

Wolffe, John. "William Wilberforce," in *The New Dictionary of National Biography*.

ACKNOWLEDGMENTS

The crafting of this revised edition is a task I have undertaken gratefully. Revising the text for better narrative flow, adding sections where my knowledge of Wilberforce had grown and introducing new illustrations, a new Preface, and an Afterword—all of these are things I had long wished to do.

Sue Brower, Bob Hudson, Greg Clouse, and their colleagues at Zondervan/HarperCollins have made this edition of *William Wilberforce: A Hero for Humanity* possible. I am in their debt. Throughout the preparation of this new edition, in everything from wise editorial counsel to page layout and the design of a new and most handsome cover, I have been a beneficiary of their commitment to excellence.

I would here like to express my deep gratitude for the many kindnesses shown me by members of the Wilberforce family. Space does not permit me to thank each of them at as much length as I might wish to; but then, I look forward to telling each of them once more how privileged I feel to have met them and to have had the gift of time in their company or to have exchanged correspondence.

I am most grateful as well for the mark of friendship Chuck Colson has shown me in writing the Foreword for this book. For his enduring gifts of wise advice, constant support, and encouragement I wish to thank Os Guinness.

When I spoke at the houses of Parliament in London last spring, William Hague honoured me with a gracious introduction to the assembled guests at Portcullis House. I thank him most sincerely, and as I do his Research Assistant Elana Cheah for her many kindnesses.

To all involved with making of *Amazing Grace*, thank you for according me the privilege of serving as the film's lead historical consultant. I shall cherish so many aspects of this experience.

Last of all, I wish to thank my wife, Kelly, and my son, Sam, for everything they are and mean to me. Their love, patience, and sacrifice have made all the difference.